THE PHONETICS OF RUSSIAN

THE PHONETICS OF RUSSIAN

THE LATE
DANIEL JONES

Formerly Professor of Phonetics
University of London

AND

DENNIS WARD

Professor of Russian
University of Edinburgh

CAMBRIDGE
AT THE UNIVERSITY PRESS
1969

CAMBRIDGE UNIVERSITY PRESS
Cambridge, New York, Melbourne, Madrid, Cape Town, Singapore,
São Paulo, Delhi, Dubai, Tokyo

Cambridge University Press
The Edinburgh Building, Cambridge CB2 8RU, UK

Published in the United States of America by Cambridge University Press, New York

www.cambridge.org
Information on this title: www.cambridge.org/9780521153003

First published 1969
This digitally printed version 2010

A catalogue record for this publication is available from the British Library

Library of Congress Catalogue Card Number: 69-10430

ISBN 978-0-521-06736-2 Hardback
ISBN 978-0-521-15300-3 Paperback

CONTENTS

v

CONTENTS

ILLUSTRATIONS

ILLUSTRATIONS

PREFACE

Professor Jones and I originally intended to do no more than revise *The Pronunciation of Russian*, which he wrote in collaboration with M. V. Trofimov and which was published in 1923. The re-writing has, however, been considerable and though it contains some of the material to be found in the earlier book, the present book is no longer simply a revised version of the earlier book. It is therefore issued as a new work, under a new title.

It is hoped that the book will be found useful not only by students of Russian who wish to learn to pronounce Russian well, or to improve their pronunciation of the language, but also by students of phonetics who wish to learn something about the phonetic system of Russian.

Apart from the earlier work by Trofimov and Jones mentioned above, four works in particular, among the many read in preparing this book, have provided valuable information. They are: *Russian Pronunciation*, by S. C. Boyanus; *Spoken Russian*, by S. C. Boyanus and N. B. Jopson; *Русское литературное произношение*[1] by R. I. Avanesov; and *Практическая фонетика и интонация русского языка*[2] by Ye. A. Bryzgunova.

Professor Jones died in 1967 and though the MS was substantially complete by 1966 declining health prevented him from reading many of the sections which I had written for Part II. Any faults which the reader finds there should be laid at my door.

I thank Dr Militsa Greene and Miss E. Vosnesensky for recording all the passages except no. 6, in chapter 26, Mr R. McWhirter for his valuable suggestions on the translations of those passages, Professor John Lyons for advice on terminology, Professor David Abercrombie for advice on terminology and on chapter 24, two of my Honours students, Mr David Hogg and Mr Robert Russell, for drawing my attention to the desirability

[1] 'Russian Literary Pronunciation.'
[2] 'Practical Phonetics and Intonation of Russian.'

ix

of a reference-chart of phonemes, my son John for help in verifying some animal-names, my wife for help with the indexes, and in particular Miss S. White for typing several of the stages through which the book has progressed. Finally, I thank our publishers for their care and patience during the long process of preparing this book for the press.

D. W.

Edinburgh, 1969

ABBREVIATIONS

acc.	accusative	nom.	nominative
dat.	dative	pers.	person
fem.	feminine	pfv.	perfective
gen.	genitive	pl.	plural
imper.	imperative	prep.	prepositional
instr.	instrumental	sh. fm.	short form
masc.	masculine	sing.	singular
neut.	neuter		

Note

The symbols used for phonetic transcription in this book are those of the International Phonetic Alphabet (IPA). Their significance becomes clear from the descriptions of the formation of the sounds which they represent. The symbol ' before a syllable indicates that the syllable is stressed ('accented'). Occasional use is made of the symbol ˌ to indicate that the following syllable receives subsidiary stress. The ligature ‿ means that the linked words are pronounced as a 'unit', with only one stressed syllable. The enclosing of a symbol in brackets means that the sound represented is pronounced in careful delivery but omitted in less careful or in rapid delivery.

PART I

PHONETIC THEORY AND TRANSCRIPTION

1

INTRODUCTION

1.1 Spoken language may be considered to be made up of successions of 'sounds'[1] emitted by the organs of speech, together with certain 'attributes'.[2]

1.2 The science dealing with speech-sounds and their attributes is called *phonetics*. The methods of studying it involve the acquisition of certain skills, and in particular ability on the part of the student to listen to and remember the sounds of foreign languages, and to learn how to perform correctly those sounds both in isolation and in connected speech.

1.3 The present manual is devoted to the phonetics of the Russian language. Its purpose is to explain to English-speaking learners of that language and to students of phonetics what Russian sounds like when spoken, how they may learn to pronounce it reasonably well, and what its phonetic system is.

1.4 To this end the learner must first *cultivate his auditory memory* for the qualities of the sounds of Russian, both singly and in combinations. This is effected by the exercise commonly known as 'ear-training'. It is described in Appendix 1. Auditory memory is also developed incidentally during the processes of learning to pronounce.

1.5 These processes are explained in chapters 12 to 22. There the learner will find detailed descriptions of the manner of forming the Russian sounds, with instructions as to how he may learn to place his tongue, lips, etc., in the necessary positions or to perform the necessary movements with them.

1.6 Then he has to learn which of the Russian sounds are the appropriate ones to use in words and sentences. This knowledge is imparted by the use of phonetic transcriptions and also, in

---

[1] Also called 'phones' or 'linear' or 'segmental' elements of speech.

[2] Also called 'prosodic' or 'suprasegmental' features of speech.

1. INTRODUCTION

this book, by a special chapter on similitudes and assimilations in addition to remarks throughout the book on the occurrence of particular sounds.

1.7 He has further to learn the Russian usages in the matter of 'sound-attributes', and in particular the stress and intonation. Some of the information may be supplied by means of rules, but in the case of stress it is best conveyed by marks in phonetic transcriptions.

1.8 In this book attention is also paid to the relations between spelling (orthography) and pronunciation in Russian. This is achieved in three ways: first, at the end of the description of each sound or phoneme the representation of that sound or phoneme in the orthography is briefly described; secondly, almost all the illustrations of sounds and phonemes are given first in phonetic transcription, then in the orthography (followed by an English translation, usually in brackets); thirdly, an appendix is devoted to a brief outline of the principles of Russian orthography.

1.9 In the chapter on vowels (chapter 12) the following general procedure is adopted: description of the formation of an allophone of the vowel-phoneme; comparison with a similar English sound or sounds, if any; remarks on difficulties which English speakers may encounter in acquiring the sound, together with suggestions for acquiring the Russian sound; a broad statement about the kind of phonetic context in which the sound occurs; representation of the sound in the orthography; list of some words illustrating the sound.

1.10 In the chapter on diphthongs (chapter 14) the Russian diphthongs are simply listed and illustrated.

1.11 The chapters on consonants (chapters 17 to 22) follow a similar procedure to that adopted in the chapter on vowels, except that the subsidiary allophones of a phoneme, if any, are described immediately after the remarks on the principal allophone and the set of illustrations is devoted to *all* the allophones, so arranged, however, that it falls into sub-sets, each illustrating one allophone. Moreover, where a consonant phoneme differs in only one major respect from another, a detailed description of its articulation is not given: it is merely recorded that its articulation is the 'same' as that of another consonant except, say, in the matter of voicing.

1.12 The influence of phonetic context and the substitution of one sound or phoneme for another which this frequently causes is made the subject of a special chapter (chapter 23—'Similitude and Assimilation'), while chapter 24 deals with the stress-accent of Russian and is an essential preliminary to chapter 25 on intonation. Finally, chapter 26 provides some common phrases and a few continuous passages for practice, in which both stress and pitch are indicated.

2

THE ORGANS OF SPEECH

2.1 It is necessary that the student of phonetics should have a fairly clear idea of the structure and functions of the organs of speech. Models of the organs of speech will be found useful. Suitable models of sections of the head, mouth, nose, larynx, etc., may be obtained from dealers in medical instruments.

2.2 Figs. 1 and 2 show all that is essential for the present book.

2.3 A detailed description of the various parts of the organs of speech is not necessary; the following points should, however, be noted.

2.4 The roof of the mouth is considered to be divided, for the purposes of phonetics, into three parts called the teeth-ridge, the hard palate, and the soft palate. The teeth-ridge is defined as the part of the roof of the mouth just behind the teeth which is convex to the tongue, the division between the teeth-ridge and the palate being defined as the place where the roof of the mouth ceases to be convex to the tongue and begins to be concave (see Fig. 1). The remainder of the roof of the mouth comprises the other two parts, the front part constituting the hard palate, and

2. THE ORGANS OF SPEECH

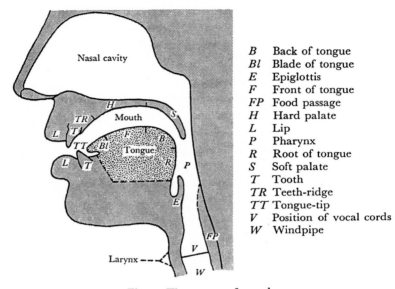

B	Back of tongue
Bl	Blade of tongue
E	Epiglottis
F	Front of tongue
FP	Food passage
H	Hard palate
L	Lip
P	Pharynx
R	Root of tongue
S	Soft palate
T	Tooth
TR	Teeth-ridge
TT	Tongue-tip
V	Position of vocal cords
W	Windpipe

Fig. 1. The organs of speech

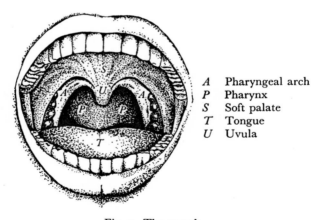

A	Pharyngeal arch
P	Pharynx
S	Soft palate
T	Tongue
U	Uvula

Fig. 2. The mouth

the back part the soft palate. These two parts should be examined carefully in the looking-glass; they may be felt with the tongue or with the finger. The soft palate can be moved upwards from the position shown in Fig. 1, and when raised to its fullest

6

extent it touches the back wall of the pharynx, as shown in Fig. 6.

2.5 The pharynx is the cavity situated in the throat immediately behind the mouth. Below it is the larynx, which forms the upper part of the windpipe (the passage leading to the lungs). The epiglottis is a sort of tongue situated just above the larynx. It is probably contracted in such a way as to protect the larynx during the action of swallowing, but it does not appear to enter into the formation of any speech-sounds.

2.6 For the purposes of phonetics it is convenient to imagine the surface of the tongue divided into four parts (see Fig. 1). The part which normally lies opposite the soft palate is called the back; the part which normally lies opposite the hard palate is called the front; and the part which normally lies opposite the teeth-ridge is called the blade. The extremity of the tongue is called the tip or point. The definitions of 'back' and 'front' are particularly important. It is sometimes convenient to use the term middle of the tongue to denote a part of the surface of the tongue including the fore part of the 'back' and the hinder part of the 'front'.

2.7 The tongue is extremely mobile. Thus the tip can be made to touch any part of the roof of the mouth from the teeth to the beginning of the soft palate. The other parts of the tongue may likewise be made to articulate against different parts of the roof of the mouth.

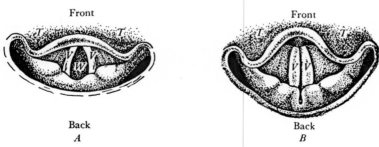

Fig. 3. The larynx as seen through the laryngoscope

A Position for breath.   *B* Position for voice.   *T* Tongue.
V Vocal cords.   *W* Windpipe.

7

2. THE ORGANS OF SPEECH

2.8   The vocal cords are situated in the larynx; they resemble two lips (see Fig. 3). They run in a horizontal direction from back to front. The space between them is called the glottis. The cords may be kept apart or they may be brought together, so as to touch and thus close the air passage completely. When they are brought near together and air is forced between them, they vibrate, producing a musical sound (see chapter 3).

2.9   In the larynx just above the vocal cords is situated another pair of lips somewhat resembling the vocal cords and running parallel to them. These are known as the false vocal cords (see § 3.1).

3

BREATH AND VOICE

3.1   The vocal cords are capable of acting in much the same way as the lips of the mouth. Thus they may be held wide apart, they may be closed completely, or they may be held loosely together so that they vibrate when air passes between them. When they are held wide apart (i.e. when the glottis is open) and air passes between them, the sound produced is called 'breath'. When they are drawn near together and air is forced between them so that they vibrate, the sound produced is called 'voice'. If the false vocal cords (§ 2.9) are drawn towards each other leaving only a narrow space for the air to pass between them, the resulting sound is one variety of whisper.

3.2   The vocal cords may be made to touch tightly along their whole length so that no air can escape at all. This is the position known as closed glottis. The explosive sound heard when this position is released is known as the 'glottal stop'.

3.3   Breath is heard most clearly in the sounds represented by h. Voice occurs as part of the articulation of numerous speech-sounds, and particularly of the vowels.

3.4   The positions of the vocal cords in the production of breath and voice are shown in Fig. 3. These diagrams show the larynx as seen from above through a laryngoscope.

3. BREATH AND VOICE

3.5 Most ordinary speech-sounds contain either breath or voice. Those which contain breath are called breathed or voiceless[1] sounds, and those which contain voice are called voiced sounds. Examples of voiceless sounds are f, s; examples of voiced sounds are v, z, b, and the vowels.

3.6 When people speak in a whisper, whispered sounds are substituted for all the voiced sounds, the voiceless sounds remaining unaltered.

3.7 It does not require much practice for a person with a fairly good ear to be able to recognize by ear the difference between voiceless and voiced sounds. Any students who have difficulty in this should practise prolonging such pairs of sounds as s, z; f, v; ʃ, ʒ; θ, ð,[2] noticing the difference between the members of each pair. They may also try the following well-known tests. (1) Stop the ears with the fingers, and pronounce the following sounds p, ɑ,[3] f, v; a buzzing sound will be heard during the utterance of ɑ and v, but not when p and f are sounded. (2) Pronounce the same sounds while touching the outside of the larynx with the fingers; the vibrations will be felt in the case of the voiced sounds. (3) Notice that voiced sounds such as ɑ, v, can be sung, while voiceless sounds cannot.

3.8 When an assimilation (chapter 23) takes place by which a voiceless sound is substituted for a voiced sound, the voiced sound is commonly said to become unvoiced or to be devocalized or, better, devoiced.

---

[1] It is sometimes convenient to use the term 'breathed' in speaking of continuant sounds and 'voiceless' in speaking of plosive consonants. It can hardly be said that during the 'stop' of a plosive consonant there is a current of air passing between the vocal cords. In what follows, however, we use only one term—voiceless.

[2] ʃ is the English sound of *sh*; ʒ is the sound of *s* in *measure*; θ and ð are the sounds of *th* in *thin* and *then*.

[3] As in *half, father*, in Received Pronunciation (RP) and many dialects of English.

4

VOWELS AND CONSONANTS

4.1 Every speech-sound belongs to one or other of the two main classes known as Vowels and Consonants.

4.2 A vowel (in normal speech)[1] is defined as a voiced sound in forming which the air issues in a continuous stream through the pharynx and mouth, there being no obstruction and no narrowing such as would cause audible friction.

4.3 All other sounds (in normal speech)[1] are called consonants.

4.4 Consonants therefore include

(1) all sounds which are not voiced (e.g. p, s, ʃ);

(2) all sounds in the production of which the air has an impeded passage through the mouth (e.g. b, l, rolled r);

(3) all sounds in the production of which the air does not pass through the mouth (e.g. m);

(4) all sounds in which there is audible friction (e.g. f, v, s, z, h).

4.5 The distinction between vowels and consonants is not an arbitrary physiological distinction. It is in reality a distinction based on acoustic considerations, namely on the relative sonority or carrying power of the various sounds. Some sounds

---

[1] Whispered speech is not considered as normal. In whispered speech 'voice' is replaced throughout by 'whisper' and every sound consists of audible friction and nothing else (except the 'stops' of voiceless plosives, which have no sound at all). The term 'whispered vowels' is commonly used to designate sounds produced with the organs in the same position as for the sounds defined as 'vowels' in § 4.2, but with 'whisper' substituted for 'voice'. There is no objection to this terminology, but it should be noted that if a whispered vowel were to occur in speech next to a voiced one, the whispered vowel would have to be regarded as a consonant. This may be seen by pronouncing a whispered ɑ immediately followed by a voiced ɑ. The result resembles hɑ with a strong kind of h. Voiceless vowels occur exceptionally in some languages (including Russian) but there is no impedance in the mouth and no audible friction in their production.

are more sonorous than others, that is to say they carry better or can be heard at a greater distance, when pronounced with the same length, stress and voice-pitch. Thus the sound ɑ pronounced in the normal manner can be heard at a much greater distance than the sound p or the sound f pronounced in the normal manner. It so happens that the sounds defined as vowels in § 4.2 are on the whole more sonorous than any other speech-sounds (when pronounced in the normal manner);[1] and that is the reason why these sounds are considered to form one of the two fundamental classes.

4.6 The relative sonority or carrying power of sounds depends on their inherent quality (tamber) and must be distinguished from the relative 'prominence' of sounds in a sequence; prominence depends on combinations of quality with length, stress and (in the case of voiced sounds) intonation. When length and stress (degree of push from the chest wall) are constant and the intonation is level, the sounds defined as vowels are more prominent than the sounds defined as consonants; 'open' vowels (§ 6.2) are mostly more prominent than 'close' vowels (§ 6.2); voiced consonants are more prominent than voiceless consonants; l-sounds and voiced nasal consonants are more prominent than other voiced consonants. The voiceless consonants have very little prominence in comparison with the voiced sounds, and the differences in prominence between the various voiceless consonants may as a rule be considered as negligible for practical linguistic purposes. It must always be remembered, however, that *more sonorous* sounds may become *less prominent*, and therefore more consonant-like, by diminishing length or stress, and that sounds of relatively small *sonority* may be made *prominent* by increasing length or stress.

4.7 It is as a consequence of the principle of relative prominence that certain short vowel-glides must be regarded as consonants. Such are the English j (as in *yard* jɑ:d) and w (as in *wait* weit). In making these sounds the speech-organs start in

---

[1] With the exception apparently of 'cardinal' i (see 'The Perceptibility of Sounds', by Stephen Jones, in *Le maître phonétique*, January 1926).

the position of i and u respectively and without remaining there any appreciable time proceed very quickly to the position of another vowel (ɑ in the case of *yard* and e in the case of *wait*). Such vowel-glides are often called semi-vowels. It must be remembered that such sounds have to be regarded as consonants on account of

(1) their gliding nature,
(2) their shortness,
(3) their lack of stress as compared with the succeeding vowel.

4.8 Certain consonants are inherently more sonorous than all others, i.e. they have greater prominence, *all other things being equal*. These include lateral consonants (l-sounds), nasal consonants (e.g. m, n) and rolled consonants (r-sounds). Such consonants as these may be distinguished from all others by the term 'sonants'.[1] The sonants of Russian, to which reference will be made in subsequent chapters, are: m, m̦ (palatalized or soft m), n, n̦ (palatalized or soft n), l, ļ (palatalized or soft l), r and ŗ (palatalized or soft r).

5

HOW TO LEARN VOWELS

5.1 Consonants are as a rule best acquired by directing attention to tactile and muscular sensations. To learn to produce foreign vowels it is needful to direct attention particularly to their acoustic qualities.

5.2 The method employed is that the learner should listen carefully to the foreign vowels and try to estimate the relations between them and those of his mother tongue or other vowels known to him. He may be assisted to some extent in his efforts to pronounce foreign vowels correctly by some knowledge of

[1] In some languages sonants may function as the peak of prominence of a syllable, in the same way as vowels, Thus, in many common pronunciations of English, the words *garden* and *kettle*, while consisting each of two syllables, have no vowel (as defined above) in the second syllable.

their organic formation, but as a rule he must rely chiefly on oral instructions from his teacher. The teacher will tell him when his attempts at reproducing the foreign vowels are successful; when his attempts are wide of the mark, the teacher can indicate to him the adjustments he must make in order to make better approximations.

5.3 If the learner is obliged to work without a teacher, it is possible for him to acquire a tolerably good pronunciation of difficult foreign vowels by having recourse to a scale of 'Cardinal Vowels', i.e. a scale of fixed vowel-sounds having known acoustic qualities and fairly well-known tongue and lip positions.

5.4 It has been found by experience that a scale of eight cardinal vowels forms a convenient basis for describing the vowels of any language. They are represented in the alphabet of the International Phonetic Association (used in this book) by the letters i, e, ɛ, a, ɑ, ɔ, o, u, and are numbered from 1 to 8.

6

THE CLASSIFICATION OF VOWELS

6.1 Vowel sounds may be classified according to the positions taken up by the tongue and lips in forming them. There are front vowels, formed by a raising of the front (§ 2.6) of the tongue in the direction of the hard palate, and there are back vowels, formed by a raising of the back (§ 2.6) of the tongue in the direction of the soft palate; there are also central vowels in forming which an intermediate part of the tongue is raised.

6.2 Vowels differ from each other also according to the degree of height to which the tongue is raised. It is customary to distinguish four such degrees: close, when the tongue is held as high as possible consistently with the sound being a vowel; open, when the tongue is quite low; half-close and half-open, when the tongue is held at intermediate heights.

6. THE CLASSIFICATION OF VOWELS

6.3 The position of the lips also plays a part in determining vowel quality. The lips may be spread or rounded or neutral.[1] Two main types of lip-rounding may be distinguished: close lip-rounding and open lip-rounding. There are also intermediate degrees of lip-rounding. Sounds of the ɪ-type have spread lips; cardinal a has neutral lips; cardinal u and ɔ have close lip-rounding and open lip-rounding respectively (Figs. 4 and 5).

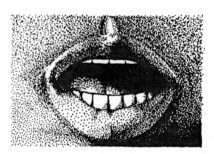

Fig. 4. Lip-positions of Cardinal ɪ and Cardinal a

6.4 A description of the 'Cardinal Vowels' referred to in chapter 5 will illustrate these ways of classifying vowels. The selection of vowels to serve as a cardinal scale has as its basis the fact that some vowels have clear and well-defined qualities, while others have more obscure sounds. The latter are chiefly those which are formed with the tongue in an intermediate vowel-position, not raised markedly at the back or at the front, and not too low down in the mouth. The most typical inter-

[1] I.e. neither spread nor rounded.

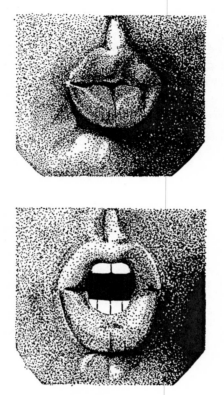

Fig. 5. Lip-positions of Cardinal u and Cardinal ɔ

mediate position gives rise to the sound known as the 'neutral vowel' or 'schwa' (phonetic symbol ə).[1]

6.5 It is from the vowels remote from schwa that it is convenient to select the chief cardinal vowels. Figs. 6 and 7 show approximately their relationships to each other. Cardinal i (no. 1) is the front vowel in forming which the tongue is raised to the highest position it can have consistently with being a vowel, the lips being spread; cardinal ɑ (no. 5) is a sound in forming which the back of the tongue is lowered as far as

[1] The English sound of ə in *about* (phonetically ə'baut) is a characteristic variety of neutral vowel.

15

possible and retracted as far as possible consistently with the sound being a vowel, and in which the lips are not rounded.

6.6 Cardinal e, ε and a (nos. 2, 3 and 4) were chosen so as to form, as well as could be judged, equal degrees of acoustic separation between each vowel and the next in the sequence i, e, ε, a, ɑ. Cardinal ɔ, o and u (nos. 6, 7 and 8) were chosen so as to continue this series of equidistant vowels.

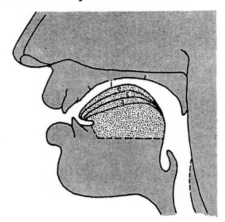

Fig. 6. Approximate tongue-positions of the Cardinal Vowels i, e, ε, a

6.7 The tongue positions of cardinals i, a, ɑ, u shown in Figs. 6 and 7 were drawn from X-ray photographs. The drawings of the remainder are approximate. The lip positions are shown in Figs. 4 and 5, which illustrate lip-positions as follows: (*a*) cardinal i (no. 1), (*b*) cardinal a (no. 4), (*c*) cardinal ɔ (no. 6), (*d*) cardinal u (no. 8).

6.8 Cardinal vowels should, if possible, be learnt from a teacher who knows them. If no teacher is available, the learner must acquire them as best he can with the aid of a gramophone record.[1]

6.9 The values of cardinal vowels cannot be explained to a reader by equating them with vowels of particular languages. The system works the other way round; the vowels of particular

[1] Linguaphone record No. ENG 252–3.

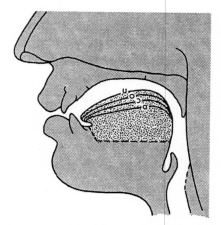

Fig. 7. Approximate tongue-positions of the Cardinal Vowels ɑ, ɔ, o, u

languages have to be identified by their relationships to the cardinal ones. Nevertheless, the beginner may form a certain rough idea of the sort of sounds the cardinal vowels are by likening them to sounds of well-known languages (always remembering, however, that there are usually variations among different speakers of a given language). Thus it may be said that:

6.10 Cardinal 1 (i) is used by many French people in the word *si*.

2 (e) is used by many French people in *thé*.

3 (ɛ) is used by many French people in *même*.

4 (a) is used by many French people in *place*.

5 (ɑ) is nearly what is obtained by taking the lip-rounding away from the English sound of *o* in *hot*.

6 (ɔ) is used by many Germans in *Sonne*.

7 (o) is used by many French people in *rose*.

8 (u) is the sound commonly used by Germans in *gut*.

6.11 There are ten secondary cardinal vowels; the first eight are formed with the same tongue-positions as the eight primary

6. THE CLASSIFICATION OF VOWELS

cardinal vowels, but have different lip-positions.[1] They are numbered 9–16. The remaining two (numbered 17 and 18) have tongue positions intermediate between those of i and u. Cardinal 17 (phonetic symbol ɨ) is said with spread lips; it is similar to one of the Russian ɨ-sounds (see § 12.19). Cardinal 18 (phonetic symbol ʉ or ü) has rounded lips. References to the other secondary cardinal vowels are not needed in this book.

6.12 A comparison of the tongue positions shown in Figs. 6 and 7 shows that the relationships between vowels may be illustrated by dots on a diagram shaped as in Fig. 8.

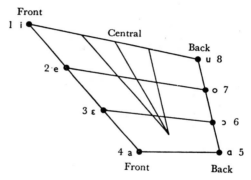

Fig. 8. Diagram illustrating the tongue-positions of the eight primary Cardinal Vowels

6.13 This figure is of an irregular shape because the dots representing the four corner vowels (i, a, ɑ, u) are placed so as to show the relative tongue positions as exhibited in the X-ray photographs. For the purposes of practical teaching it is convenient to substitute the shape illustrated in Fig. 9, which is easier to draw.

[1] Cardinal 9 (phonetic symbol y) is a closely lip-rounded i; it is near to the French vowel in *lune*. Cardinal 10 (phonetic symbol ø) is a closely lip-rounded e; it is near to the French vowel in *peu*. Cardinal 11 (phonetic symbol œ) is derived from ɛ by adding 'open' lip-rounding; its sound has resemblance to that used by French people in *œuf*.

6. THE CLASSIFICATION OF VOWELS

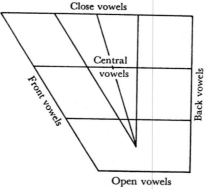

Fig. 9. Conventionalized vowel-diagram

7

HOW TO DESCRIBE CONSONANTS

7.1 Most consonants fall into well-defined classes, classes which are clearly separated from neighbouring classes by differences in place or manner of articulation.

7.2 In describing the consonants of Russian the following terms relating to place of articulation are needed:

bi-labial: formed by the two lips (examples: p, m);[1]

labio-dental: formed by the lower lip against the upper teeth (examples: f, v);

dental: formed by the tip of the tongue against the upper teeth (example: l);

denti-alveolar: formed by the tip of the tongue against the upper teeth and the blade against the teeth-ridge (examples: t, d);

alveolar: formed by the tip or blade of the tongue against the teeth-ridge (examples: s, z);

post-alveolar: formed by the tip of the tongue against the back part of the teeth-ridge (examples: ʃ, ʒ);

palatal: formed by the front of the tongue against the hard palate (example: j);

[1] Unless otherwise indicated, the examples refer to *Russian* sounds.

velar: formed by the back of the tongue against the soft palate (examples: k, g).

7.3   In this book the following terms relating to the manner of forming consonants are needed:

plosive: formed by complete closure of the air-passage during an appreciable time; the air is compressed (generally by action of the lungs) and on release of the closure issues suddenly, making an explosive sound or 'plosion' (example: t);

fricative: formed by narrowing the air channel to such an extent that the air in escaping produces audible friction, i.e. some kind of hissing or buzzing (example: s);

affricate: formed as plosive consonants but with slower separation of the articulating mechanism, so that the corresponding fricative is audible as the separation takes place (example: English sound of *ch* in *chain*);

nasal: formed by a complete closure in the mouth, the soft palate being however lowered so that the air is free to pass out through the nose (example: n, ŋ);[1]

lateral: formed by placing an obstacle in the centre of the air channel, but leaving a free passage for the air on one or both sides of the obstacle (example: l);

rolled: formed by a rapid succession of taps of some elastic organ (example: Italian r);

flapped: formed by the same kind of action as rolled consonants but consisting of one single tap (example: Spanish sound of r in *pero*);

semi-vowel: a voiced gliding sound in which the speech organs start by producing a weakly articulated vowel of comparatively small inherent sonority and immediately change to another sound of equal or greater prominence (example the English sound of *y* in *yard*).

7.4   The terms *labialized, velarized* and *labio-velarized* are explained in chapter 15, the term *palatalized* in chapter 16, and one or two other terms are explained as they arise.

---

[1] ŋ is the phonetic symbol for the English sound of *ng* in *sing*.

8

PRINCIPLES OF TRANSCRIPTION, PHONEMES

8.1 In § 1.6 mention was made of the use of phonetic transcriptions. The student of a spoken foreign language has to learn not only to pronounce the sounds but also 'to use the right sound in the right place' in words and in connected speech. Phonetic transcriptions of words and connected texts help him to do this.

8.2 A phonetic transcription is commonly thought to mean a system of alphabetic writing based on the principle 'one sound one symbol'. A little consideration will, however, show that this rough definition needs modification, and that in practice it is often necessary to introduce conventions which have the effect of utilizing a symbol to denote more than one sound.

8.3 A simple example illustrating the principle is furnished by the k-sounds of English and other languages. It is not difficult to perceive that the k-sounds in the English words *key, curve* and *cot* differ from each other, and one can easily feel that the tongue articulates the three sounds against three different parts of the palate. Yet no one would think it necessary to write these three k's with separate letters in a phonetic transcription; we symbolize all the sounds by the same letter (k), with the convention that the sound used in each case is the one appropriate to the following vowel.

8.4 When, as in this example, two or more distinguishable sounds count for linguistic purposes as if they were one and the same, they are said to belong to a single 'phoneme'.

8.5 A phoneme may be described roughly as a family of sounds in a given language consisting of an important sound of that language together with other related sounds which 'take its place' in particular phonetic contexts. The sounds comprised in a phoneme are called its 'members' or 'allophones'. Thus

21

the three varieties of k mentioned in § 8.3 are three allophones of the English k-phoneme.

8.6 A more striking instance illustrating the phoneme principle is found in the use of the sounds of n and ŋ (§ 7.3) in different languages. In the Italian language n-sounds are very common; ŋ-sounds also occur, but only when k or g follows—positions which n does not occupy in any word. This usage means that the n and ŋ sounds belong to a single phoneme in Italian. It means further that broad (phonemic) writing of the Italian words *banca* and *lungo*, for instance, would be 'banka, 'lungo; to write 'baŋka, 'luŋgo would be a narrow (allophonic) representation of the words.

8.7 n and ŋ sounds also occur in English, but the manner of using them differs from that found in Italian. The use of the ŋ-sounds[1] is not prescribed by phonetic context as it is in Italian, since there are contexts in English which admit both sounds. In particular, both can occur between vowels (e.g. in *sinner* 'sɪnə and *singer* 'sɪŋə) and finally (e.g. in *sin* sɪn and *sing* sɪŋ). These examples show that the sounds do not belong to one phoneme in English, and that therefore they must be represented by separate letters in phonetic transcriptions of our language.

8.8 In Russian, ŋ-type sounds do not occur at all, not even before k or g. Thus банк *bank* is pronounced with an ordinary n-sound: bank.

8.9 It will be seen from the examples in § 8.7 (and from others which will appear later on in the book) that it is phonemes which have the function of differentiating one word from another. Two allophones of a single phoneme are not capable of doing this.[2]

8.10 A system of phonetic transcription may therefore be more properly described as an alphabetic method of writing which

---

[1] We say the 'ŋ-sounds', and not simply 'ŋ', to allow for the slight differences of ŋ-type sound employed when different vowels are adjacent (e.g. in *sing* and *song*).

[2] For detailed information concerning the theory of phonemes readers are referred to D. Jones, *The Phoneme, its Nature and Use* (Heffer, Cambridge). See also K. L. Pike's *Phonemics* (University of Michigan Press).

provides a letter[1] to represent each phoneme of the language to be transcribed, and in which additional symbols are available for indicating allophones when desirable.

8.11 When a transcription represents phonemes only, it is said to be 'broad' or 'phonemic'. When a transcription is such that it represents not only the phonemes of a language but also some of the allophones, it is said to be 'narrow' or 'allophonic'.

8.12 The style of transcription used in this book for representing the pronunciation of Russian is narrow in several respects. We have chosen this style because some of the conventions that would have to be understood in a broad (phonemic) form of notation are complicated and difficult for the learner to remember.

9

DIGRAPHS

9.1 Although systems of phonetic writing have as their basis the principle 'one letter per phoneme' (supplemented in the case of narrow transcriptions by additional letters to represent some of the allophones), cases sometimes arise when it is convenient to denote a phoneme (or a sound) by a sequence of two letters. Such a sequence is called a 'digraph'. Thus it is customary when writing English phonetically to represent the English sounds of *ch* and *j* (as in *chalk, jaw*) by digraphs such as tʃ, dʒ.[2] Similarly in phonetic transcriptions of German it is usual to represent the German sound of *z* (as in *Zahn*) by the digraph ts.

9.2 The purpose of using digraphs is to keep the number of letters as small as may be, and to avoid the introduction of complicated letters which are awkward to write or which may render phonetic texts difficult to read.

---

[1] Or digraph (see chapter 9).
[2] Some transcribers prefer to use single letters (such as the IPA c, ɟ). When the digraph tʃ is used, the sequence t plus ʃ (as in *lightship*) has to be shown by inserting a hyphen—'lait-ʃip.

PART II

THE PHONETICS OF RUSSIAN

10

TYPES OF RUSSIAN PRONUNCIATION

10.1 There are different types of Russian pronunciation, just as there are different types of English pronunciation. In a book of this kind, intended for the English-speaking student of Russian, it would be inappropriate to describe various types of Russian pronunciation. It is necessary to describe one type of pronunciation only and the type of pronunciation chosen is that which might be called 'contemporary standard'. It is the 'average' pronunciation of the educated inhabitants of Moscow or Leningrad and has no features which could be said to be characteristic of any particular district. This type of pronunciation is taken as the educated 'norm' throughout the Soviet Union and has been described by R. I. Avanesov[1] in the Soviet Union, for example, and, in this country, by the late S. Boyanus.[2]

10.2 A few features of this type of pronunciation call for comment here. First, in this type of pronunciation the letter щ has the phonetic value of ʃtʃ (a 'palatalized ʃ' followed by a sound similar to tʃ, in which the stop element, represented by t, is weak) or ʃʃ (a long 'palatalized ʃ'). Either of these pronunciations of щ is regarded as correct, but it is customary for any one speaker to use only one of them. Certain combinations of letters may also, in certain circumstances, have these alternative pronunciations. More details are given in §§ 18.87–94. Secondly, in one variant of this type of pronunciation, the sounds ɛ and e occur only in stressed syllables. In unstressed syllables they are replaced by the sounds ɩ and ᴉ, according to rules which are given below (§ 23.18). This type of pronunciation is known as иканье ('ikənji) and is taken as the norm in this book. In another variant of this type of pronunciation sounds of the e-type do occur in unstressed syllables. This variant is known as

---

[1] In his *Русское литературное произношение* (Moscow, 1964).
[2] In his *Russian Pronunciation* (Lund Humphries and Co.; London, 1955).

éканье ('jɛkənjʲ) and further reference is made to it below (§§ 12.72–6). Reference is also made below (§§ 18.96, 97) to the possible occurrence of зз (a long 'palatalized з'), in addition to зз, as the pronunciation of the letter-combinations зж and жж in certain circumstances.

10.3 With these provisions, it may be said that the type of pronunciation described in this book is uniform. The description is, moreover, based on what might be called a fairly careful manner of speaking: it does not generally take into account features of pronunciation which may occur when speech is rapid.

11

GENERAL NOTES ON THE RUSSIAN VOWELS AND CONSONANTS

11.1 A striking feature of the vowel system of Russian is that while there are only five vowel phonemes (which may be represented in broad transcription by the symbols i, e, a, o, u) many more than five different vowel sounds can easily be perceived. This is because the phonemes comprise an unusual number of allophones. This is particularly true of the phonemes i and a.

11.2 The phonetic contexts which determine the use of the various allophones may be complicated and difficult for the learner to remember at first. They consist in the main of the natures of adjoining consonants and of the degrees of stress (or more precisely of the location of the accent; see chapter 24).

11.3 To help the learner to become familiar with the working of these phonetic contexts we have found it advisable to make use in part of a 'narrow' notation for the vowels, indicating the most noteworthy allophones by special symbols. Thus, throughout the book we make use of four symbols for members of the i-phoneme (i, ι, ɨ, ʲ), two for members of the e-phoneme (e, ɛ), four for members of the a-phoneme (a, æ, ʌ, ə), two for members of the o-phoneme (o, ö) and two for members of the u-phoneme (u, ü). When discussion of special points occurs, a few further symbols are used.

11.4 The Russian consonant phonemes do not show such striking allophonic variation. By and large it is true to say that each of the Russian consonant phonemes has several members, determined by the nature of the surrounding sounds, as are the k's of English mentioned above (§ 8.3). However, these allophones differ from each other only slightly for the most part and, with few exceptions, will arise automatically if the surrounding sounds are formed correctly. Attention is drawn to these exceptions where necessary in the description of Russian consonants in the relevant chapters.

12

THE RUSSIAN VOWELS IN DETAIL

The Russian i-phoneme

12.1 The Russian i-phoneme has four easily discernible members: two stressed members, i and ᵻ, and two unstressed, ι and ɩ. A fifth member, stressed ɪ, is also described in this book (§ 12.11).

i

12.2 *Formation of the Russian sound* i
   (1) *height of tongue:* nearly close (§ 6.2);
   (2) *point of tongue which is highest:* centre of front (§ 2.6);
   (3) *position of lips:* spread or, in a more rapid colloquial style, neutral.

12.3 i is a close, front unrounded vowel.

12.4 The Russian sound i is about the same as the English sound of *ee* in the pronunciation of those who do not use a diphthong for the English sound.[1] The Russian i is a pure vowel and must be carefully distinguished from the common diph-

[1] In pronouncing a diphthong the tongue does not remain in one position throughout the duration of the sound but starts in one position and proceeds to another.

thongal pronunciations of English *ee*, the most typical of which is ʊi. A diphthong similar to this occurs in Russian in unstressed positions, that is, ɪj (see §§ 14.8, 11).

12.5 English speakers whose diphthongization of the i-sound in *see* is only slight may obtain the pure Russian i by taking care to keep the tongue, lips and lower jaw motionless throughout the sound. They should repeat the vowel a number of times (i i i i i...), looking at the mouth in a mirror to make certain there is no motion of the lips and lower jaw.

12.6 Those who pronounce English *ee* as ʊi or some such diphthong would do well to learn ɪ̵ (see § 12.11), before learning the Russian i. A slight relaxation of muscular tension will then suffice to produce the Russian i. Here again the student should look at his mouth in a mirror, to make certain that there is no motion of tongue, lips or lower jaw during the pronunciation of i. While testing for diphthongization of i, however, he must be careful not to set up the habit of unduly prolonging the Russian i (see §§ 24.41, 42).

12.7 The tendency of English people to diphthongize i is particularly noticeable in final position. Special care must therefore be taken to avoid diphthongizing the i in such Russian words as tɾi три (three), dɲi дни (days), which must not sound like tɾʊi, dɲʊi.

12.8 Speakers of Scottish English usually have no trouble in achieving the Russian sound i, since they do not normally diphthongize i, as do many speakers of Southern (RP) English.

12.9 The Russian sound i occurs only in stressed syllables.[1] The only consonants that can precede it are the soft consonants but it does not occur *between* two soft consonants (here the sound ɪ̵ occurs; see § 12.11). It occurs initially only after a pause in speech, no matter how slight, or after a soft consonant. Hence it occurs initially in words spoken in isolation. It is represented only by the letter и.

---

[1] It is to be understood that all statements about Russian sounds in this book, unless otherwise stipulated, refer only to the style of pronunciation taken as a basis for the present description (see §§ 10.1–3).

12.10 *Words illustrating the sound* i

'p̡ivə	пиво	(beer)
b̡il	бил	(struck)
'ţinə	тина	(slime)
'şilə	сила	(strength)
tʃin	чин	(rank)
ķit	кит	(whale)
tɾi	три	(three)
d̡ɲi	дни	(days)
'imə	имя	(name)
'ivə	ива	(willow)
isp	изб	(huts, *gen. pl.*)
isk	иск	(lawsuit)
il	ил	(silt)
i̡m	ильм	(elm)

i˄

12.11 This is practically cardinal i, the closest possible variety of i (see Fig. 6). It is a variety in which the tongue is raised higher than in the i-sound described in the preceding paragraphs. Some writers on phonetics would call it a particularly 'tense' i. In discussing points of Russian phonetic theory the sound may be written i˄ (˄ signifies 'with tongue raised higher'); in the phonetic transcriptions given here it is written simply i and is to be understood as occurring only between two palatalized consonants in stressed syllables.

12.12 The sound i˄ does not occur in English. It is heard in French as the normal i-sound of that language.

12.13 English people who have difficulty in making a very close i—and there are many of them—should try the expedient of pronouncing a continuous fricative j (not the ordinary semi-vowel j), holding it on for several seconds; the friction must be heard continuously throughout the sound. This fricative consonant should be practised till it can be said without using much force of the breath; then the amount of friction may be diminished; when the friction is so diminished as to be practically inaudible in comparison with the sound of the voice, a very close i, as in ḷiʈ лить (to pour), will result.

12.14 Some English people are able to acquire a very close i by trying to pronounce an i-sound with considerable muscular tension of the tongue. It is a good plan to try to stiffen and push forward the outside of the throat, placing the finger about half-way between the chin and the larynx to test it.

12.15 The sound iᴸ is represented only by the letter и.

12.16 *Words illustrating the sound* iᴸ

ɲiʈ	пить	(to drink)
ɦiʈ	бить	(to strike)
ḷiʈ	лить	(to pour)
ɲiʈ	нить	(thread)
ʂʈiḷ	стиль	(style)
ʃɲiḷ	шпиль	(spire)
ʂiɳ	синь	(blue colour)

ɨ

12.17 *Formation of the Russian sound* ɨ
  (1) *height of tongue:* close;
  (2) *point of tongue which is highest:* a point approximately at the division between front and back *or* a point further back than this (see below);
  (3) *position of lips:* spread or, in a more rapid colloquial style, neutral.

12.18 ɨ is a close, non-front, unrounded vowel.

12.19 Two different varieties of ɨ can easily be discerned. In one variety the point of the tongue which is highest is in the front part of the area which is designated 'central' on the vowel quadrilateral (Fig. 8). This variety occurs after dental, alveolar, post-alveolar and velar consonants (t, d, n, s, z, r, ts, ʃ, ʒ, k, ɡ and x). Since this variety occurs after a greater number of different consonants than the other it may, as the occasion arises, be described as the principle variety of ɨ.

12.20 When it is both preceded *and* followed by one of the consonants listed above the sound ɨ is produced somewhat further forward in the mouth. This is particularly noticeable when both the surrounding consonants are dental or alveolar, as in sɨn сын (son), tɨn тын (fence). Following soft consonants also produce this fronting effect on ɨ.

12.21 The other variety occurs after labial and labio-dental consonants (p, b, m, f and v) and also after l. In this variety the part of the tongue which is highest is at the back of the central area. In discussing fine points of Russian pronunciation this variety of ɨ may be symbolized by ɨ˗ (signifying a retracted ɨ) but this symbol is not used in the transcriptions in this book. This variety of ɨ is slightly diphthongized, beginning at a point even further back than ɨ˗, almost as far back as ɯ (an 'unrounded u') and moving immediately towards the ɨ˗ position.

12.22 When ɨ˗ occurs at the end of a word, the tongue moves even further forward, through the position of ɨ˗ to a truly central or even pre-central position, so that a very narrow transcription of the sound would be ᵘᶸˑɨ˗ɨ˖.[1] This fronting effect is also produced by a following soft consonant.

12.23 Sounds of the ɨ-type are difficult for most speakers of English, since in most varieties of English there is no sound of this type. In London dialectal speech, however, a sound of the ɨ-type occurs as the first part of the diphthong which occurs in such words as *boot, soon* (bɨüt, sɨün).[2] If the learner has this kind of diphthong he may use the first part of it as a means of achieving the different varieties of Russian ɨ-sound. He will, however, have to raise the tongue slightly in order to achieve the stressed ɨ-sounds of Russian.

12.24 For others, the following ways of learning Russian ɨ are suggested. Spread the lips as for i and then try, *while still keeping the lips spread*, to say u (the vowel in *too, moon*, etc.). It is essential to keep the lips in the i-position during this exercise; they must not move in the least degree. It will be found helpful to watch the lips in a mirror.

[1] The symbol ˖ means 'fronted', i.e. pronounced somewhat further forward in the mouth than the symbol to which it is attached normally indicates.
[2] The symbol ü represents a fronted (or 'advanced') u (see §§ 12.179–181).

12. THE RUSSIAN VOWELS IN DETAIL

12.25 If the learner's variety of English u-sound is one with advanced tongue-position,[1] the result of the above exercise will be to produce a sound of the ɨ-type. If his English u-sound is a true back vowel, the vowel resulting from this exercise will be ɯ ('unrounded u'). To reach a central ɨ from this, the learner must modify the sound in the direction of i. He should practise doing this in the presence of the teacher, who will tell him when he has achieved the required sound.

12.26 Another method is to start from the English word *book*, keeping the tongue in the position for the learner's normal pronunciation of this word but having the lips spread, instead of rounded. The result of this exercise will be a sound very near to an 'unstressed variety of ɨ' (see §§ 12.41–43). If the tongue is then raised nearer the palate (or, as some would put it, if the vowel is pronounced more 'tensely'), the resulting sound will be very near to or identical with the retracted variety of ɨ which occurs after labial consonants (see § 12.21). Central and pre-central varieties of ɨ can then be achieved by moving the tongue slightly in the direction of i.

12.27 It will be found a good exercise to practise alternating i and ɯ, and to try to make a sound which is acoustically half-way between the two. The result will be what might be called a 'cardinal' ɨ, from which varieties of Russian ɨ can be reached.

12.28 The principle of *vowel pitches* will be found of use by some in connexion with the acquisition of Russian ɨ. Let the learner whisper an u, an ɯ and an i in succession and note the differences in the musical pitches of the vowels. If his u is cardinal, he will probably find it to have a pitch about E. Cardinal ɯ will be found to have a whisper-pitch almost an octave above this, i.e. about E♭. Cardinal i has a

[1] Many Scots speakers pronounce u with quite an advanced tongue-position.

pitch in the neighbourhood of G . A central ɨ has a

pitch half-way between the pitches of ɯ and i, i.e. about

B . The retracted Russian ɨ˕ (§ 12.21) has a pitch

about three semi-tones below this, i.e. about A♭ .

12.29   The learner may make use of these facts in the following way. Having practised whispering u, ɯ and i until he can hear the pitches, he learns to whisper a scale of notes between ɯ and i; he must be careful in doing this to keep his lips spread.[1] He can then stop on any required note, keep his mouth perfectly still and produce voice. The result will be one of the vowel-sounds intermediate between ɯ and i.

12.30   The Russian sounds of the ɨ-type occur only in stressed syllables. They are always preceded by a hard consonant. In a sentence, such a hard consonant may be the final consonant of the preceding word, provided there is no pause between that word and the following word.

12.31   The sound ɨ is written by the letter ы and also by the letter и (after ш, ж, ц within a word and also after any consonant letter which represents a hard consonant at the end of a preceding word, where the words are 'closely bound').

12.32   *Words illustrating different varieties of* ɨ

tɨ	ТЫ	(you)
dɨm	ДЫМ	(smoke)
ʒɨl	ЖИЛ	(lived)
pʲiʃɨ	ПИШИ	(write, *imper.*)
sɨn	СЫН	(son)
tɨn	ТЫН	(fence)

[1] If he rounds his lips, he will get clearer pitches, but they will belong to other sounds, that is, sounds on the scale u–ü–y (see § 6.11).

krɨs	крыс	(rats, *gen. pl.*)
tsɨrk	цирк	(circus)
'dɨnə	дыня	(melon)
ʒɨʒn̩	жизнь	(life)
ʃɨț	шить	(to sew)
rɨț	рыть	(to dig)
bɨt	быт	(mode of life)
pɨl	пыл	(ardour)
bɨl	был	(was)
mɨt	мыт	(strangles, moult)
vɨ	вы	(you)
mɨ	мы	(we)
bɨț	быть	(to be)
pɨļ	пыль	(dust)
mɨț	мыть	(to wash)
's ɨgərˌɪm	с Игорем	(with Igor)

ɪ

12.33 *Formation of the Russian sound* ɪ
  (1) *height of tongue:* nearer to half-close than to close;
  (2) *point of tongue which is highest:* a point between centre of front and the point of division between front and back;
  (3) *position of lips:* spread or, in a more rapid, colloquial style, neutral.
Some writers on phonetics would call this sound a 'lax' i.

12.34 ɪ is a half-close, retracted-front, unrounded vowel.

12.35 Russian ɪ is similar to the most usual Southern English 'short' sound of *i* (as in *sit*). It is somewhat more i-like than this English sound.

12.36 The Russian sound ɪ does not present difficulty to most English people, because it is practically identical with the vowel most frequently heard in English words such as *sit, pin*. Speakers of dialectal English who use a 'central' vowel approaching ɨ (as sometimes in Scotland) or a vowel of the e-type in these English words must learn to use a more i-like sound in Russian.

12.37 When ɪ occurs finally in Russian, as in 'fskorɪ вскоре

36

(soon), 'poşɩ после (after), it has the same value as in other positions. Many English people are liable to substitute an e-like or even an ɛ-like sound in such cases (as they do in the final syllables of such English words as *pity, very*). It is also necessary to distinguish final ɩ from final ɩj; compare ʌ'ʃeɲɩ олени (stags) with ʌ'ʃeɲɩj оленей (of stags).

12.38 The sound ɩ occurs only in unstressed syllables. The only consonants that can precede it are the soft consonants. It occurs initially only after a pause in speech, no matter how slight, or after a word ending in a soft consonant. Hence it occurs initially in words spoken in isolation. It is represented by the letters и, e and э. In positions before the stress the letter я also represents ɩ and so does the letter a, if preceded by ч or щ.[1]

12.39 *Words illustrating the sound ɩ*

ɩʧ'ʧi	идти	(to go)
ɩz'bɨ	избы	(hut, *gen. sing.*)
ʧɩs'ḳi	тиски	(vice)
prɩ'tʃinə	причина	(cause)
pɩ'ʃɨ	пиши	(write, *imper.*)
'bɨʃɩ	были	(were)
'ʒɨʒɲɩ	жизни	(life, *gen. sing.*)
'jezdɩʧ	ездить	(to travel)
şɩmɩ'na	семена	(seeds)
pɩrɩmɩ'ʃi	перемели	(grind, *imper.*)
'poʃɩ	поле	(field)
'ḅerɩk	берег	(shore)
ɩʃɩk'tritʃɩs(t)və	электричество	(electricity)
ɩʃɩ'vatər	элеватор	(grain-elevator)
jɩ'zɨk	язык	(tongue)
pɩ'ʧi	пяти	(five, *gen.*)
tʃɩ'sɨ	часы	(watch, clock)
dva tʃɩ'sa	два часа	(two o'clock)
ʃtʃɩ'şĺiyɩts	счастливец	(lucky man)
ʃtʃɩ'dɩʧ	щадить	(to spare)

[1] Except in such loan-words as чарльстон tʃarĺs'ton (charleston), чартизм tʃar'ʧizm (chartism), чартист tʃar'ʧist (chartist).

12. THE RUSSIAN VOWELS IN DETAIL

12.40 A closer variety of ι than that described above may be heard as the first part of the diphthong ιj. This is most evident where -ий is written at the end of words, as in 'ʂredɲιj средний (average), 'armιj армий (armies, *gen. pl.*). At normal conversational speed, however, this final diphthong is not usually pronounced. Instead a pure vowel of the ι-type is pronounced and this may become very i-like: 'ʂredɲι·, 'armι·. In such a case a vowel of the ι-type (*sci.* ι·) is represented by two letters -ий. The question of this diphthong ιj is discussed again under *Diphthongs* (see § 14.13).

ɩ

12.41 *Formation of the Russian sound* ɩ

(1) *height of tongue:* nearer to half-close than close;

(2) *point of tongue which is highest:* the point of division between front and back;

(3) *position of lips:* spread or, in a more rapid, colloquial style of pronunciation, neutral.

12.42 ɩ is a half-close, central, unrounded vowel.

12.43 This sound may be described as a variety of ɨ in which the tongue takes up a somewhat lower position than in the pronunciation of the stressed varieties of ɨ. Some writers would call this sound a 'lax' ɨ. After the affricate consonant ts some speakers pronounce an even more open vowel, approaching the vowel ə. A similar sound may also be heard in very weakly stressed syllables.

12.44 The sound ɩ resembles the sound of *e* in the German word *bitte*, in the pronunciation of many native speakers of German. A very similar sound is heard in some dialectal varieties of English in a diphthong of the type ɩö.[1] In London dialect, for instance, *two boots* is pronounced ttö bɩöts (təö bəöts may also be heard).

12.45 The vowel ɩ may be acquired

(1) by aiming at a sound half-way between a (central) stressed ɨ and ə (the vowel represented by *a* in *about*), or

---

[1] ɷ is an 'advanced and lowered' u. ö is a more advanced (*sci.* central) variety of this.

(2) by pronouncing ɨ in a lax manner, i.e. by reducing the amount of muscular tension of the tongue, or

(3) by pronouncing the vowel of the English word *book* with spread lips (see § 12.26) and then moving the tongue slightly further forward.

12.46 The sound ɪ occurs only in unstressed syllables. It is always preceded by a hard consonant, which may be the final consonant of a preceding word, provided that there is no pause between the two words (cf. § 12.30).

12.47 The sound ɪ is represented in spelling by ы and э, and also, after ш, ж and ц, by и and е. It is also represented after other hard consonants by и in some abbreviated compounds (such as госиздат—see below) and by и and э at the beginning of a word when the preceding word ends in a hard consonant and there is no pause intervening between the two words.

12.48   *Words illustrating the sound* ɪ

bɪ'la	была	(was, *fem.*)
dɪ'mok	дымок	(puff of smoke)
dɪ'ra	дыра	(hole)
klɪ'ķi	клыки	(tusks)
bɪ'ķi	быки	(bulls)
'krɪsɪ	крысы	(rats)
'dɪrɪ	дыры	(holes)
'ʒonɪ	жены	(wives)
'oftsɪ	овцы	(sheep, *pl.*)
sɪkʌ'nomɪʦ	сэкономить	(to economize, *pfv.*)
ʃt'p̡i	шипи	(hiss, *imper.*)
ʒt'ɣi	живи	(live, *imper.*)
tsɪyɪ̡ɪ'zatstjə	цивилизация	(civilization)
'p̡laʃɪt	пляшет	(dances)
ʒt'na	жена	(wife)
tsɪ'na	цена	(price)
s ɪ'vanəm	с Иваном	(with John)
k ɪ'vanu	к Ивану	(towards John)
ʌt ɪ̡ɪ'vatərə	от элеватора	(from the grain-elevator)

39

gəstz'dat   Госиздат   (State Publishing House)

The Russian e-phoneme

12.49 In the type of pronunciation described in this book (иканье 'ikənjɩ—see § 10.2) the Russian e-phoneme has only stressed members: e and sounds of the ɛ-type. The use of these members of the e-phoneme is determined by the factors stated in §§ 12.52, 62, 69. In another type of pronunciation unstressed members of the e-phoneme occur. Some further remarks on this type of pronunciation are made below (§§ 12.71–6). The sounds of the ɛ-type are described first.

ɛ˔

12.50 *Formation of the Russian sound* ɛ˔

(1) *height of tongue:* about midway between half-close and half-open;

(2) *point of tongue which is highest:* centre of front;

(3) *position of lips:* spread or, in a more rapid colloquial style, neutral.

12.51 ɛ˔ is a front, unrounded vowel, midway between half-close and half-open.

12.52 The Russian ɛ˔-sound is much the same as the 'average' Southern English vowel in *get, bed*. It differs from the English vowel, however, in having a slight diphthongal quality in certain positions (§ 12.56). The sound ɛ˔ occurs only after soft consonants and is never followed by a soft consonant.

ɛ

12.53 *Formation of the Russian sound* ɛ

(1) *height of tongue:* half-open or very slightly below half-open;

(2) *point of tongue which is highest:* centre of front, or a point just behind centre of front;

(3) *position of lips:* spread or, in a more rapid colloquial style, neutral.

12.54 ɛ is a half-open, front unrounded vowel.[1]

---

[1] It is about Cardinal Vowel no. 3 (Fig. 8), or very slightly lower than this.

12. THE RUSSIAN VOWELS IN DETAIL

12.55   The Russian ɛ-sound is much the same as the first part of the diphthong heard in the Southern English pronunciation of the word *air*. The sound ɛ never occurs after soft consonants and never before soft consonants. Some writers on Russian phonetics consider that it is slightly retracted from a fully front position. This is most evident after the consonants ʃ, ʒ and ts.

12.56   Both Russian ɛ˔ and Russian ɛ are often slightly diphthongal, moving in the direction of ə (the vowel represented by *a* in *about*).[1] This diphthongal quality should not be so exaggerated that a diphthong of the nature of the English diphthong ɛə (as in *air*) results.

12.57   The diphthongal quality of ɛ˔ and ɛ is most evident in open syllables.[2] In closed syllables,[2] the diphthongal quality is very slight and may be entirely absent.

12.58   If the English-speaking learner is from the South of England it is probable that the vowel he pronounces in such words as *get*, *bed*, is very close to the Russian ɛ˔ (apart from the diphthongal quality of the latter). To acquire the Russian ɛ he must try to make his vowel in *get* more open. The student from the North of England may have a more open vowel in *get* than the Southern English speaker. This will be near to Russian ɛ. To acquire the Russian ɛ˔ he must make his normal English ɛ more close. The Scots speaker is likely to have a vowel in *get*, *bed* as close as that of the Southern English speaker, or even closer. Starting from this vowel, he will have to aim at a slightly more open vowel for Russian ɛ˔ and an even more open vowel for Russian ɛ.

12.59   It is not too difficult for English speakers to acquire the pronunciation of Russian ɛ-sounds in closed syllables, as in ŋɛ˔t нет (no). When, however, the Russian ɛ-sounds occur in open syllables, as in 'dɛ˔lə дело (affair), English learners may be apt to replace it by the diphthong they use in such words as *day* dei/dɛi/dɛe. It is particularly important to avoid this mistake.

[1] Another way of putting this is to say that ɛ˔ and ɛ have an 'ə off-glide'.
[2] An open syllable is one that ends in a vowel; a closed syllable is one that ends in a consonant.

12. THE RUSSIAN VOWELS IN DETAIL

Russian ε-sounds are not diphthongs of the ei/εi/εe-type. Moreover, a diphthong similar to ei exists in Russian and must not be confused with sounds of the ε-type.

12.60 To avoid the use of a diphthong of the ei-type for the Russian ε-sounds, the learner should concentrate his attention on his vowel in *get* and learn to isolate it. He must be able to hold on to this vowel without making the slightest change in the position of his tongue, lips or lower jaw. He should repeat the sound a number of times (εεεεε...), looking at his mouth in a mirror, so as to make certain that there is no motion. He must always bear in mind that the only Russian words containing anything approaching his vowel in *day* are those which are written in this book with ej, as in dι'ţej детей (children, *gen. pl.*).

12.61 Most Scots and Northern English speakers do not pronounce a diphthong in such words as *day, name* and do not therefore require to perform the exercise described in the preceding paragraph.

12.62 Both ε‌ɪ and ε occur only in stressed syllables. The Russian sound ε‌ɪ occurs only after soft consonants and is never followed by a soft consonant. The sound ε occurs only initially or after a hard consonant and is never followed by a soft consonant. The sound ε‌ɪ is represented by the letter e, the sound ε also by the letter e and, initially, the letter э.

12.63 *Words illustrating (a) the sound ε‌ɪ; (b) the sound ε*[1]

(a)	ţε	те	(those)
	fşε	все	(all)
	v‿u'm̩ε	в уме	(in the mind)
	'd̪ɛlə	дело	(affair)
	'ɣɛrə	вера	(belief)
	ŋɛt	нет	(no)
	ţεx	тех	(those, *gen.*)
	jɛl	ел	(ate, *masc.*)
	jɛm	ем	(I eat)
	jɛst	ест	(eats)

[1] In the transcriptions the symbol ε is used both for ε and for ε‌ɪ.

42

	ɣɛrx	верх	(top)
	'm̥ɛstə	место	(place)
(b)	'ɛtət	этот	(this, *nom. sing. masc.*)
	'ɛxə	эхо	(echo)
	'ɛrə	эра	(era)
	ʃɛst	шест	(pole)
	ʒɛst	жест	(gesture)
	tsɛl	цел	(whole)

e

12.64 *Formation of the Russian sound* e

(1) *height of tongue:* half close;

(2) *point of tongue which is highest:* centre of front;

(3) *position of lips:* spread or, in a more rapid, colloquial style, neutral.

12.65 e is a half-close, front, unrounded vowel.

12.66 Russian e is about Cardinal Vowel no. 2 (see Fig. 8). There is no sound like it in educated Southern English.[1] The sound is a pure vowel and it must be carefully distinguished from diphthongs of the types ei, ɛi, which are commonly used in such English words as *day*. Diphthongs of the type ei exist in Russian in addition to the pure vowel e (§§ 14.8, 11).

12.67 The acquisition of this sound is often a matter of considerable difficulty to the Southern English speaker. One way of learning it is to start from the normal Southern English ɛ, as in *get*, and then to aim at a sound which is much more i-like in acoustic effect than ɛ is. Great care must be taken to avoid substituting one of the numerous diphthongs heard in such English words as *day*, *name* (e.g. ei, ɛi, or ɛe). The learner should look at his mouth in a mirror while practising the Russian sound e, to satisfy himself that there is no motion whatever of tongue, lips or lower jaw. The Russian word for 'day' is ɟɛɲ; it must not be made to sound like ɟeiɲ or ɟɛiɲ.

12.68 In initial position Russian e may be slightly retracted

[1] For those who know French it may be of help to know that Russian e is about the same as French '*e*-acute'.

43

from a fully front position. After one of the consonants ʃ, ʒ and ts, this slight retraction from a fully front position is more discernible.

12.69 The sound e occurs only in stressed position. It is always followed by a soft consonant. The sound is represented by the letter e and, in initial position, by the letter э.

12.70 *Words illustrating the sound* e

jeḷ	ель	(fir-tree)
jeṣṭ	есть	(there is)
ṣeṣṭ	сесть	(to sit down)
d̪yeᶉ	дверь	(door)
ᶉetʃ[1]	речь	(speech)
d̪eɳ	день	(day)
p̪eṭ	петь	(to sing)
tʃeṣṭ	честь	(honour)
'eṭɪ	эти	(these)
'eṭɪkə	этика	(ethics)
ʃeṣṭ	шесть	(six)
ʒeṣṭ	жесть	(tin)
tseḷ	цель	(aim)

Unstressed e

12.71 It can be seen from some of the words illustrating the sound ɪ that this sound occurs in unstressed syllables where the orthography has the letter e (§§ 12.38, 39). These words illustrate a feature of the type of pronunciation described in this book known as иканье 'ikənjɪ, in which the phoneme e is replaced in unstressed positions by members of the phoneme i, namely the sound ɪ initially and after soft consonants, or the sound ᵻ after hard consonants. The phonemes a and o are also affected by the phenomenon of иканье 'ikənjɪ, a fuller description of which is given in chapter 23.

12.72 There is, however, another type of pronunciation, which is described by some Soviet phoneticians[2] and which is taught

---

[1] tʃ is a soft consonant (§§ 16.2 and 19.20, 21, 24).

[2] E.g. R. I. Avanesov.

in Russian schools, and which does not have the feature of иканье ˈikənjɪ. This type of pronunciation has the feature known as еканье ˈjɛkənjɪ and is distinguished by the fact that members of the phoneme e *do* occur in unstressed positions. In other words the phoneme e is not replaced by members of the phoneme i in unstressed positions. Moreover, where, in the иканье ˈikənjɪ type of pronunciation, the phonemes a and o are, in certain unstressed positions, replaced by members of the i-phoneme, they are replaced in the еканье ˈjɛkənjɪ type of pronunciation by unstressed members of the e-phoneme.

12.73 In this type of pronunciation, therefore, unstressed ɪ and unstressed ɪ are distinguished from unstressed members of the e-phoneme. After soft consonants the unstressed member of the e-phoneme is a sound of the e-type but is retracted from the fully front position. After hard consonants and initially the unstressed member of the e-phoneme is a sound of the ɛ-type but is not as open as stressed ɛ and is retracted from the front position. It may help the learner to think of these unstressed members of the e-phoneme as a short, lax e with an ɪ-like quality after soft consonants and as a short, lax ɛ with an ɪ-like quality after hard consonants and initially.

12.74 The distinction between unstressed ɪ and ɪ on the one hand and unstressed members of the e-phoneme on the other hand is most clearly heard in immediately pretonic syllables, thus prɪˈdaʦ придать (to add to) but prɛˈdaʦ[1] предать (to betray). The distinction can however be heard in positions further removed from the stress, as in tʃɪstʌˈta чистота (cleanliness) but tʃɛˈstʌˈta частота (frequency).[2]

12.75 It must be said that at normal conversational speed the distinction between unstressed members of the i-phoneme and unstressed members of the e-phoneme tends to disappear and the иканье ˈikənjɪ type of pronunciation dominates, particularly in positions which are several syllables away from the

---

[1] The symbol eʰ represents a retracted e.
[2] In иканье ˈikənjɪ pronunciation, both придать and предать are pronounced prɪˈdaʦ and both чистота and частота are pronounced tʃɪstʌˈta.

stressed syllable. This mingling of the иканье 'ikənjʋ and еканье 'jɛkənjʋ types of pronunciation appears to be indefinable, depending as it does on various factors, such as speed of pronunciation, location of the stressed syllables, etc. Considerable research would be necessary before a definitive statement about the mingling of the two types of pronunciation could be made, if any at all could be made. It is for this reason that the authors of this book decided to take as the basis for their description the uniform иканье 'ikənjʋ type of pronunciation.

12.76 Learners who wish to adopt the еканье 'jɛkənjʋ type of pronunciation must avoid making their unstressed members of the e-phoneme too e-like or ɛ-like. On the other hand, those who adopt the иканье 'ikənjʋ type of pronunciation must avoid making their ʋ too like stressed i and their ɩ too like stressed ɨ.

The Russian a-phoneme

12.77 The Russian a-phoneme has three easily discernible members in stressed position (symbolized in this book by a, æ and ɑ·) and two easily discernible members in unstressed positions (symbolized by ʌ and ə). Their use is determined by the considerations stated in §§ 12.83, 92, 98, 105, 112, 113, 117, 118.

a

12.78 *Formation of the Russian sound* a
  (1) *height of tongue:* open;
  (2) *point of tongue which is highest:* a point a little further back than centre of front;
  (3) *position of lips:* neutral.

12.79 a is an open, front, unrounded vowel.

12.80 The Russian a-sound lies between the usual Southern English vowels in *man* (mæn) and *calm* (kɑ:m). It is near the 'average' values of the first elements of the English diphthongs ai and au (as in *high* (hai) and *how* (hau)).

12.81 Some English speakers use a sound not far from Russian a in words like *calm, father*. Such a pronunciation is typical of many Scots speakers of English. The Russian a has a tongue-position a little further back than the most usual Northern English vowel in *man* (Cardinal Vowel no. 4, see Fig. 8). Some of those English speakers who have in words like *calm, father* a vowel which is nearer to Cardinal Vowel no. 5 than to Russian a, may have approximately the Russian a in a certain class of words of which *glass, plant* are typical. If they have not, they may learn to produce this Russian sound a by aiming at a sound more a-like or (if they do not know cardinal a) more æ-like, than their vowel in *calm*.

12.82　Above all, English speakers must avoid substituting æ for Russian a in closed syllables, as in tak так (so), brat брат (brother). They must avoid substituting a sound of the ɑ type in open syllables, as in dva два (two), 'pravə право (right).

12.83　The sound a occurs only in stressed syllables. There are two stressed positions where it does not occur. First, it does not occur between two soft consonants. Here the sound æ occurs (see § 12.92). Secondly, it does not occur either initially or after a hard consonant if it is followed by the hard consonant l. Here the sound ɑ˖ occurs (see § 12.98).

12.84　When a is preceded by a soft consonant or is followed by a soft consonant it is slightly advanced, its quality lying between 'normal' a and the sound æ. In these positions it is approximately Cardinal Vowel no. 4.

12.85　The sound a is represented by the letters a and я.

12.86　*Words illustrating the sound* a

at	ад	(hell)
'atəm	атом	(atom)
da	да	(yes)
dva	два	(two)
bɪ'la	была	(was, *fem.*)
kak	как	(how)
dar	дар	(gift)
ʒar	жар	(heat)
ʃak	шаг	(step)
mɪ'ɲa	меня	(me, *gen. and acc.*)
tɪ'ḇa	тебя	(you, *gen. and acc.*)

ɥas	вяз	(elm)
'm̦asə	мясо	(meat)
'm̦atə	мята	(mint)
'ʈagə	тяга	(draught)
maʈ	мать	(mother)
maʂ	мазь	(ointment)
znaʈ	знать	(to know)
ʒaļ	жаль	(it's a pity)

æ

12.87 *Formation of the Russian sound* æ

(1) *height of tongue:* about half-way between half-open and open;

(2) *point of tongue which is highest:* centre of front;

(3) *position of lips:* neutral.

12.88 æ is a front vowel, half-way between half-open and open, with unrounded lips.

12.89 Russian æ is very similar to the most usual Southern English vowel in *man, bad,* etc. It should not, however, be made long or diphthongized as this vowel is in English by some speakers, i.e. it must not become æː or æə as in mæːn, bæːd, mæən, bæəd. Nor must it be made too ɛ-like.

12.90 Northern English speakers and others who use a vowel near to Cardinal a (Cardinal Vowel no. 4) should aim at a sound slightly more ɛ-like than their normal a. If, however, they find difficulty in pronouncing æ they may use their normal a, which is near enough to the Russian æ.

12.91 English speakers who normally use æ in *man, bad,* etc., must be careful never to use æ in Russian other than in cases of the type described in § 12.92 and illustrated in § 12.93.

12.92 The sound æ occurs only in stressed syllables. It is always preceded *and* followed by a soft consonant. It is represented by the letter я and also, after the letters ч and щ,[1] by the letter a.

---

[1] Both of which always represent soft consonants.

12.93   *Words illustrating the sound* æ

m̡æt̡	мять	(to crumple)
̡pæt̡	пять	(five)
ʂæt̡	сядь	(sit down!)
ʐæt̡	зять	(son/brother-in-law)
m̡ætʃ	мяч	(ball)
tʃæʂt̡	часть	(part)
̡pʃ'tʃæt̡	пищать	(to squeak)

ɑ+ (or ɑ⊦)

12.94   *Formation of the Russian sound* ɑ+[1]

(1) *height of tongue:* open;

(2) *point of tongue which is highest:* a point somewhat further forward than centre of back;

(3) *position of lips:* neutral.

12.95   ɑ+ is a back, open vowel with neutral lips.

12.96   Russian ɑ+ is not far from the most usual Southern English sound of *a* in *calm, father,* etc. It is further forward than Cardinal Vowel no. 5 (Fig. 8).

12.97   English speakers who normally use a fully back vowel in such words as *calm* kɑ:m, *father* 'fɑːðə must make this vowel slightly more a-like to acquire Russian ɑ+. Both they and those who use a slightly advanced variety of ɑ must take care not to lengthen the Russian vowel ɑ+.

12.98   The sound ɑ+ occurs only in stressed syllables when the sound ı follows. If a soft consonant precedes the vowel the effect of the ı on the vowel is just about neutralized by that of the soft consonant, so that in such words as 'ʋalt̡j вялый (flaccid) the vowel has about the value described in §§ 12.78–80.

12.99   The sound ɑ+ is represented only by the letter a.

12.100   *Words illustrating the sound* ɑ+[2]

| pal | пал | (fell, *masc.*) |
| 'palkə | палка | (stick) |

---

[1] For ⊦ see note 1, p. 33.

[2] Transcribed here and elsewhere as a. It will be clear from the considerations stated in § 12.98 when the symbol a represents the sound ɑ+.

znal	знал	(knew, *masc.*)
bral	брал	(took, *masc.*)
dal	дал	(gave, *masc.*)

ʌ (or aᴗ⊢)

12.101 *Formation of the sound* ʌ

(1) *height of tongue:* slightly lower than half-open;

(2) *point of tongue which is highest:* a point just behind the point of division between front and back or, in other words, the forepart of the back;

(3) *position of lips:* neutral.

12.102 ʌ is an advanced back vowel, slightly more open than half-open, with neutral lips.

12.103 Some speakers have an ʌ-sound which is slightly more a-like. The sound must not, however, be made *too* a-like, i.e. it must not be made identical in quality with stressed a.

12.104 The vowel in such English words as *cup*, kʌp, *tuck* tʌk is very similar in the pronunciation of many English speakers to Russian ʌ. There is, however, some variation in the pronunciation of the English vowel ʌ. Some speakers, especially in the South of England, have a vowel which is distinctly a-like while in the North of England a sound nearer to ə (as in *about* ə'baut) is heard.[1] Neither of these two extremes is correct for Russian ʌ. English learners whose ʌ is very a-like must modify this sound in the direction of ə. Conversely, English learners whose ʌ is ə-like or who in fact use ə instead of ʌ must aim at a sound midway between ə and the ɑ of *calm* kɑːm. Alternatively, both types of English learners, and others, may try to acquire the Russian sound ʌ by starting from the English sound ɔː as in *sawn* sɔːn, advancing slightly the highest point of the tongue and removing the lip-rounding. The Russian vowel must not be lengthened, of course.

12.105 The sound ʌ never occurs in stressed syllables and is

---

[1] The sound heard in Northern English *dialect* pronunciation of such words as *cup*, *tuck* is a back, *rounded* vowel, ranging from half-open in some dialects to almost close in others.

never preceded by a soft consonant in the same word. It occurs only before the stress: *immediately* before the stress ('pretonic' position), or as the first sound in a word,[1] or as either one of a sequence of two vowels where the letter a or the letter o is written.[2] The sound ʌ is represented by the letters a and o.

12.106 *Words and phrases illustrating the sound* ʌ

ʌdvʌ'kat	адвокат	(solicitor)
ʌftʌ'mat	автомат	(automaton, slot-machine)
ʌdnʌ'vo	одного	(of one)
ʌpʌz'dal	опоздал	(was late, *masc.*)
ʌ'ņi	они	(they)
ʌtʃɪ'saʈ	очесать	(to comb)
glʌ'za	глаза	(eyes)
sʌ'ma	сама	(self, *fem.*)
ʃʌ'ḷiʈ	шалить	(to play pranks)
ʒʌ'ra	жара	(hot weather)
nʌ'ga	нога	(foot)
dʌ'ma	дома	(houses)
xʌ'ḍiʈ	ходить	(to go)
vʌʌbrʌ'ʒaʈ	воображать	(to imagine)
nʌu'gat	наугад	(at random)
vʌʌpʃ'tʃɛ	вообще	(in general)
sʌʌ'tyɛt-s(t)vəvəʈ	соответствовать	(to correspond)
sʌu'tʃas(t)vəvəl	соучаствовал	(participated, *masc.*)
pʌ‿ʌdnʌ'mu	по одному	(one each)
u‿ʌdnʌ'vo	у одного	(one has)
nʌ‿ʌstrʌ'vax	на островах	(on the islands)

12.107 In such words as жара, шалить (§ 12.106), i.e. where the orthography has a after ш or ж in pretonic position, the older Moscow pronunciation had the sound ɨ, thus ʒɨ'ra, ʃt'ḷiʈ. This pronunciation is no longer heard in the usual speech of educated

---

[1] But note that in 'closely bound' units of preposition and following word any vowel occurring at the beginning of such following word in the written form is *not* phonetically initial. (Cf. examples in § 12.106 and § 12.116.)

[2] As the first of two such vowels in sequence before the stress, however, some speakers pronounce ə instead of ʌ.

12. THE RUSSIAN VOWELS IN DETAIL

persons, and though some Soviet writers on phonetics state that
a is still pronounced ι in a few words (such as жалеть, ӡt'ʆeʦ
to regret and лошадей ləʃt'dej, gen. pl. of *horse*), there is no
doubt that this feature of Russian pronunciation is becoming
rarer.

ə

12.108 *Formation of the Russian sound* ə
  (1) *height of tongue:* somewhat lower than midway between
       half-close and half-open;
  (2) *point of tongue which is highest:* the point of division between
       front and back;
  (3) *position of lips:* neutral.

12.109 ə is a central vowel, midway between half-close and
half-open, with neutral lips.

12.110 The Russian sound ə, as in 'daмə дама (lady), presents
no difficulty for most English speakers, being much the same as
the usual English sound attached to the letter *a* in *along* ə'lɔŋ.
This vowel is not so open as the sound used by *some* English
speakers in final position in such words as *china, sofa, supper,*
which is almost ʌ.

12.111 Many Scots speakers do not have the sound ə. In the
second syllable of *china* they have ʌ, in the second syllable of
father and *pitted* they have ι, and in the second syllable of *pitied*
they have an e-like vowel. In order to acquire the sound ə, if
they are unable to do so by imitation, they should try to make
their ʌ in *china* more ι-like, keeping the lips neutral, however,
and not producing a clearly ι-like sound.

12.112 The sound ə occurs both before the stress and after the
stress ('post-tonic'). Before the stress it cannot be preceded by
a soft consonant, nor can it occur immediately before the stress
or as the first sound in a word or as one of a sequence of two
vowels before the stress (see footnotes, p. 51).

12.113 It occurs therefore in pre-pretonic syllables after a hard
consonant, but not as one of a sequence of two vowels. In post-
tonic positions there are no such restrictions on the occurrence
of ə—it occurs after hard consonants or soft consonants.

12.114 There is some slight variety in the quality of ə because of the influence of surrounding sounds. In positions before the stress when r follows, for example, the sound ə often seems more ʌ-like in the pronunciation of some speakers. In post-tonic syllables, between two soft consonants, the sound ə is often more ɩ-like. This is more discernible if the following syllable contains the vowel ɩ. Until more research has been done on the various qualities of ə it is impossible to be more definite and the learner will do best to aim at the central vowel described in § 12.108. A slight advancing of this vowel towards ɩ will in any case probably arise automatically when the speaker aims at a central vowel between two soft consonants in post-tonic positions.

12.115 The sound ə is represented in positions before the stress by the letters o and a (but not when the latter is preceded by ч or щ; see § 12.38) and in post-tonic positions by the letters a, я and o. In the older Moscow style of pronunciation the letter e was pronounced as (j)ə in the nom. sing. neut. ending of the noun and adjective (e.g. 'vzmorjə взморье *sea-shore,* 'krasnəjə красное *red,* 'starəjə старое *old,* 'pţitʃjə птичье *bird's*) and in двое *two,* трое *three* ('dvojə, 'trojə). Such pronunciations may still be heard. After hard consonants too the letter e in post-tonic positions may be pronounced as ə in the nom.-acc. sing. of neuter nouns (сердце 'şɛrtsə *heart,* солнце 'sontsə) and occasionally elsewhere, especially if there is a following hard consonant (вышел 'viʃəl *went out,* скошено 'skoʃənə *reaped*).

12.116 *Words and phrases illustrating the sound* ə

gəlʌ'va	голова	(head)
gərʌ'da	города	(towns)
məlʌ'ko	молоко	(milk)
stərʌ'na	сторона	(side)
skəvərʌ'da	сковорода	(frying-pan)
pərʌ'xot	пароход	(steamer)
s əblʌ'kof	с облаков	(from the clouds)[1]
s əpɩl'şinəm	с апельсином	(with an orange)[2]

[1] Cf. ʌblʌ'ka облака (clouds).

[2] Cf. ʌpɩl'şin апельсин (orange).

ʌt ədnʌˈvo	от одного	(from one)[1]
ˈdamə	дама	(lady)
ˈranə	рано	(early)
ˈɛtəvə	этого	(this, *gen. masc. and neut.*)
ˈnasmərk	насморк	(cold in the head)
təbuˈrɛtkə	табуретка	(stool)
ˈznaɱə	знамя	(banner)
ˈiɱə	имя	(name)
ˈkrasnəjə	красная	(red, *nom. sing. fem.*)
ˈstarəjə	старая	(old, *nom. sing. fem.*)
ˈploʃtʃəʈ	площадь	(square)
ˈploʃtʃədɪ	площади	(squares)
ˈnoṣət	носят	(they carry)
ˈvoḓət	водят	(they lead)

Distribution of the sounds ʌ and ə

12.117 The formation of the sounds ʌ and ə usually presents no difficulty to English-speaking learners. Because of their English speech habits, however, such learners may make mistakes in the distribution of these sounds in Russian words. In English the position immediately in front of the stress is very weakly stressed and it is here that the sound ə very often occurs in English words (e.g. pærəˈdɔksɪkəl *paradoxical*, əˈpɔlədʒaɪz *apologize*). It is precisely here, in the immediately pretonic position, which is *the second most heavily stressed syllable* in Russian words,[2] that the Russian sound ə does *not* occur. The member of the a-phoneme that occurs here is ʌ (§ 12.105).

12.118 Conversely, many long English words have a secondary stress two or more syllables before the main stress and here various vowels, including ʌ, but *not* ə, occur (e.g. ˌvʌlnərəˈbɪlɪtɪ *vulnerability*, ˌkɔnsənˈtreɪʃn *concentration*). Such positions in Russian words are more weakly stressed than the immediately pretonic position and it is precisely in these positions that the Russian sound ʌ does not occur (except in the circumstances

---

[1] Cf. ʌdnʌˈvo одного (one, *gen. masc. and neut.*).

[2] This does not apply to those compound words which have two stresses (see chapter 24).

described in § 12.105). Here the member of the a-phoneme that occurs is ə.

12.119 What this amounts to is this: English learners often tend to pronounce ə in immediately pretonic position, where ʌ is required, and to pronounce ʌ in pre-pretonic positions, where ə is required. They must beware of saying gʌlə'va for gəlʌ'va, stʌrə'na for stərʌ'na, etc. In order to ensure against such mis-pronunciations, the learner should devote particular attention to the first seven examples in § 12.116, find other examples of words with similar vowel distributions and practise all these words until the correct distribution of ʌ and ə becomes automatic.

The Russian o-phoneme

o

12.120 *Formation of the Russian sound* o
  (1) *height of tongue:* between half-open and half-close but nearer to half-open than to half-close;
  (2) *point of tongue which is highest:* centre of back;
  (3) *position of lips:* medium lip-rounding.

12.121 o is a back vowel, slightly less than half-open, with medium lip-rounding.

12.122 Some Russian speakers use an opener sound than the one described above, the tongue-position being slightly lower than that of Cardinal Vowel no. 6 (Fig. 8). Learners would do better however to aim at the closer variety of o.

12.123 The principal member of the Russian o-phoneme can-not be identified with any English vowel. The nearest is the sound of *aw* (as in *saw*), but the difference is considerable. The most usual English sound of *aw* (ɔ:) has a tongue-position some-what lower than that of Cardinal Vowel no. 6 (Fig. 8).

12.124 The Russian normal o must be carefully distinguished from the various diphthongs used by different English speakers in such words as *home*, *go*; also from the various values given by different English speakers to the 'short' *o* in such words as *hot*, *long*.

12. THE RUSSIAN VOWELS IN DETAIL

12.125   The opener o-sound used by some Russian speakers (as mentioned in § 12.122) is not far removed from the 'average' English vowel in *hot*.

12.126   Many English speakers find difficulty in learning to produce the Russian o-sound. One method of acquiring this sound is as follows. If the learner has in his pronunciation of the word *saw* (sɔ:) a vowel somewhat more open that Cardinal Vowel no. 6, he should try to make this vowel closer, i.e. raise the tongue slightly in the direction of o (Cardinal Vowel no. 7), at the same time making the lips slightly more rounded.

12.127   If the learner has already learnt to make o (Cardinal Vowel no. 7), he may be able to acquire the Russian o by aiming at a sound intermediate between cardinal o and his English vowel in *saw*.

12.128   Another method is to start by placing the lips in close rounded position and to try simultaneously to produce the English vowel of *saw*. The learner must try various adjustments of the tongue and lips, practising the sound in the presence of his teacher, who will tell him when he hits upon the right shade of sound.

12.129   Some Southern speakers of English, especially in London and its environs, have a vowel in such words as *saw* which is closer and more rounded than that described above (§ 12.120). It is somewhat closer than Russian o. Hence, if it is modified by being made slightly more open and less rounded, it will approximate to Russian o.

12.130   In Scotland the sound ɔ in words spelt with *aw*, *au* and *ou* (as in *thought*) and in some words spelt with *or*[1] is short and slightly more open. On the other hand, the sound ɔ: is generally replaced in Scotland by a short vowel o, nearly as close as Cardinal Vowel no. 7, in words spelt with *ore*, *oar*, *our* (as in *course*), *oor* (as in *floor*) and in some words spelt with *or*.[1] Scots speakers will therefore have to bear these facts in mind when following the methods described in §§ 12.126, 127 for acquiring the Russian o-sound.

---

[1] See Daniel Jones, *The Pronunciation of English* (4th edition), p. 40.

12. THE RUSSIAN VOWELS IN DETAIL

12.131 Having learnt to produce the Russian o-sound in the manner described above, the student should proceed to the further refinement of making the sound slightly diphthongal, as it undoubtedly is in many positions. This phenomenon may also be thought of as consisting of an 'off-glide' after the vowel o. (There is also an 'on-glide' to this vowel in certain positions; see below, §§ 12.134, 135.)

12.132 In open final position, as in ʌ'kno окно (window), and before a hard consonant, as in rot рот (mouth), the vowel o has an off-glide in the nature of a still more open o-sound, below the position of Cardinal Vowel no. 6 and with a slightly advanced tongue-position. At normal conversational speed the lip-rounding of this off-glide is frequently lost and the glide is similar in quality to ə, thus oᵊ. Students would do best to aim at this kind of off-glide, taking care not to prolong it or give it undue prominence. Russian o should not become a diphthong of the type used by some English speakers in such words as *course* [kɔəs], *hoarse* [hɔəs].[1]

12.133 Before a soft consonant, as in 'koɲ конь (*horse*), the off-glide is in the nature of an i-sound, as the tongue begins to move into the position for the soft consonant. Again, the off-glide must not be exaggerated so that the o-sound with i-glide is replaced by a diphthong of the type oj, which also occurs in Russian (§§ 14.8, 11). If the student is producing both the vowel and the soft consonant correctly the i-glide often arises automatically, but the teacher should verify its presence.

12.134 The on-glide before o is heard most clearly in absolute initial position, as in 'oknə окна (*windows*), or after the labials p, b, m, f, v and the velars k, g, x. It is similar in quality to an u-sound. To an English speaker 'mogut могут (*they can*), for example, may sound like 'mʷogut but the u-glide must not be exaggerated into the English bi-labial semi-vowel w nor into an independent syllable with an u-vowel.

12.135 After a soft consonant the on-glide before o is in the

---

[1] It should be noted that in 'modern' RP such words as these are more often pronounced with a 'pure' vowel—kɔːs, hɔːs.

57

nature of an i-sound, as in ļon лен (*flax*). If the soft consonant is produced in the correct manner the i-glide will often arise automatically. The glide must not be exaggerated so that it becomes an independent syllable. The pronunciation ļi'on or ļι'on for ļon, is incorrect.

12.136 After a soft consonant, the beginning of the vowel o may be slightly fronted. Conversely, before a soft consonant, the end of the vowel may be slightly fronted. Such fine shades of pronunciation as these usually arise automatically when the student has mastered and is pronouncing easily the Russian sound o and the soft consonants.

12.137 With the exceptions noted below (§§ 12.153–8) the sound o occurs only in stressed syllables. In unstressed syllables it is replaced by a member of the a-phoneme or a member of the i-phoneme (see chapter 23 and Appendix 2, §§ 23.19–22). The only stressed position in which o does not occur is that between two soft consonants. Here the sound ö occurs (§§ 12.159–66).

12.138 The sound o is represented by the letters o and e. The letter e, when it represents o, is regularly provided with a diaeresis (ë) only in elementary text-books and many dictionaries. Otherwise ë is written only to avoid ambiguity (e.g. всё fşo *everything*, but все fşɛ *everybody*).

12.139 *Words illustrating the sound* o

'obə	оба	(both)
'okələ	около	(around)
'obləkə	облако	(cloud)
dno	дно	(bottom)
pəlʌ'tno	полотно	(linen)
tot	тот	(that)
dom	дом	(house)
'vorən	ворон	(raven)
vol	вол	(ox)
mok	мог	(could)
kot	кот	(tom-cat)
'goləs	голос	(voice)

oʂ	ось	(axle)
'oɬɡə	Ольга	(Olga)
'oʐɪrə	озеро	(lake)
'doɬə	доля	(portion)
koɳ	конь	(horse)
roɬ	роль	(role)
'botʃkə	бочка	(tub)
voɳ	вонь	(stink)
fʂo	все	(all)
'ɳobə	небо	(palate)
'jolkə	елка	(fir-tree)
joʃ	еж	(hedgehog)

The sound o in the position of subsidiary stress

12.140 Certain classes of words in Russian are pronounced with two stressed syllables. The second in sequence of two such stressed syllables bears a heavier stress than the first. In this book the heavier of two such stresses is called the 'major' stress and the lighter one is called the 'subsidiary' stress. Major stress is marked in this book in the normal way (with a raised tick), subsidiary stress with a lowered tick.

12.141 Each of the stressed syllables in a word with two stresses acts as the main stress in that part of the word in which it occurs, so that the quality of the vowels in the unstressed syllables around the main stress is, as in words with one main stress, determined by the position of the unstressed syllable in relation to the position of the main stress.

12.142 The sound o occurs in the position of subsidiary stress, as well as in the position of major stress. When it occurs in the position of subsidiary stress the sound o is usually pronounced without the off-glides described in §§ 12.132, 133.

12.143 Compound words in which the first element is трех-,[1] or четырех- always have a subsidiary stress. Thus ˌtroxtʃɪsʌ'voj трехчасовой (three-hour), ˌtroxjɪ'zitʃnɪ(j) трехъязычный (tri-lingual), tʃɪtɪˌroxmɪ'trovɪ(j) четырехметровый (four-metre), tʃɪtɪˌrox'taktnɪ(j) четырехтактный (four-beat).

---

[1] But *not* тре-.

12. THE RUSSIAN VOWELS IN DETAIL

12.144 With the exception of stʌˈɭeʈɪ(j)ɪ столетие (centenary) and related words, compound words in which the first element is сто- are also usually pronounced with a subsidiary stress: ˌstomɪˈtrofkə стометровка (hundred-metre sprint), ˌstoˈgradusnɪ(j) стоградусный (centigrade). Compounds in which the first element is a numeral ending in сот also have subsidiary stress: pɪʈɪˌsotmɪˈtrovɪ(j) пятисотметровый (five-hundred-metre). The few compounds with the initial element девяносто- also have subsidiary stress: dɪvɪˌnostəˈɭeʈɲɪ(j) девяностолетний (ninety-year).

12.145 Many long compound words with the linking vowel written o or e have a subsidiary stress, particularly those which pertain to the spheres of technology and science, or are not common in everyday speech. Thus:

səmʌˌɭotəstrʌˈ(j)eŋ(ɪ)jɪ	самолетостроение	(aircraft-construction)
pərʌˌvozərɪˈmontnɪ(j)	паровозоремонтный	(locomotive-repair)
vɪˌsokətʃɪsˈtotnɪ(j)	высокочастотный	(high-frequency)

12.146 The more familiar such words become to the general public, the more likely they are to be pronounced without a subsidiary stress. Thus, while законосообразный (in accordance with the law) is pronounced zʌˌkonəsʌʌˈbraznɪ(j), законодательный (legislative), being much more familiar, is pronounced zəkənʌˈdaʈɪɭnɪ(j).

12.147 Hyphenated compounds, in most of which both parts are declined, also have a subsidiary stress: ˌʃkoləɪnʈɪrˈnat школа-интернат (boarding-school), vʌˌgonɾɪstʌˈran вагон-ресторан (dining-car).

12.148 Co-ordinate compound adjectives[1] usually have a subsidiary stress. Thus: ˌtʃornəˈbɛlɪ(j) черно-белый (black and white), ɪkskurʂɪˌonətuˈɾistskɪ(j) экскурсионно-туристский (tourist and excursion).

---

[1] That is those whose meaning is equivalent to 'x *and* y' (see D. Ward, *The Russian Language Today*, pp. 154–5).

12.149 Abbreviated compounds[1] have one stress if they are well-known words in everyday use, e.g. kʌl'xos колхоз (collective farm), otherwise they have two stresses. Thus: ˌobl'sut облсуд (district court).

12.150 The 'abutted' compounds[2] which the creation of abbreviated compounds has given rise to usually have a subsidiary stress. Thus: ˌbortprəvʌ'ɖɲik бортпроводник (steward), ˌsport'klup спортклуб (sports club).

12.151 Words formed with the initial elements фото- and мото- have a subsidiary stress if they are new words or not familiar, everyday words. Thus:

ˌfotəbu'magə	фотобумага	(photographic paper)
ˌfotəgrʌ'ɣurə	фотогравюра	(photogravure)
but fətʌ'ʂɲiɱək	фотоснимок	(photograph)
ˌmotə'ʃʆɛm	мотошлем	(crash-helmet)
ˌmotəp̡ɩ'xotə	мотопехота	(motorized infantry)
but mətʌ'tsɨkl	мотоцикл	(motor-cycle)

12.152 Some compound words may have *three* stresses: a major and two subsidiary stresses. The major stress is the last of the three. Thus: ˌtɽoxˌsod-'znatʃnɨ(j) трехсотзначный (having three hundred digits).

Unstressed o

12.153 In a few words of foreign origin the sound o occurs in unstressed syllables. It is then pronounced without an off-glide.

12.154 Among such words are:

do'ʂjɛ	досье	(dossier)
koɱüɲɩ'kɛ[3]	коммюнике	(communiqué)
konso'mɛ[3]	консоме	(consommé)
o'teʆ[3]	отель	(hotel)
'raɖɩo	радио	(radio)
kʌ'kao	какао	(cocoa)

[1] That is those in which at least one element is in the form of an abbreviation.

[2] That is those which consist apparently of two nouns in full simply agglutinated, without a linking-vowel (see D. Ward, *The Russian Language Today*, pp. 144–5).

[3] Note hard consonant before ɛ/e.

12. THE RUSSIAN VOWELS IN DETAIL

12.155 The pronunciation of o in unstressed syllables persists much longer in some words than in others, which are more rapidly adapted to the Russian phonetic system. The words модель (model) and модерн (modern), for instance, are pronounced either with unstressed o or with ʌ in the first syllable: moˈdeļ/mʌˈdeļ,[1] moˈdɛrn/mʌˈdɛrn.[1]

12.156 The pronunciation of some words with unstressed o is heard only in a bookish or pedantic style: thus поэт (poet), поэзия (poetry), фонетика (phonetics) are normally pronounced pʌˈɛt, pʌˈeẕịə, fʌˈŋeṭịkə.

12.157 The letter o in foreign names, other than those of Slavonic origin, is often pronounced as o in unstressed syllables, with the exception noted below (§ 12.158). Examples are:

mopʌˈsan	Мопасан	(Maupassant)
voļˈtɛr[1]	Вольтер	(Voltaire)
ʃoˈpɛn[1]	Шопен	(Chopin)
golsuˈorṣị	Голсуорси	(Galsworthy)
borˈdo	Бордо	(Bordeaux)

12.158 In unstressed final closed syllables, however, ə is pronounced where o is written, as in ˈbrajtən Брайтон (Brighton), ˈlondən Лондон (London).

ö

12.159 *Formation of the Russian sound* ö
(1) *height of tongue:* a little below half-close;
(2) *point of tongue which is highest:* the point of division between front and back;
(3) *position of lips:* medium lip-rounding.

12.160 ö is a half-close, central vowel with medium lip-rounding.

12.161 Varieties of ö occur as the first element of some of the numerous diphthongs heard in such English words as *home, go*.

12.162 Those who use the diphthong öü in such English words as *home, go*, have only to isolate the first element of this diphthong to make Russian ö, as in ŋịˈṣöṭị несете (you are carrying).

---

[1] Note hard consonant before ɛ/e.

12. THE RUSSIAN VOWELS IN DETAIL

12.163 Though the diphthong öü is only used by a minority of English people,[1] yet there are a great many who use a diphthong of which the first element is a variety of o approaching ö. Many of these will be able to acquire a sufficiently near approximation to Russian ö by isolating the first element of their English o-diphthong. The very advanced vowel which some people use and which is near to ø[2] will not do, however, for Russian ö. People who habitually use a sound near to ø in the pronunciation of *home, go* will have to aim at a sound midway between this and Russian o in respect of the tongue-position. The respective tongue-positions of Russian o and ö are shown in Fig. 10.

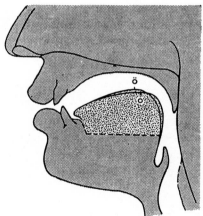

Fig. 10. Tongue-positions of Russian o and ö compared

12.164 Those whose English o-diphthong begins with a fully back vowel may acquire a fairly good ö by adding lip-rounding to the sound ə (§ 12.108). They may also proceed as follows. Add close lip-rounding to Cardinal Vowel e (Fig. 8), thus producing the sound which is written phonetically ø; then aim at a sound half-way between this and cardinal o; the exercise must be practised in the presence of the teacher, who will tell the learner when he hits upon the right intermediate sound.

[1] See D. Jones, *The Pronunciation of English*, §§ 171–2.
[2] This vowel is approximately the sound of *eu* in French *peu*.

12. THE RUSSIAN VOWELS IN DETAIL

12.165 The sound ö occurs only in stressed syllables, *between two soft consonants.* It is written e (or ë. See § 12.138.)

12.166 *Words illustrating the sound* ö

'ţöţə	тетя	(aunt)
ɲɩ'şöţɩ	несете	(you are carrying)
vʌ'ʐɱöţɩ	возьмете	(you will take)
zʌ'şɲöţɩ	заснете	(you will fall asleep)

The Russian u-phoneme

u

12.167 *Formation of the Russian sound* u
 (1) *height of tongue:* nearly close;
 (2) *point of tongue which is highest:* centre of back;
 (3) *position of lips:* close lip-rounding.

12.168 u is a close, back rounded vowel.

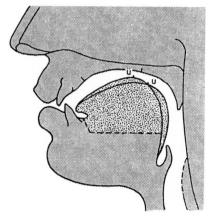

Fig. 11. Tongue-positions of u and ü compared

12.169 The sound u, the principal member of the Russian u-phoneme, is about the same as one of the numerous English sounds of *oo* in *too, food,* namely the one which is pure (i.e. not diphthongized) and which is a true back vowel without any trace of 'advancing' (see §§ 12.173, 179, 180 and Fig. 11). The

64

Russian u, however, is short, not long, as the English *oo* sound often is.

12.170   This u must be carefully distinguished from the more usual English sounds of 'long' *oo*, which are diphthongized (§ 12.171) and more or less 'advanced' (§ 12.173). It must also be distinguished from the advanced but pure sounds of *oo* heard in various Scottish forms of pronunciation.

12.171   The chief mistake which English people are liable to make in regard to the Russian normal u is to diphthongize it; in other words they do not keep the speech-organs motionless in the appropriate position, but they allow them to move from one position to another. The diphthongization in this case is chiefly a matter of lip-action; the lips start with very little rounding and gradually come together into the close rounded position. One form of this diphthong may be written ɒu; thus many English people are liable to pronounce ʂɩˈʒu сижу (I sit) as ʂɩˈʒɒu.

12.172   To cure this fault the English learner must put his lips into the close rounded position (Fig. 5) at the very beginning of the u-sound, and he must take care that they do not move while the sound is being held. He should repeat the sound a number of times (uuuuuuu...), looking at his mouth in the mirror to ensure that there is no motion.

12.173   Many English people mispronounce the Russian normal u by advancing the tongue-position, as well as by diphthongizing in the manner just described. An extreme form of this pronunciation is the diphthong ɩö found in the London dialect pronunciation of such words as *too, food*.

12.174   By keeping the lips motionless in close rounded position such a diphthong will be converted into a pure vowel of the ü type. The difference in tongue-position between ü and u is shown in Fig. 11. To get the tongue into the proper back position for the Russian normal u, the student must first learn to make some variety of fully back o-sound. Cardinal o (Cardinal Vowel no. 7) is the best for this purpose, but Russian normal o would also do fairly well.[1] He must then aim at making a sound which is more u-like than his advanced u or ü. He must perform the exercise in the presence of his teacher, who will tell him as soon as the right shade of sound has been attained.

12.175 The same exercise must be practised by Scottish learners who do not possess in their natural speech any variety of back u, but have instead a pure sound of the ü-type.

12.176 The sound u occurs only in stressed syllables. It does not occur between two soft consonants. Here the sound ü (§§ 12.179–86) occurs.

12.177 The sound u is written by the letter y or the letter ю.

12.178 *Words illustrating the sound* u

um	ум	(mind)
'uxə	ухо	(ear)
'ugəl	угол	(corner)
'uʐʟl	узел	(knot)
'uʟɪtsə	улица	(street)
sʟ'ʒu	сижу	(I am sitting)
ʟ'du	иду	(I am coming)
ɲʟ'su	несу	(I am carrying)
gəvʌ'ru	говорю	(I say)
xʌ'tʃu	хочу	(I want)
ʃju	шью	(I sew)
tut	тут	(here)
dup	дуб	(oak)
pʌ'kupkə	покупка	(purchase)
pərʌ'ʃut	парашют	(parachute)
ʈuk	тюк	(bale)
'rumkə	рюмка	(wine-glass)
ʟuk	люк	(hatch)
puʈ	путь	(path, way)
ʈʟ'nuʈ	тянуть	(to pull)
guʂ	гусь	(goose)

[1] Without the on-glide and off-glide described in §§ 12.132–5.

12. THE RUSSIAN VOWELS IN DETAIL

ü

12.179 *Formation of the Russian sound* ü

(1) *height of tongue:* nearly close;

(2) *point of tongue which is highest:* the point of division between front and back (see Fig. 11);

(3) *position of lips:* close lip-rounding.

12.180 ü is a close, central, rounded vowel.

12.181 ü does not exist in the most usual type of educated Southern English. In the dialect of London, and to a certain extent in the speech of educated Southerners, ü or a sound approaching it occurs in words like *too, food,* as the second element of a diphthong of the type ɨü or ʌö (see §§ 12.192–4). In Scotland the sound ü is often heard as a pure vowel in the same words; also in *book, good,* etc.

12.182 Those Scottish speakers who have an ü in their pronunciation of English pronounce *book* with much the same vowel as that used by Russians in the pronunciation of kⱡütʃ. Those Londoners who have a diphthong of the ɨü or ʌö type in their speech can acquire an ü by saying their *oo* sound (as in *too*) with close lip-rounding from the very beginning of the sound.

12.183 Those whose English vowel in *too* is a true back vowel or nearly so may learn to make ü in one of two ways.

(1) They may learn to make a Cardinal ɨ (by the methods outlined in §§ 12.25–9) and then add lip-rounding to it.

(2) Or they may add lip-rounding to ɨ (thus producing approximately the French sound of *u*, as in *lune*, phonetically y), and then aim at a sound half-way between this and u; the teacher should be present to say when the right shade of sound has been reached.

12.184 To some the principle of vowel pitches will prove of assistance. Whispered cardinal u has a pitch about E ; whispered cardinal y (i.e. the vowel obtained by adding close lip-rounding to cardinal i) has a pitch about D ; whispered middle ü has a pitch half-way between these two, i.e. about Eb . In whistling, the various pitches are obtained by variations in the position of the tongue; in other words by putting the tongue in the position for various vowels. Hence the student may learn to make ü by whistling gently the note Eb ,[1] and then keeping his mouth still in this position and producing voice.

12.185 ü occurs only in stressed syllables, *between two soft consonants*. It is written ю or, after ч and щ, y.[2]

12.186 *Words illustrating the sound* ü

klütʃ	ключ	(key; spring)
ʈül	тюль	(tulle)
'lüʈɩk	лютик	(buttercup)
'lüdɩ	люди	(people)
'tʃüdɩtsə	чудится	(it seems)
tʃüjəʈ[3]	чуять	(to sense)
'ʃtʃürɩʈ/'ʃʃürɩʈ	щурить	(to screw up one's eyes)
'ʃtʃütʃɩ(j)/ʃʃütʃɩ(j)	щучий	(of a pike)

ꞷ (or u˕+)

12.187 This is a variety of u in which the tongue-position is somewhat lower and slightly more advanced than for u. Some writers would call this sound a 'lax' u. In discussing points of Russian phonetic theory the symbol ꞷ may be used but for the

---

[1] This note will be situated at about the middle of his range of whistled notes. (Many people are liable to estimate the pitch of a whistled note at an octave below what it really is.)

[2] Since ч and щ always represent soft consonants, it is a convention of Russian orthography that one writes after ч and щ the vowel letters a, e, и, o and y (see Appendix 2, p. 297).

[3] The sound j has the same effect on preceding vowels as does a soft consonant.

phonetic transcriptions in this book it is sufficient to write u, the phonetic value of which is then determined by the principles given in §§ 12.176, 190.

12.188 Russian ɷ is much the same as the usual Southern English vowel in *put, book* and it therefore presents no difficulty to Southern English learners.

12.189 Most Scottish speakers, however, do not have the sound ɷ, but use instead the sound ü (§§ 12.179, 181) or u. If they have the sound u, they may acquire the sound ɷ either (1) by making a sound more o-like and with less lip-rounding than their u, or (2) by making a sound more ə-like than their u, or (3) by trying to pronounce u in a very lax manner, i.e. reducing the amount of muscular tension in the tongue and lips. If, on the other hand, they have the sound ü, they should approach ɷ by first acquiring the sound u and then modifying in one or other of the ways just described.

12.190 ɷ occurs only in unstressed syllables and never between two soft consonants. It is written y or ю.

12.191 *Words illustrating the sound ɷ[1]*

ugʌ'lok	уголок	(nook)
u'rok	урок	(lesson)
u'ʒɛ	уже	(already)
u'mɨ	умы	(minds)
'pravdu	правду	(truth, *acc. sing.*)
'ɽɛʒu	режу	(I cut)
'domu	дому	(house, *dat. sing.*)
u'ŋizʮ	унизить	(to humilate)
'znaju	знаю	(I know)
dʮ'ɽɛɣŋu	деревню	(village, *acc. sing.*)
ku'sok	кусок	(piece)
ru'ka	рука	(hand)
du'ʃa	душа	(soul)
lu'ga	луга	(meadows)
ʂu'da	сюда	(here, hither)
ŋu'ans	нюанс	(nuance)

[1] Transcribed as u in the examples and elsewhere in this book.

12. THE RUSSIAN VOWELS IN DETAIL

ö (or ü̇ɾ)

12.192 This is a variety of u-sound in which the tongue is more advanced than for o, or lower than for ü. Its formation might be described as

(1) *height of tongue:* slightly higher than half-close;

(2) *point of tongue which is highest:* the point of division between front and back or possibly a point slightly in advance of this;

(3) *position of lips:* nearly close lip-rounding.

12.193 ö (or ü̇ɾ) is a half-close, central, rounded vowel.

12.194 The sound ö does not occur in the most usual type of educated Southern English. A sound practically identical with it is found in one form of the diphthong in words like *too, food* as pronounced by some London dialect speakers, i.e. ꞇö. The Russian ö sound, however, is short and must not be prolonged.

12.195 There are several ways in which this sound may be reached. The tongue-position is very close to that of ꞇ ('unstressed ɪ'), so that if lip-rounding is added to ꞇ the sound ö or a very close approximation to it will be produced. (It should be remembered that with this sound, as with o, lip-rounding is more lax than with u or ü.)

12.196 It may be reached by trying to pronounce ü according to the manner described in §§ 12.182–4 but with a slightly lower tongue-position. Some writers would say that ö is a 'lax' ü, and one may attempt to reach ö by pronouncing ü in a more 'lax' fashion.

12.197 o pronounced in a more forward position in the mouth becomes, in effect, ö.

12.198 ö occurs only in unstressed syllables and only between soft consonants. It is written ю or, after ч and щ, y.[1]

12.199 In discussing points of phonetic theory the symbol ö (or ü̇ɾ) may be used, but for most purposes it is sufficient to use either ü or, in a broader style of transcription, u, for this sound,

---

[1] See footnote 2, p. 68.

its occurrence being clear from the statement given in § 12.198 above. In the examples given below (§ 12.200) and elsewhere in this book the symbol ü is used.

12.200   *Words illustrating the sound ö*

jü'ʈitsə[1]	ютиться	(to huddle)
ʈü'ʃak	тюфяк	(mattress)
ʈüɽ'ma	тюрьма	(prison)
kʃü'tʃa	ключа	(key, *gen. sing.*)
ʃü'dej	людей	(people, *gen. pl.*)
tʃü'ʈjo	чутье	(scent)
ʂü'ʂukəʈ	сюсюкать	(to lisp)
ʂʃüdɪ'noj	слюдяной	(of mica)

13

THE RUSSIAN SEMI-VOWEL j

13.1   Semi-vowels are sounds requiring a motion on the part of the organs of speech (see §§ 4.7, 7.3). They cannot be prolonged. Thus semi-vowels differ from vowels proper and from nasal, lateral and fricative consonants, which require the maintenance during an appreciable period of a definite position of the organs of speech. Semi-vowels function as consonants.

13.2   The Russian language contains only one semi-vowel, that is, the sound here written j. English has two semi-vowels—j and w. In forming a normal j the organs of speech start at or near the position of the vowel i (§ 12.2) and immediately proceed in the direction of some other vowel. Thus the symbol j in the group ja denotes the gliding sound formed as the tongue passes from at or near the i-position to the a-position. The symbol j in the group ju denotes the very different gliding sound formed as the tongue and lips pass from at or near the i-position to the u-position.

---

[1] The sound j has the same effect on following vowels as does a soft consonant.

71

13. THE RUSSIAN SEMI-VOWEL j

13.3 When it is desired to represent with special precision the starting-point of a semi-vowel, this may be indicated by placing the mark ⌣ over the symbol of the vowel at which the glide commences. Thus ĭa would mean a preceded by a vowel-glide beginning at i; ῐa would mean a preceded by a vowel-glide beginning at ɩ. These would be more precise ways of representing two varieties of ja.

13.4 The starting-point of the semi-vowel j may vary within certain limits without affecting the general character of the sound. Thus ĭa, ῐa and ĕa are not easy to distinguish from each other by ear; and even ɛ̆a has an effect not very different from ĕa. The vowel-glides in ĭa, ῐa, and ĕa are, in fact, so much alike, that for practical linguistic purposes they may be considered identical, and represented by the symbol j.

13.5 The starting-point of a j preceding or following cardinal i is just above that of cardinal i, i.e. the position of a slightly fricative j.

13.6 In Russian the sound j normally starts at or near i. When, however, j occurs between two vowels, the tendency in Russian is to reduce the motion of the tongue to a minimum. This is particularly the case when the second vowel or both vowels are unstressed. Thus in pɪˈredɲəjə передняя (lobby) the tongue does not nearly reach the i-position between the two vowels ə; a very slight raising and fronting of the tongue from the ə-position is sufficient to produce a j-glide.

13.7 When at least one of two such unstressed vowels is a high close vowel, it is quite common to omit the intervocalic j altogether. Thus, at normal conversational speed, ujɪzˈʒatʲ уезжать (to go away) is usually pronounced uɪzˈʒatʲ and verb-forms such as ˈduməjɪʃ думаешь (you think), ˈduməjɪt думает (thinks), ˈduməjim думаем (we think), ˈduməjɪtʲɪ думаете (you think) are usually pronounced respectively ˈduməiʃ, ˈduməɪt, ˈduməɪm, ˈduməɪtʲɪ.[1] It is for this reason that in this book the

---

[1] The last form is distinguished from the imperative ˈduməjtʲɪ думайте (think!) largely by having one more syllable, but only a slight further acceleration turns ˈduməɪtʲɪ into ˈduməĭtʲɪ, i.e. ˈduməjtʲɪ, which is then indistinguishable from the imperative.

sound j between two vowels is sometimes written in brackets, to indicate that the tongue may not reach the i-position or that the sound may be omitted altogether. The lapse of intervocalic j may also be heard in circumstances other than those just indicated. For instance, bʌl'ʃajə большая (big, *nom. sing. fem.*) may be pronounced bʌl'ʃaə.

13.8 In this book the non-syllabic i of Russian diphthongs is treated as a member of the j-phoneme and the diphthongs are accordingly written aj, oj, etc. (see chapter 14).

13.9 It is appropriate here to refer to the j-glide which occurs after palatalized consonants. It is pointed out in § 17.50 that in forming p before vowels the height of the front of the tongue probably depends on the following vowel: the less close any front vowel after p the less is the raising of the front of the tongue in forming p. The same applies to other palatalized labial and labio-dental consonants. If the student tempers the raising of the front of the tongue to the following front vowel he will avoid a too obvious j-glide between the consonant and the following vowel. Before the back vowels u and o a tongue-position near to that of cardinal e will help to avoid a too obvious j-glide. The student should note too that before i and ɪ there is little or no glide after palatalized labial and labio-dental consonants. After such consonants in final position the glide is of the minimum length to make its presence audible.

13.10 The Russian normal j may be considered identical with the English normal j as in *yes* jɛs.

13.11 No words for practice of the semi-vowel j are given here, since words with j occur throughout the book.

14

THE RUSSIAN DIPHTHONGS

14.1 A diphthong is a vocalic gliding-sound, in which the organs of speech start in one vowel-position and proceed by the shortest route to the position of another vowel without any

14. THE RUSSIAN DIPHTHONGS

intervening fall in prominence followed by a rise. A diphthong on its own, or with preceding consonant(s), constitutes one syllable. If two vowels are uttered in sequence and, while the vocal cords continue to vibrate, the prominence of the second vowel then rises, the two vowels are members of different syllables.

14.2 In describing a diphthong, it is necessary to state (1) the position where the diphthong begins, and (2) the position where the diphthong ends. Hence the most convenient way of symbolizing a diphthong is by means of two symbols, for the initial and finàl positions respectively, e.g. ai or ae as in *height*, *white*, etc. When the need arises, diphthongs may be distinguished from a succession of two vowels by inserting a ligature, thus a͡i or a̯i.

14.3 A diphthong may proceed from a vowel of greater inherent sonority to a vowel of lesser inherent sonority, in which case it is known as a 'falling' diphthong, or from a vowel of lesser sonority to a vowel of greater sonority, in which case it is known as a 'rising' diphthong. This gives rise to another method of transcribing diphthongs, in which the less sonorous element is marked, as in aĭ or ăe.

14.4 All Russian diphthongs are falling diphthongs, since they start from one or other of the vowel-positions described in chapter 12 and move to a vowel-position which is high, close, front and unrounded. This is the position of the Russian stressed vowel i. Thus the diphthongs in the Russian words бой (battle) and дай (give!) might be written oi and ai respectively. When the starting-point of a Russian diphthong is itself i then the tongue is raised slightly higher for the final position of the diphthong as in ķïї кий (cue).

14.5 The Russian consonant j (chapter 13) and the final element of Russian diphthongs ï may be regarded as members of one phoneme, the distribution of which is determined by the 'rule' that ï occurs as the second element of a diphthong whereas consonantal j occurs either before a vowel (as in jɛst ест, eats) or between two vowels (as in rʌ'jon район, region).

14. THE RUSSIAN DIPHTHONGS

14.6 Both consonantal j and the diphthongal element ǐ are transcribed broadly in this book, as j. This has the added advantages:

(1) that a diphthong transcribed by means of a vowel symbol and the symbol j will not be misconstrued as a sequence of two vowels;

(2) that it underscores the fact that the second element of the Russian diphthongs is high and close;

(3) that it underscores the fact that the second element of Russian diphthongs is short.

14.7 Once the student has learnt to produce the vowels described in chapter 12, he should have no difficulty in producing the Russian diphthongs. English-speaking students are, however, likely to make two mistakes in pronouncing the Russian diphthongs. First, they may make the second element insufficiently close. The second element of the diphthongs in English *die*, for example, is ɩ (daɩ) or e (dae) or even ɛ (daɛ). The second element of the Russian diphthongs must be high and close, like the stressed Russian i (see above, § 12.2). Secondly, the English-speaking student may tend to prolong the second element of a diphthong when it is at the end of a word. The second element of Russian diphthongs *must* be kept short.

14.8 The following diphthongs occur in Russian: ij, ɨj, ʉj, ʊj, ej, aj, æj, ʌj, əj, oj, öj, uj, üj, ɒj and öj.

14.9 The vowels ɛ⊦ and ɛ cannot occur as the first element in a Russian diphthong, since they do occur before soft consonants (§ 12.62) and j has the same effect on preceding vowels as does a soft consonant. Students must take care therefore not to use a diphthong similar to that heard in many pronunciations of the word *day* (dɛɩ).

14.10 Diphthongs are represented in Russian writing by one of the vowel letters и, ы, е, э, а, я, о, у or ю followed by the letter й.[1]

---

[1] Between two vowel letters, however, the letter й represents *consonantal* j (see § 14.5).

14.11 *Words illustrating the Russian diphthongs*

1. ij

ķij	кий	(cue)
ʌnˈɡļijsķɩj	английский	(English)
ḅɩļˈɡ̧ijsķɩj	бельгийский	(Belgian)

2. ɨj

ˈvɨjʈɩ	выйти	(to come out)
ˈvɨjdu	выйду	(I shall come out)

3. ɩj[1]

tʃɩjˈkofsķɩj	Чайковский	(Chaikovsky)
kļɩjˈmo	клеймо	(brand)
dɩjsˈtyiʈɩļnə	действительно	(indeed)
ˈvikļɩjm̧ɩʈ	выклеймить	(to brand)
ˈvɨp̧ɩjʈɩ	выпейте	(drink up!)
ˈvɨļɩjʈɩ	вылейте	(pour out!)
ˈmɨşļɩj	мыслей	(thoughts, *gen. pl.*)
ˈuļɩj	улей	(beehive)
ˈşiɲɩj	синий	(blue)
ˈɲisķɩj	низкий	(low)
ˈstroɡ̧ɩj	строгий	(severe)
ˈʈixɩj	тихий	(quiet)
ɡʌˈɾætʃɩj	горячий	(hot)
ˈarm̧ɩj	армий	(armies, *gen. pl.*)

4. ɪj

ˈkrasnɪj	красный	(red)
ˈḅɛlɪj	белый	(white)
ˈslabɪj	слабый	(weak)
ˈsyɛʒɪj	свежий	(fresh)
ˈm̧enʃɪj	меньший	(lesser)

5. ej

ļüˈḑej	людей	(people, *gen. pl.*)
kʌˈp̧ejkə	копейка	(copeck)
druˈʐej	друзей	(friends, *gen. pl.*)
ˈp̧ejʈɩ	пейте	(drink!)
ˈḑejstvəvəʈ	действовать	(to act)

[1] See 'Further Remarks on Diphthongs' below (§ 14.13).

6. aj

'dajʈʟ	дайте	(give!)
'tajnə	тайна	(secret)
urʌ'ʒaj	урожай	(harvest)
maj	май	(May)
'gajkə	гайка	(nut)

7. æj

tʃæj	чай	(tea)
'tʃæjɳʟk	чайник	(tea-pot)
ɳʟgʌ'dæj	негодяй	(good-for-nothing)
prʌʃ'tʃæjʈʟ	прощайте	(farewell)
stɾʟ'ļæjʈʟ	стреляйте	(shoot!)

8. ʌj

tʌj'ga	тайга	(*taiga*)
pʌj'du	пойду	(I shall go)
dvʌj'ŋik	двойник	(double)
nʌj'du	найду	(I shall find)
pʌj'koνɾj	пайковый	(ration, *adj.*)
vʌj'na	война	(war)

9. əj

'dɛləjʈʟ	делайте	(go!)
pʌ'duməjʈʟ	подумайте	(just imagine!)
'z daməj	с дамой	(with a lady)
s sʌ'bakəj	с собакой	(with a dog)
v gʌʂ'ʈinəj	в гостиной	(in the drawing-room)

10. oj

boj	бой	(battle)
stoj	стой	(stop!)
pʌ'koj	покой	(peace)
'dvojkə	двойка	(deuce)
gus'toj	густой	(thick)
'kojkə	койка	(bunk)

11. öj

ş şʟ'mjöj	с семьей	(with the family)
ȥ ȥʟm'ļöj	с землей	(with land)
stru'jöj	струей	(in a jet)
zaɾöj	зарей	(dawn, *instr. sing.*)

14. THE RUSSIAN DIPHTHONGS

12. uj

'dujʈɩ	дуйте	(blow!)
pətsɩ'luj	поцелуй	(kiss)
'bujnɛj	буйный	(tempestuous)
ʌbrʌ'zujʈɩ	образуйте	(form!)

13. üj

ḍüjm	дюйм	(inch)
pɩɽɪnʌ'tʃüjʈɩ	переночуйте	(spend the night!)
'kļüjʈɩ	клюйте	(peck!)

14. ɔj (transcribed here as uj)

uj'ʈi	уйти	(to go away)
uj'du	уйду	(I shall go away)
pəḅɩ'ʂɛdujʈɩ	побеседуйте	(have a chat!)

15. öj (transcribed here as üj)

ḍüj'mofkə	дюймовка	(inch-plank)
'vɨpļüjʈɩ	вылюйте	(spit out!)

Further remarks on diphthongs

14.12 Speakers who have a variety of e in unstressed position (§§ 12.72–4) have an additional unstressed diphthong ej (narrowly eɼj), pronounced where the orthography has ей, as in мыслей, улей, etc. Speakers who do not otherwise have a variety of e in unstressed position may also pronounce ей in unstressed position as ej, for the sake of grammatical differentiation.

14.13 At normal conversational speed the adjectival endings written -ый and -ий are frequently pronounced not as diphthongs but as simple vowels, ɩ and ɪ respectively. For this reason these endings are transcribed elsewhere in this book as ɩ(j) and ɪ(j).[1]

14.14 Some speakers pronounce the diphthong əj instead of ɪj in the adjectival ending written -ый, as in 'krasnəj красный (red), 'ḅɛləj белый (white). This is now not so common as formerly.

[1] Final ɪj in nouns may also be reduced to ɪ, as in 'armɪ(j) (see § 12.40).

14. THE RUSSIAN DIPHTHONGS

14.15 Similarly, the pronunciation of the adjectival ending written -ий as əj or ɯj after velar consonants, as in 'uskəj узкий (narrow), 'strogəj строгий (severe), 'ţixəj тихий (quiet), is less common now than the pronunciation ɯj with preceding soft velar consonant—'uskʲɯ(j), 'strogʲɯ(j), 'ţixʲɯ(j).

15

LABIALIZATION AND VELARIZATION

15.1 The hard (non-palatalized) consonants of Russian are particularly affected by a following u, o or ɨ. This is to say that special allophones of the hard consonants occur before these vowels.

15.2 Before u and o the allophones are accompanied by lip-rounding ('labialization'), which is somewhat greater before u than before o, and by a raising of the back of the tongue into the u-position ('velarization'). Consonants formed in this way are said to be 'labio-velarized'.

15.3 Before u the acoustic effect of this 'labio-velarization' may not be discernible to the untrained ear, since the lip-rounding and raising of the back of the tongue continue unchanged throughout the formation of the consonant and the following u. Before o the effect of labio-velarization is more easily discernible. It was pointed out in § 12.134 that the initial phase of the vowel o, other than after soft consonants, has a greater degree of lip-rounding and a slightly higher tongue-position than the main phase of the vowel. The greater degree of lip-rounding and the higher tongue-position are present in the articulation of a hard consonant preceding o. Consequently, when a hard consonant is followed immediately by the vowel o there is a 'glide' in the nature of an u-sound or the English sound w.

15.4 This glide should on no account be exaggerated. It is most noticeable after labial, labio-dental and velar consonants, as in the following examples:

15. LABIALIZATION AND VELARIZATION

pot	пот	(sweat)
bok	бок	(side)
mok	мог	(could)
fon	фон	(background)
von	вон	(over there)
kot	кот	(cat)
got	год	(year)
xot	ход	(move(ment))

15.5   In forming the sound ɨ the lips are not rounded (§ 12.17) and consonants occurring before ɨ are not labialized. The back of the tongue is, however, raised in or near the ɨ-position. Consonants formed with the additional articulation of a raising of the back of the tongue are said to be 'velarized'.

15.6   After labial and labio-dental consonants the initial phase of the vowel ɨ is articulated with the highest part of the tongue at a point further back than in the articulation of ɨ after, say, t or d (see § 12.21). At the same time the raising of the back of the tongue which is an essential feature of the articulation of this kind of ɨ is present during the articulation of the preceding labial or labio-dental consonant.[1]

15.7   The acoustic effect of the transition from a labial or labio-dental consonant to the following ɨ is that of a glide, in the nature of a very retracted ɨ (phonetic symbol ɯ). This may also strike the English-speaking learner as being like an English w from which, somehow, the lip-rounding has been removed. The glide should on no account be exaggerated.

15.8   Examples of words where a labial or labio-dental consonant precedes the vowel ɨ are:

pɨl	пыл	(ardour)
bɨl	был	(was)
mɨl	мыл	(washed)

---

[1] It is as if the consonant and the vowel mutually influenced each other. In terms of a phonetic theory somewhat different from that which underlies the present description, this could be expressed by saying that the feature of velarization (raising of the back of the tongue) extends through the entire complex of consonant and vowel (and 'belongs', so to speak, neither to the consonant nor to the vowel).

15. LABIALIZATION AND VELARIZATION

| 'fɪrkəʈ | фыркать | (to snort) |
| vɨl | выл | (howled) |

15.9 Before unstressed ɫ the velarization effect is not very strong and may conveniently be ignored for present purposes. It should be noted that the word был, quoted as an example above, is very often unstressed and pronounced bɫl.

15.10 In the pronunciation of some speakers labial and labio-dental consonants, especially the former, seem to be slightly *labialized* (i.e. accompanied by lip-rounding) as well as velarized before ɨ, so that the glide is slightly more like an English w. Again, the glide must not be exaggerated.

16

PALATALIZED CONSONANTS AND THEIR PHONETIC REPRESENTATION

16.1 As the Russian language contains a considerable number of consonants known as 'palatalized' or 'soft' consonants, it is appropriate here to make a few preliminary remarks about the nature of such consonants and their phonetic representation.

16.2 In the pronunciation of palatalized consonants the hard palate plays a fundamental part. By raising the front of the tongue so as to touch or almost to touch the hard palate a palatalized consonant is produced. This raising of the front of the tongue may accompany another articulation without otherwise changing it, as in the pronunciation of palatalized p, b, m, f, v, where the labial or labio-dental articulation is normal but is accompanied by simultaneous raising of the front of the tongue. Or it may, so to speak, merge with another articulation, so that a 'combined' articulation is produced, as in the pronunciation of palatalized t, d, n in Russian, where the blade of the tongue is placed on the teeth-ridge and the front of the tongue is raised towards the hard palate, so that most of the fore part of the tongue, including the blade and the front, acts as a single articulating organ. For this reason, the consonant tʃ is regarded as a palatalized consonant in Russian, the fact that, unlike other palatalized consonants in Russian, it has no non-palatalized counterpart being irrelevant.

16.3 Finally, palatalization may be manifested as an advanced or fronted articulation. Thus palatalized k, g and x are pronounced with the back of the tongue touching or nearly touching the soft palate over a considerable area, reaching as far forward as the junction with the hard palate, whereas 'hard' (non-palatalized) k, g and x are formed against a much more restricted area of the soft palate, towards the back part of its extent.

16.4 Palatalized consonants in Russian are frequently followed by a slight 'glide', like a j-sound, and known as an 'off-glide'. The occurrences and nature of these off-glides are described in the appropriate sections dealing with the individual consonants. Between a vowel and a following palatalized consonant there is often an 'on-glide', like a faint suggestion of an i-like vowel gliding from the vowel into the consonant. This should never be exaggerated so that a diphthong results. Indeed, if the student pronounces the palatalized consonants correctly the on-glides will usually arise automatically.

16.5 There are several ways of registering palatalized consonants, including the digraphic method (consisting, for example, of a normal consonant letter followed by j), the use of normal consonant letters slightly modified, and the use of specially designed letters. In this book we adopt largely the second method: palatalized consonants are indicated by a normal consonant letter with a small j attached to it at the lower right-hand corner. Thus, ɟ represents 'palatalized d', ʂ represents 'palatalized s', ɡ represents 'palatalized g' and so on. Palatalized ʃ and ʒ, however, are indicated by special symbols in which the lower curl is brought round to form a loop and tail, thus: ʆ, ʓ.

16.6 Since the affricate consonant tʃ (chapter 19) is palatalized and has no non-palatalized counterpart we have not considered it necessary either to adopt a special letter or to modify the constituent parts of this digraph. Where it is necessary to distinguish the palatalized consonant tʃ from the sequence of hard t plus hard ʃ a hyphen is inserted between the two symbols, thus: t-ʃ.

17

THE RUSSIAN PLOSIVE CONSONANTS

17.1 The articulation of a complete plosive consonant consists of two parts, the *stop* and the *release*.

17.2 The *stop*—is the action of holding the articulating organs in the position of contact. A stop has an appreciable length.

The *release*—of the articulating organs causes a sudden rush of air. The sound produced by this sudden emission of air is called the *plosion*. A plosion may be regarded as an instantaneous sound; it has no appreciable length.

Aspiration of voiceless plosives

17.3 Voiceless plosive consonants are said to be aspirated when between the instant of separation of the articulating organs and the commencement of a following vowel there is a perceptible interval during which breath is issuing from the mouth while the vocal cords have not yet begun to vibrate.

17.4 In English, p, t and k are with most speakers somewhat aspirated when followed by a stressed vowel and not preceded by s. Thus, when the words *pin, tea, come* are stressed the initial consonants are (with most speakers) somewhat aspirated. When special accuracy is required, the fact of aspiration may be indicated in phonetic transcription by inserting a small ʰ. Thus the English word *tea* might be written phonetically tʰiː or tʰʮi.

17.5 In Russian and many other languages (e.g. French) voiceless plosive consonants are normally not aspirated.[1]

---

[1] Restricting the term 'aspiration' to the insertion of ʰ *before vowels*. There is always a kind of aspiration when such sounds occur finally or are exploded before other consonants.

17. RUSSIAN PLOSIVE CONSONANTS

17.6　It is as a rule a matter of some difficulty for English people to learn to pronounce voiceless plosive consonants without aspiration. It is best to start practising with the syllable pa, observing that the effect of it (if the p is quite unaspirated) is something like the noise made by a cork being drawn out of a bottle. If the correct sound cannot be attained by simple imitation, the student should

(1) try to pronounce pa with a sound intermediate between his English p and his English b,

(2) try holding the breath just before pronouncing the syllable pa.

17.7　To get rid of the aspiration of t and k is more difficult, but the correct pronunciation may be attained by similar methods. For the Russian unaspirated t, practise the syllable ta with a sound intermediate between the English t (t^h) and d, but with the tip and blade of the tongue in the positions described in § 17.68. For unaspirated k, practise the syllable ka with a consonant intermediate between the English k (k^h) and g. In both cases some students will find it helpful to hold the breath just before pronouncing the syllable.

17.8　It is worthy of note that the aspiration of p, t, k in English is less marked in unstressed position. In fact many English people actually use the unaspirated sounds in such words as *happy, matter, letter, locket*. When preceded by the sound s, as in *span, stand, scan*, the consonants p, t, k are unaspirated before stressed vowels in the pronunciation of many English speakers. Many English speakers also use unaspirated consonants when the following vowel belongs to a separate word; thus many would use an unaspirated t in *blacked in* (blækt in) while they would use an aspirated t in *black tin* (blæk tin). These facts may be made use of in acquiring the Russian unaspirated sounds.

17.9　The Russian affricates ts and tʃ appear to have no perceptible aspiration following the fricative elements.

17. RUSSIAN PLOSIVE CONSONANTS

Voiced plosives

17.10 In the case of voiceless consonants, such as p, nothing whatever is heard during the stop. In voiced consonants, such as b, voice is heard during the stop. This voice may sound throughout the whole stop, or it may sound during a part of it only. Usage in regard to this varies in different languages.

17.11 When voice sounds throughout the stop, the consonant is said to be *fully voiced*. When voice sounds during only a part of the stop, the consonant is said to be *partially voiced*.

17.12 The Russian voiced plosive consonants (b, ḅ, d, ḍ, g, g̦) and the affricates dz and dʒ appear to be fully voiced in all circumstances.

17.13 In English, the consonants b, d, g are, with most speakers, fully voiced only when they occur between two other voiced sounds in connected speech. In other positions, and notably when initial or final, the voicing is only partial.

17.14 Some English speakers are unable, without special practice, to make the voiced sounds b, d, g at all. In speaking English they substitute the sounds known as 'unvoiced b, d, g' (phonetically ḅ, ḍ, g̦). In these sounds there is no voice at all during the stop; the voice begins at the instant of separation of the articulating organs. The sounds are very similar to the unaspirated p, t, k; the only difference is that ḅ, ḍ, g̦ are pronounced with less force of the breath than unaspirated p, t, k.

17.15 Those who use ḅ, ḍ, g̦ in English often have considerable difficulty in learning to make the properly voiced sounds required for Russian and other languages.

17.16 The best way of setting about learning to make fully voiced plosives is to start with b and endeavour to make the voice sound *during the stop*. Some English learners are able to do this as soon as the manner of forming the sound has been explained to them.

17.17 If the attempt is unsuccessful, the following method should be tried. Pronounce a long ə: (as in the English word *fern*); then, while holding on this sound, gradually draw the lips towards each other until the air-passage is all but closed. The result will be a fully voiced 'bi-labial *v*' (phonetically β). Practise this sound until it can be produced correctly without hesitation. Then pronounce the sound and press the lips together with the fingers so as to make the closure complete. It will be found that the voice still sounds, but the air, instead of issuing between the lips, simply enters the mouth and causes the cheeks to be puffed out. Repeat this exercise several times, taking care that the sound causes the cheeks to be well puffed out each time. Then try to do the same thing holding the lips together by their own muscular action without the aid of the fingers. The result will be an exaggerated form of the stop of a fully voiced b. Repeat the sound again several times, taking care that the sound causes the cheeks to be well puffed out each time. Then try to make the same sound in the normal way, that is, using such muscular pressure as will prevent the cheeks from puffing out.

17.18 The puffing out of the cheeks may be used by those who are studying alone as a test for whether the sound is correctly formed or not. Anyone who cannot make the sound in such a way as to cause the cheeks to be puffed out may be certain that he is not making it correctly.

17.19 It is helpful to some to notice that the stop of b or any other voiced consonant may be sung on different notes. It is a useful exercise to practise singing a tune on this sound.

17.20 When a good voiced b has been acquired by means of the foregoing exercises, and the learner can easily feel the mechanism by which the full voicing is produced, the other voiced plosives (d, g, and eventually also ḅ, ḍ, g̣, and the affricate dʒ) should be tried. The learner must apply to them the same mechanism as that which he uses in pronouncing fully voiced b.

17.21 The following exercises will be found useful in connexion with the acquisition of fully voiced plosive consonants.

    (1) pmpmpmpm... without moving the lips (the pm being as in the normal pronunciation of the English word *topmost*);

(2) bmbmbmbm... without moving the lips (the bm being as in the normal pronunciation of the English *submit*);

(3) tntntntn... without moving the tongue (the tn being as in the most usual pronunciation of the English word *mutton*);[1]

(4) dndndndn... without moving the tongue (the dn being as in the normal pronunciation of the English word *suddenly*);[2]

(5) bbbbb... without moving the lips (i.e. repetition of the stop of b);

(6) ddddd... without moving the tongue (i.e. repetition of the stop of d);

(7) kŋkŋkŋkŋ...[3] with wide open mouth and without moving the tongue;

(8) gŋgŋgŋgŋ... with wide-open mouth and without moving the tongue;

(9) ggggg... without moving the tongue (i.e. repetition of the stop of g).

17.22   It is desirable to practise exercises (3), (4) and (6) with the tip of the tongue against the teeth (as in Russian t, d), as well as with the tip of the tongue against the teeth-ridge (as in English).

17.23   Russian words for practising the voiced plosive consonants are given in this chapter below.

17.24   It is worthy of note that voiced plosive consonants do not occur before a pause in Russian.

Incomplete plosive consonants

17.25   To pronounce a complete plosive consonant two things are essential:

(1) contact must be made by the articulating organs,

(2) the articulating organs must subsequently be separated.

Thus in pronouncing p the lips are first closed and then opened.

---

[1] I.e. with no vowel between the t and the n.
[2] I.e. with no vowel between the d and the n.
[3] ŋ is the English sound of *ng* as in *hang*.

17. RUSSIAN PLOSIVE CONSONANTS

17.26 Sometimes plosive consonants are not fully pronounced. This happens, for instance, in English when a plosive consonant is immediately followed by another plosive consonant. Thus in the most usual pronunciation of the word *act* (ækt) the tongue does not leave the roof of the mouth in passing from the k to the t; there is therefore no plosion to the k; only the stop of it is pronounced.

17.27 In Russian the plosive consonants do not lose their plosions when followed by another heterorganic plosive or affricate.[1] Thus the italicized sounds in the following words have a distinct plosion before the following consonant is formed:

kʌˈroρkə	коробка	(box)
ˈpʈitsə	птица	(bird)
kuρˈtsu	купцу	(merchant, *dat. sing.*)
ˈotpusk	отпуск	(leave of absence)
tkatʃ	ткач	(weaver)
ˈʃtʃotkə	щетка	(brush)
ʌdˈgatkə	отгадка	(answer)
ˈsvaɟbə	свадьба	(wedding)
fʂɩgˈda	всегда	(always)
gɟɛ	где	(where)

17.28 When, however, two identical plosives occur together there is only one plosion. The stop element is held on for twice the normal length before the closure is released, as in:

ʌpˈpatʃkəʈ	обпачкать	(to stain)
ʌtˈtudə	оттуда	(thence), etc.

Abnormal plosion

17.29 Plosive consonants are sometimes exploded elsewhere than at the point of primary articulation. Such abnormal plosions may be (1) nasal or (2) lateral.

17.30 Thus in the group tn pronounced as in the English word

---

[1] 'Heterorganic' means 'formed in a different manner (*sci.* in a different part of the mouth and/or by different organs or parts thereof)'. The converse is 'homorganic'.

mutton ('mʌtn),[1] the mouth closure is retained throughout the two sounds, and the plosion is produced by the air suddenly escaping through the nose at the instant when the soft palate is lowered for forming the nasal consonant.

17.31 In the group dl pronounced as in the English word *middle* (mɪdl), the tip of the tongue does not leave the teeth-ridge, but the d is simply exploded laterally.

17.32 Cases like this occur also in Russian. Examples of this are:

pɪ'tno	пятно	(spot)
'bɛdnɪ(j)	бедный	(poor)
vərʌ'ʈɳik	воротник	(collar)
'peʈlə	петля	(loop)
fu'ʈlar	футляр	(case)

17.33 In Russian, nasal plosion is confined to cases where both the plosive and the nasal consonant have the same primary articulation.[2] In English, however, nasal plosion occurs also in such groups as kn, tm (as in *Hackney* (hæknɪ), *utmost* ('ʌtmoust)). English learners have therefore to be careful to give proper plosion to the plosive consonants in such Russian words as:

pʌ'dm̩otkə	подметка	(sole of boot)
zʌ'ʈm̩en(ɪ)jɪ	затьмение	(eclipse)
'g̑ibnuʈ	гибнуть	(to perish)
'kɳigə	книга	(book)
sɪ'dmoj	седьмой	(seventh)

The Russian plosive consonant phonemes

17.34 According to the analysis which underlies the description of Russian phonetics in this book, there are eleven plosive consonant phonemes in Russian p, p̦, b, b̦, t, ʈ, d, d̦, k, k̦ and g.[3] Attention is called to allophonic variation only where necessary.

---

[1] Very many English speakers do not use t at all in words of this kind, but replace it by the 'glottal stop', thus 'mʌʔn. Students must make sure which form they use.

[2] I.e. are homorganic (see footnote 1, p. 88).

[3] Although k and k̦ are considered to be distinct phonemes (see § 17.122), g̑ is considered to be an allophone or member of the phoneme g (see § 17.131).

17. RUSSIAN PLOSIVE CONSONANTS

Formation of the Russian plosive consonants in detail

p

17.35   The principal allophone of the Russian p-phoneme is formed as follows:

(1) *articulating organs:* the two lips, the tongue being in position for whatever vowel follows the p or for ə;

(2) *state of air-passage:* completely closed at the point of articulation; when closure is released, air escapes suddenly, producing plosion;

(3) *position of soft-palate:* raised, so that air cannot issue through the nose;

(4) *state of larynx:* vocal cords apart, in position for breath.

17.36   Russian p is a voiceless bi-labial plosive consonant.

17.37   Labio-velarized varieties of p occur before u and o, and velarized varieties before ɨ (see chapter 15). These varieties of p-sounds are subsidiary allophones of the p-phoneme.

17.38   The phoneme p does not occur before voiced consonants other than sonants. It is represented in spelling by the letter п and also, before voiceless consonants and at the end of a word, by the letter б.[1]

17.39   *Words illustrating the phoneme* p

'palkə	палка	(stick)
ʌ'pasnɨ(j)	опасный	(dangerous)
pətʌ'lok	потолок	(ceiling)
'kapļə	капля	(drop)
'optəm	оптом	(wholesale)
'kŗɛpķɨ(j)	крепкий	(strong)
'pţitsə	птица	(bird)
pʃt'ɲitsə	пшеница	(wheat)
puţ	путь	(path)
pus'toj	пустой	(empty)
pot	пот	(sweat)
sapok	сапог	(shoe)

---

[1] For cases where the letter б at the end of a word represents the consonant b see § 17.43 below.

pɨɭ	пыль	(dust)
'pɨtkə	пытка	(torment)
kʌ'ropkə	коробка	(box)
'jupkə	юбка	(skirt)
ʌpstu'paȶ	обступать	(to surround)
klop	клоп	(bug)
xⱡɛp	хлеб	(bread)
lop	лоб	(forehead)

b

17.40 The allophones of the b-phoneme differ from those of the p-phoneme (§§ 17.35–7) in that the vocal cords are close together and vibrating throughout the duration of the labial closure.

17.41 The principal allophone of the b-phoneme is a voiced, bi-labial plosive consonant.

17.42 Labio-velarized allophones of b occur before u and o, and velarized before ɨ (see §§ 15.3–6).

17.43 The phoneme b occurs at the end of a word only

(1) when the word is the preposition об and the next word begins with a vowel, as in ʌ'b ɛtəm, об этом (about this);[1]

(2) when the word is not an auxiliary word such as a preposition but is closely bound with a following word beginning with a voiced consonant (other than j, v, ɣ or a sonant).

Such following word is usually a particle, as in 'grob bɨ греб бы (would row), though it may also be the past tense of the verb 'to be', especially when this, as is frequently the case, is unstressed. Thus: 'lob bɨl лоб был (forehead was). Very occasionally word-final b may occur in front of other words beginning with a voiced consonant. With these exceptions, the phoneme b does not occur at the end of a word or before voiceless consonants.

17.44 In the pronunciation of many speakers b does not occur

[1] Note that here hard b occurs before a member of the phoneme e. Cf. ʌ'ȵɛtəm обетом (vow, *instr.*).

before m̩—instead the phoneme ɓ occurs. Some speakers sometimes practise the same 'substitution' of ɓ for b before ɣ.

17.45 The phoneme b is represented in spelling by the letter б. It may occasionally be represented by the letter п, as in the last three examples given below, when a word ending with the letter п is closely bound, phonetically, with a following word (usually a particle—sometimes the past tense of the verb 'to be') beginning with a voiced consonant.

17.46 *Words illustrating the phoneme* b

'bazə	база	(base)
gu'ba	губа	(lip)
bərʌ'da	борода	(beard)
brat	брат	(brother)
'dobrɪ(j)	добрый	(kind)
'g̦ibnuʈ	гибнуть	(to perish)
'obmərək	обморок	(swoon)
ʌ'bman	обман	(deception)
ʌ'bm̩ɛn	обмен	(exchange)
ʌblʌ'daʈ	обладать	(to possess)
'bukvə	буква	(letter)
'obuʃ	обувь	(footwear)
bok	бок	(side)
rʌ'botə	работа	(work)
bɨk	бык	(bull)
bɨt	быт	(mode of life)
ʌ'b ɛtəm	об этом	(about this)
ʌb t'vaɳɪ	об Иване	(about John)
ʌ'kr̦ɛb bɪ	окреп бы	(would grow strong)
ʌ'șlɛb bɪ	ослеп бы	(would go blind)
'klob bɪl	клоп был	(bug was)

17.47 The Russian p and b are identical with the normal English p and b respectively (as in *part*, *boat*), with the restrictions that in Russian p is not aspirated before vowels, b is voiced throughout and both consonants are labiovelarized or velarized in the circumstances described above (§§ 17.37, 42). Once the student has learnt to avoid aspiration of voiceless plosives in general and to make voiced consonants in general voiced throughout, he should have no difficulty in pronouncing Russian p and b.

ꞔ

17.48 The Russian ꞔ ('soft p') differs from the Russian p in that the tongue is in the position for j throughout the formation of the consonant.

17.49 Russian ꞔ is a voiceless, palatalized (soft) bi-labial plosive consonant.

17.50 The position of the tongue in the formation of ꞔ probably depends on the following vowel: the more open the vowel, the less likely is the tongue to reach the high, close position of the consonant j. As the closure of the lips is released, the tongue begins to move into the necessary position for the following vowel. When the following vowel is i or ɪ the tongue is already in or almost in the necessary position and there is no appreciable glide between ꞔ and a following i or ɪ. Before other vowels there is a slight glide, less obvious before e and ɛ, more obvious before other vowels. This glide is in the nature of a j-sound. It must on no account be exaggerated to give the effect of ꞔ followed by the consonant j. (The sequence ꞔ + j does occur; see § 17.55.)

17.51 When ꞔ occurs at the end of a word, several different effects are produced, according to what follows. If the next word begins with a vowel and there is no pause between the words, a glide occurs as described in the preceding paragraph, as in 'goluꞔ 'ɛtəvə tʃɪlʌ'ɣɛkə голубь этого человека (this man's pigeon).

17.52 If there is a pause after a word ending in ꞔ—and this is particularly the case at the end of a sentence—there is a glide after the ꞔ, but it is voiceless, similar in sound to the consonant in the German word *ich* (phonetically ç, see Fig. 23). The sound ç is a voiceless fricative. It is obtained by raising the tongue higher than the j-position until there is audible friction, the vocal cords however being in the open position, so that there is no voice. The voiceless off-glide of pre-pausal ꞔ has very little friction and is very short. Final, pre-pausal ꞔ must not sound like the sequence of consonants, ꞔ + ç.

17.53 A similar voiceless glide occurs after final ʙ when the next word, following without a pause, begins with a plosive, since any plosive in Russian is separately released before another, unlike plosive (see § 17.27). The glide after ʙ here, however, is not so obvious as the glide after pre-pausal ʙ. An example of ʙ in this position is provided by 'goluʙ 'ʦotkɪ голубь тетки (my auntie's pigeon).

17.54 If, however, the next word begins with a consonant before which the closure of ʙ is not released, such as m, there can be no glide. The softness of ʙ is then revealed, where it is preceded by such stressed vowels as a, o or u, by the presence of a very short i-glide between the vowel and the ʙ. The obligatory occurrence before a soft consonant of the e-allophone of the e-phoneme (§ 12.69) also reveals the softness of ʙ in these circumstances. After i and ɪ there is no discernible glide before ʙ while after ɨ, ɤ and other unstressed vowels the glide is faint or barely discernible.

17.55 When ʙ is followed by the consonant j, as in ʙjot пьет (drinks), some speakers pronounce the sequence ʙj with a short voiceless glide, as described in § 17.52, between the ʙ and the j. In the pronunciation of other speakers this voiceless glide between ʙ and j is not so obvious. Nevertheless, such speakers distinguish the sequence ʙo, for example, as in 'ʙostrɤ(j) пестрый (motley), from the sequence ʙjo, as in ʙjot. It is clear from this that the glide between ʙ and a following vowel must not be exaggerated until it sounds like the consonant j.

17.56 English speakers do not usually experience difficulty in making the sound ʙ, since it consists simply of the articulation of p with the simultaneous articulation of the sound j. They may, however, tend to exaggerate the glide before vowels and thus make the first syllable of 'ʙostrɤ(j) sound like the beginning of the word ʙjot, or the beginning of the word 'ʙatkə пятка (heel) sound like the beginning of the word 'ʙjant(j) пьяный (drunk).

17.57 Apart from consciously trying to keep the glide short, the learner may find it helpful not to raise the tongue too high in producing the softness of ɲ (see § 17.50). It may also help, if the learner constantly produces a strong j-glide between ɲ and a following vowel, to start from, e.g. ɲjot, where the consonant j is essential to correct pronunciation of the word, and then practice reducing the j until it no longer sounds like a separate consonant but is merely a short glide.

17.58 The sound ɲ does not occur before voiced consonants other than j and the sonants. It is represented in spelling by the letter п followed by one of the vowel letters е, и, ю, я or the soft sign, ь. At the end of a word it may also be represented by the letter б followed by the soft sign.

17.59 *Words illustrating the phoneme* ɲ

ɲiʈ	пить	(to drink)
nʌ'ɲitək	напиток	(drink)
kʌ'ɲilkə	копилка	(money-box)
ɲɩʈɩ'lɛtkə	пятилетка	(five-year plan)
ɲɩ'sok	песок	(sand)
ɲeʈ	петь	(to sing)
ɲetʃ	печь	(stove)
ɲɛl	пел	(sang)
us'ɲɛl	успел	(succeeded)
ɲæʈ	пять	(five)
ʌ'ɲæʈ	опять	(again)
'ɲatkə	пятка	(heel)
'ɲatɩ(j)	пятый	(fifth)
ɲotr	Петр	(Peter)
'ɲostrɩ(j)	пестрый	(motley)
ɲu'rɛ	пюре	(purée)
'goluɲ	голубь	(pigeon)
sʈeɲ	степь	(steppe)
'nastɩɲ	насыпь	(embankment)
toɲ	топь	(boggy ground)
'goluɲ 'ɛtəvə tʃɩlʌ'γɛkə	голубь этого человека	(this man's pigeon)
toɲ kʌ'torəjə	топь, которая	(the boggy ground which)

17. RUSSIAN PLOSIVE CONSONANTS

'golup məjɪvo	голубь моего	(my brother's
'bratə	брата	pigeon)
pjot	пьет	(drinks)
pju	пью	(I drink)
pjant(j)	пьяный	(drunk)

ḅ

17.60 The phoneme ḅ differs from the phoneme p (§§ 17.48, 49) in that the vocal cords are close together and vibrating throughout the duration of the consonant.

17.61 The phoneme ḅ is a voiced, palatalized (soft) bi-labial plosive consonant.

17.62 The remarks made in § 17.50 on the height of the tongue in the pronunciation of p and the nature of the glides between that consonant and a following vowel apply also to the consonant ḅ. The phoneme ḅ may also occur before other consonants. There is then no glide between ḅ and the following consonant (with the exception noted below, § 17.63), the softness of ḅ being revealed either in the off-glide of the preceding vowel (cf. § 17.54) or in the occurrence of the close member of the e-phoneme (cf. § 12.69).

17.63 The glide between ḅ and a following vowel must not be exaggerated (cf. § 17.55 above). When ḅ is followed by the consonant j, some speakers have a glide between the ḅ and the j, as in ḅjot бьет (strikes). This glide is the voiced correspondent of the glide described in § 17.52 above and can be obtained by raising the tongue from the j-position until there is audible friction, while the vocal cords continue to vibrate, producing a voiced glide. Other speakers do not produce audible friction in the sequence ḅj. They have instead a glide like a very short i-sound.

17.64 The remarks made in §§ 17.56, 57 apply, *mutatis mutandis*, to the pronunciation of ḅ. The word ḅjot may be used as a starting-point in the exercise to reduce the j in order to arrive at, for example, the middle syllable of rɪ'ḅonək ребенок (child), the word ḅju бью (*I strike*) as a starting-point for the first two sounds of ḅust бюст (bust).

17. RUSSIAN PLOSIVE CONSONANTS

17.65 The phoneme ḅ does not occur before voiceless consonants. It occurs at the end of a word only when that word is closely bound, phonetically, with a following word beginning with a voiced consonant (other than j, v, ɣ or a sonant). Such following word is usually a particle, or the unstressed past tense of the verb 'to be' (see some of the examples below), or very occasionally some other word.

17.66 The phoneme ḅ is represented in spelling by the letter б followed by one of the vowel letters е, и, ю, я, or the soft sign, ь. At the end of a word it may also be represented by the letters пь in the circumstances described in the preceding paragraph.

17.67 *Words illustrating the phoneme* ḅ

ḅiţ	бить	(to strike)
ʌ'ḅidə	обида	(insult)
'leḅɪţ	лебедь	(swan)
ḅɪ'şɛdə	беседа	(chat)
'ḅeɾɪk	берег	(shore)
ʌ'ḅɛt	обед	(dinner)
ɾɪ'ḅatə	ребята	(lads)
gəlu'ḅatə	голубята	(young pigeons)
ɾɪ'ḅonək	ребенок	(child)
'ḅodrə	бедра	(hips)
ḅust	бюст	(bust)
yɪşţɪ'ḅül	вестибюль	(vestibule)
'goluḅ bɪ	голубь бы	(pigeon would)
şţeḅ bɪ'la	степь была	(steppe was)
ḅjot	бьет	(strikes)
ḅju	бью	(I strike)
vərʌ'ḅja	воробья	(sparrow, *gen.*)

t

17.68 The principal allophone of the Russian t-phoneme is formed as follows:

(1) *articulating organs:* tip of tongue touching front teeth in angle formed by upper incisors and teeth-ridge; blade of tongue against forward part of teeth-ridge (Fig. 12);

(2) *state of air-passage:* completely closed at point of articulation; when closure is released, air escapes suddenly, producing plosion;

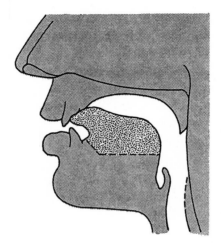

Fig. 12. Tongue-position of Russian t and d

(3) *position of soft palate:* raised, so that air cannot issue through the nose;

(4) *state of larynx:* vocal cords apart, in position for breath.

17.69 The principal allophone of the Russian t-phoneme is a voiceless, denti-alveolar plosive consonant.[1]

17.70 Except before the sound θ (i.e. the sound represented by the letters *th* in *think*), the English t is alveolar and *apical* in most accents of England, i.e. it is formed with the *tip* of the tongue against the teeth-ridge just at or slightly in front of the angle where it begins to rise up towards the hard palate

[1] There are slight differences in the articulation of t from speaker to speaker. Some speakers, for example, pronounce a purely dental t, in which the tongue-tip touches the upper incisors (about half-way down their back surface) but the blade makes no contact with the teeth-ridge. A quite common alternative pronunciation of t is with the blade only, making contact with the front part of the teeth-ridge and roots of the upper incisors, while the tongue-tip is lowered to the roots of the lower incisors.

17. RUSSIAN PLOSIVE CONSONANTS

(Fig. 13). Consonants formed with the tip of the tongue are called 'apical' consonants, whereas consonants formed with the blade of the tongue are known as 'laminal' consonants. English t is apical, Russian t as described in § 17.68 'apico-laminal' (i.e. both apical and laminal).

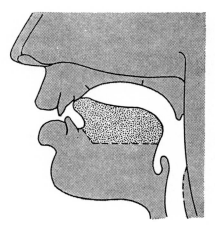

Fig. 13. Tongue-position of alveolar t and d

17.71 In § 17.5 it was pointed out that voiceless plosives in Russian are not normally aspirated, whereas they are in English, in certain circumstances. Care must be taken therefore not to aspirate Russian t. If necessary the student should remind himself of this point and of the apico-laminal formation of Russian t by marking every t in the phonetic transcription of a passage he is practising.

17.72 The Russian t-phoneme does not occur before voiced consonants other than j, v, y and the sonants, nor before the palatalized consonants ţ, ş, tʃ, ɟ, ļ and ņ and the vowel phoneme e.

17.73 Subsidiary allophones which are labio-velarized occur before u and o and a velarized allophone occurs before ɨ (chapter 15). Before n and l occur allophones which have nasal and lateral release respectively (§§ 17.29–32).

99

17.74 The phoneme t is represented in spelling by the letter т and before voiceless consonants and at the end of a word, also by the letter д. For cases where the letter д at the end of a word represents the phoneme d, see below, § 17.81.

17.75 *Words illustrating the phoneme* t

tak	так	(thus)
tam	там	(there)
'patəkə	патока	(treacle)
tut	тут	(here)
prʌs'tudə	простуда	(cold)
tot	тот	(that)
pʌ'tom	потом	(then)
tɨ	ты	(thou)
bu'tɨlkə	бутылка	(bottle)
'buttə	будто	(as if)
ʌttʌ'vo	оттого	(therefore)
ʌt'tudə	оттуда	(thence)
ʌttʌs'kaʈ	оттаскать	(to drag away)
trut	трут	(they rub)
trʌ'va	трава	(grass)
'utrə	утро	(morning)
ʌ'trostək	отросток	(shoot)
ʌt-sʈ'laju[1]	отсылаю	(I send away)
pʌt-'sluʃəl[1]	подслушал	(eavesdropped)
nʌt-'smotr[1]	надсмотр	(supervision)
ʌt'tsa	отца	(father, *gen. sing.*)
pʌt'tsɣetʃɩvəʈ	подцвечивать	(to dye)
ʌbɣɩt-'ʃalʈ(j)[2]	обветшалый	(decrepit)
ʌt'-ʃeḷɳɩk[2]	отшельник	(hermit)
tku	тку	(I weave)
tknul	ткнул	(prodded)
'satkə	садка	(planting)
'otpusk	отпуск	(leave)

[1] The hyphen in these words is to show that a sequence of t + s is pronounced, not the single consonant ts (chapter 19).

[2] The hyphen in these words is to show that a sequence of (hard) t + (hard) ʃ is pronounced, not the single (soft) consonant tʃ (chapter 19).

17. RUSSIAN PLOSIVE CONSONANTS

ʌtprɪ'gaʈ	отпрягать	(to unharness)
ʌtmɪ'vaʈ	отмывать	(to wash away)
ʌ'tm̩ɛtkə	отметка	(mark)
ʌtnʌ'ʃu	отношу	(I carry away)
'plotnɪ(j)	плотный	(compact)
bʌl'tnuʈ	болтнуть	(to blurt out)
kʌ'tla	котла	(boiler, *gen. sing.*)
ʌtlʌ'ʒu	отложу	(I shall put off)
m̩ɪ'tla	метла	(broom)
rot	рот	(mouth)
got	год	(year)
ŋɛt	нет	(no)
yit	вид	(view)
pətpɪ'raʈ	подпирать	(to prop up)

d

17.76   The allophones of the phoneme d differ from the allophones of the phoneme t (§§ 17.68–9, 73) in that the vocal cords are together and vibrating throughout the duration of the sounds.

17.77   Thus the principal allophone of the d-phoneme is a voiced, denti-alveolar plosive consonant.

17.78   Subsidiary allophones are labio-velarized before u and o, velarized before ɨ and those occurring before n and l have nasal and lateral release respectively.

17.79   Russian d differs from English d in the same way that Russian t differs from English t (see § 17.70 and Figs. 12 and 13).

17.80   The phoneme d does not occur before voiceless consonants nor before d̦, z̦, n̦, l̦ and e.

17.81   When the next word begins with a voiced consonant other than d̦, z̦, n̦ or l̦, then the phoneme d occurs at the end of the simple prepositions written над (above), под (below), перед/пред (in front of) and the compound preposition written из-под (from under). It also occurs at the end of the preposition written от when the next word begins with a voiced consonant other than d̦, z̦, j, v, y or a sonant. In the same phonetic circumstances a final letter д or т is usually pronounced d before a particle or the unstressed past tense of the verb 'to be', and may occasionally be so pronounced elsewhere. Otherwise d does not occur at the end of a word.

17.82 The phoneme d is represented in spelling by the letter д and also, before voiced consonants other than those just enumerated, by the letter т.

17.83 *Words illustrating the phoneme* d

da	да	(yes)
u'dar	удар	(blow)
damə	дама	(lady)
ʌ'ḥidə	обида	(insult)
dom	дом	(house)
u'dobnə	удобно	(convenient)
dup	дуб	(oak)
'vozdux	воздух	(air)
dɨm	дым	(smoke)
sʌ'dɨ	сады	(gardens)
nəddʌ'vaҭ	наддавать	(to add)
ʌd'daҭ	отдать	(to give up)
'poddənstvə	подданство	(citizenship)
ʌdgəvʌ'ɽiҭ	отговорить	(to dissuade)
pədgʌ'toүɪҭ	подготовить	(to prepare)
'od-zɪf[1]	отзыв	(testimonial)
pəd-zəgʌ'lovək[1]	подзаголовок	(subheading)
nʌ'd-zor[1]	надзор	(supervision)
drʌ'va	дрова	(firewood)
'dramə	драма	(drama)
үɪ'dro	ведро	(bucket)
pəd-ʒɪ'gaҭ[2]	поджигать	(to kindle)
'tod ʒɪ	тот же	(the same)
d-ʒut[2]	джут	(jute)
'd-ʒunglɪ[2]	джунгли	(jungle)

[1] The hyphen here indicates the sequence d + z as distinct from the voiced allophone (dz) of the phoneme ts (§ 19.13).

[2] d-ʒ indicates the sequence d + ʒ as distinct from the voiced allophone (dʒ) of the phoneme tʃ (§ 19.27).

dno	дно	(bottom)
ʌ'dno	одно	(one)
'ɣidnt(j)	видный	(prominent)
prtdlʌ'ʒit	предложить	(to propose)
nʌ'dlom	надлом	(fracture)
pʌ'dlok	подлог	(forgery)
nʌ'dm̩ennt(j)	надменный	(arrogant)
pʌ'dm̩otkə	подметка	(sole of shoe)

ʈ

17.84   The Russian phoneme ʈ ('soft t' or 'palatalized t') has a principal allophone which is formed as follows:

(1) *articulating organs:* blade of tongue against teeth-ridge and front of tongue close to front part of hard palate[1] (the tip of the tongue is usually lowered, making contact or near-contact with the base of the lower front teeth (see Fig. 14);[2]

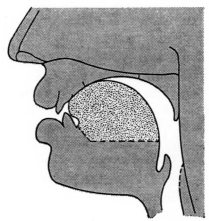

Fig. 14. Tongue-position of Russian palatalized alveolar ʈ and ɖ

(2) *state of air-passage:* completely closed at point of articulation; when closure is released, air escapes suddenly, producing plosion;

---

[1] Contact of the foremost part of the front of the tongue with the foremost part of the hard palate is not uncommon.

[2] Less commonly, the tongue-tip is behind the upper front teeth, but there is usually no contact with the front teeth.

(3) *position of soft palate:* raised, so that air cannot issue through the nose;

(4) *state of larynx:* vocal cords apart, in position for breath.

17.85 The principal allophone of ţ is a voiceless, palatalized alveolar plosive consonant.

17.86 In forming ţ, all the articulating parts of the tongue reach their respective positions as nearly as possible simultaneously. In the plosion of ţ, the closure made by the blade against the teeth-ridge is released just before the front of the tongue moves away from the hard palate. As a result of this the blade and front of the tongue are, for a fraction of a second, in a position similar to that for Russian ş, and a *very* short fricative element, like Russian ş, is heard.

17.87 This short fricative element, which must on no account be exaggerated so that ţş (which *does* occur in Russian; see § 17.90) instead of ţ is pronounced, varies somewhat from speaker to speaker, such that in the pronunciation of some speakers it is hardly discernible at all.[1]

17.88 When ţ is followed by a vowel there is, in addition to the possible fricative element, a very slight j-glide between ţ and the following vowel. This j-glide also varies in prominence from speaker to speaker but is never so prominent that ţo, for example, sounds like ţjo. (The sequence ţj does occur and is illustrated below, § 17.97.) The j-glide is least discernible before i, where indeed it may not be discernible at all.

17.89 Before a pause (as for example at the end of an utterance), air may continue to issue briefly through the mouth after the closure of ţ has been released but while the front of the tongue is still raised towards the hard palate. The result of this is the involuntary production of a 'voiceless j', i.e. the voiceless fricative consonant ç (as in German *ich*, iç; see Fig. 23). This

---

[1] The degree of prominence of this fricative element depends on the order in which the various articulating parts of the tongue are released and the intervals between these releases. It may also be that the fricative element is more obvious when ţ is pronounced with the tongue-tip behind the upper front teeth. This is a matter which needs to be investigated.

sound should not be exaggerated: indeed no attempt should be made deliberately to pronounce it.

17.90 It was pointed out in § 17.28 that when there are two identical plosives in sequence there is only one release. Thus in ʌ̡t̡t̡ˈnul оттянул (drew off), there is only one release, the closure being held for twice the normal length of time. t̡ is not independently released before s̡ either, so in ʌˈt̡s̡udə отсюда (hence), for example, the t̡ proceeds straight into the s̡ and there is no fricative off-glide to the t̡. Before plosives other than t̡, however, and before ɣ, m and m̡, the plosive t̡ does have its own plosion.

17.91 Before n̡ and l̡ subsidiary allophones of t̡ occur which differ from t̡ as described above in having nasal and lateral plosion respectively. In the sequences t̡n̡ and t̡l̡ therefore there is no independent release of t̡ and therefore no fricative element.

17.92 Before the soft affricate consonant tʃ (chapter 19) an allophone of t̡ is used which is formed in the same way as the stop-element of tʃ, that is to say with the tongue-tip touching the teeth-ridge and the blade against the back part of the teeth-ridge. The t̡ in the sequence t̡tʃ is not separately released, i.e. the initial stop-element of tʃ is held on for twice its normal length to produce t̡tʃ.[2]

17.93 The acoustically nearest English equivalents to Russian t̡ and d̡ (see below, §§ 17.98, 99) are, respectively, the tj and dj heard in *tulle* (tjuːl) and *dune* (djuːn). There are, however, considerable differences between Russian t̡ and English tj for example and the use of the latter for Russian t̡ is not satisfactory. The principal allophone of Russian t̡, as described above, is laminal whereas t in English tj is apical. Some speakers pronounce t in English tj more like the Russian t̡ in the sequence t̡tʃ (see § 17.92).

17.94 It may, however, help English speakers who find difficulty in achieving Russian t̡ and d̡ from the descriptions given in §§ 17.84, 98 to start from the English combinations of phonemes, tj and dj, respectively, heard in the words *tune* and

---

[1] See § 19.25.

dune. They must then try to produce the plosive element with the tip of the tongue behind the lower teeth and the blade against the teeth-ridge, and make the j-element very short, trying to combine it as closely as possible with the preceding stop element. The short fricative element must also be borne in mind. The student should note that there are, for example, considerable differences in the initial consonants between, on the one hand, Russian ʈüļ тюль (tulle) and 'ɖun дюн (dunes, *gen. pl.*) and on the other hand, English *tulle* and *dune.*

17.95   The phoneme ʈ does not occur before voiced consonants other than j, v, ɣ and the sonants. Nor does the phoneme ʈ occur before the voiceless consonants p, s, t and ʃ.

17.96   The phoneme ʈ is represented in spelling by the letter т followed by one of the vowel letters и, е, я or ю, or the soft sign, ь. The letter т also represents ʈ when it is not followed by one of the letters just listed but when the next sound is ʈ, ş, ɳ, ļ, tʃ, or ʃ and, in some words, when the next sound is ɱ or ɣ. At the end of a word, ʈ may also be represented by the letter д followed by the soft sign. The letter д also represents ʈ in the middle of a word when the next sound is ʈ, ş, tʃ or ʃ. In such instances a soft sign follows д in one or two words.

17.97   *Words illustrating the phoneme* ʈ

'ʈixə	тихо	(quietly)
ʈɪ'ļɛga	телега	(cart)
ʈeɳ	тень	(shadow)
pʌş'ʈeļ	постель	(bed)
'ʈɛlə	тело	(body)
'ʈanuʈ	тянут	(they pull)
'ʈagə	тяга	(draught)
'ʈotkə	тетка	(auntie)
'ʈoplɪ(j)	теплый	(warm)
ʈüɽ'ma	тюрьма	(prison)
ʈuk	тюк	(bale)
maʈ	мать	(mother)
krʌ'vaʈ	кровать	(bedstead)
glaʈ	гладь	(smooth surface)

ʌʈʈɩˈnul	оттянул	(drew off)
ˈbuʈʈɩ	будьте	(be!)
ˈbuʈkə	будь-ка	(just be!)
ˈoʈʈɩ̥ɴ̩l	оттепель	(thaw)
pəʈʈɩˈraʈ	подтирать	(to wipe)
ʌˈʈṣuda	отсюда	(hence)
ʌˈʈṣetʃ	отсечь	(to chop off)
ˈbaʈkə	батька	(dad)
ʈʃu	тьфу	(pshaw!)
ʈɣerʳ[1]	Тверь	(Tver)[2]
ʈɣordɩ(j)[1]	твердый	(hard)
ʈma	тьма	(darkness)
rʌˈboʈɴ̩k	работник	(worker)
ʌʈɴɩṣˈʈi	отнести	(to carry off)
ʈla	тля	(aphis)
ˈɴeʈlə	петля	(loop)
ˈoʈtʃɩstvə	отчество	(fatherland)
ʌʈˈtʃot	отчет	(report)
pʌʈˈtʃas	подчас	(at times)
tʃüˈʈjo	чутье	(sense)
tʃüˈʈja	чутья	(sense, *gen. sing.*)

ɖ

17.98 The allophones of the phoneme ɖ differ from those of the phoneme ʈ (§§ 17.84, 85) in that the vocal cords are close together and vibrating throughout the duration of the sounds.

17.99 Thus, the principal allophone of the ɖ-phoneme is a voiced, palatalized alveolar plosive consonant (see Fig. 14).

17.100 The remarks made in §§ 17.86–8 about the slight fricative element of ʈ and the j-glide before a following vowel apply also to ɖ, except that the slight fricative element is *voiced* and is rather like Russian ʒ (§§ 18.65, 66).

17.101 In a sequence of two ɖ's there is only one release: the stop is held on for twice the normal length of time. ɖ is not

---

[1] Hard t is also heard in these words in the pronunciation of younger speakers. Such pronunciation may ultimately become the 'norm'.

[2] Now called kʌˈlʲinɩn Калинин (Kalinin).

independently released before ʐ—the ḍ proceeds straight into the ʐ and there is no fricative off-glide to the ḍ. Before plosives other than ḍ and before y and m̩ the plosive ḍ does have its own release.

17.102 As in the case of ṭ, there are subsidiary allophones of ḍ occurring before n̩ and ḷ and having nasal and lateral release respectively.

17.103 On an English sound near to Russian ḍ and on adapting this sound to Russian ḍ see §§ 17.93, 94.

17.104 The phoneme ḍ does not occur before voiceless consonants nor before voiced hard consonants in one and the same word. It occurs at the end of a word when the word is one of the prepositions written над (above), под (below), перед/пред (in front of) or из-под (from under) and the next word begins with ḍ, ʐ, n̩, or ḷ, as in pəḍ ḍɪˈɾeyjəm̩ɪ под деревьями (under the trees). It also occurs at the end of the preposition written от when the next word begins with ḍ or ʐ. It is also usual at the end of any word where дь or ть is written and the next word is a particle beginning with a voiced consonant other than v, y, j or a sonant or is the unstressed past tense of the verb 'to be', and it may occasionally occur before other words beginning with a voiced consonant other than v, y, j or a sonant. Otherwise ḍ does not occur at the end of a word.

17.105 The phoneme ḍ is represented in spelling by the letter д followed by one of the vowel letters е, и, ю or я, or the soft sign, ь. Without a following soft sign, д also represents ḍ when the next consonant in a word is ḍ, ʐ, n̩ or ḷ and in some words when the next consonant is y or m̩. The letter т may also represent the phoneme ḍ when the next consonant in a word is ḍ or ʐ. At the end of a word the letters д or т, and the letter-sequences дь or ть represent ḍ in the circumstances described in the preceding paragraph.

17.106 *Words illustrating the phoneme* ḍ

ˈḍivə	диво	(marvel)
ḍɪˈɾeyn̩ə	деревня	(village)

17. RUSSIAN PLOSIVE CONSONANTS

'dets	дети	(children)
den	день	(day)
tʃü'dɛsnt(j)	чудесный	(marvellous)
brʌ'dagə	бродяга	(tramp)
'doʃtvə	дешево	(cheap)
'duʒtnə	дюжина	(dozen)
'duʒt(j)	дюжий	(sturdy)
ʌd'dɛl	отдел	(section)
pʌd'dɛlət	подделать	(to forge)
'svadbə	свадьба	(wedding)
u'sadbə	усадьба	(homestead)
dγɛ¹	две	(two)
dγer¹	дверь	(door)
'dγigət¹	двигать	(to move)
ʃü'dmilə¹	Людмила	(Liudmilla)
'dmitrt(j)¹	Дмитрий	(Dmitry)
pədʒt'meʃnt(j)	подземельный	(underground)
nədʒt'rat	надзирать	(to supervise)
pədŋt'mat	поднимать	(to raise)
dŋa	дня	(day, *gen. sing.*)
'sredŋt(j)	средний	(average)
dʃt'na	длина	(length)
dʃt	для	(for)
prʌ'dʃit	продлить	(to prolong)
'podʃt	подле	(beside)
'mad bt	мать бы	(mother would)
'djavəl	дьявол	(devil)

k

17.107 The principal allophone of the Russian k-phoneme is formed as follows:

(1) *articulating organs:* back of tongue against central and forward parts of soft palate (see Fig. 15), the lips being in a neutral position;

(2) *state of air-passage:* completely close at place of articula-

¹ Hard d is also heard in these words in the pronunciation of younger speakers. Such pronunciation may ultimately become the 'norm'.

tion; when closure is released, air escapes suddenly, producing plosion;

(3) *position of soft palate:* raised, so that air cannot issue through the nose;

(4) *state of larynx:* vocal cords apart, in position for breath.

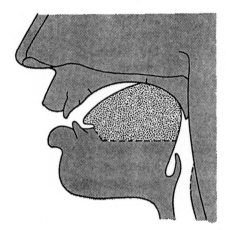

Fig. 15. Tongue-position of 'average' k and g

17.108 This allophone of k is a voiceless velar plosive consonant.

17.109 The subsidiary allophone of k occurs before u and o and is labialized (see chapter 15). In the few loan-words where k occurs before *unstressed* o, such as konso'mɛ консоме (*consommée*), there is, however, no labialization.

17.110 The principal allophone of k presents no difficulty to English speakers. The labialized allophone can be acquired by adding lip-rounding to the English k. Care must be taken, however, not to allow kot кот (tom-cat), for example, to sound like kwot.

17.111 While the labialized allophone of k occurs only before u and o, the principal allophone occurs elsewhere: at the end of a word, before other voiceless consonants, before v, ɣ, and the sonants and before a (see, however, §§ 17.113–14).

17. RUSSIAN PLOSIVE CONSONANTS

17.112   When k occurs before other, different plosives it has its own plosion (see § 17.27). This is also the case when it occurs before v, ɣ, m, m̥, n and ŋ.

17.113   The phoneme k occurs before the phonemes i and e only at the junction of two words, as follows.[1] When the preposition к (towards, to) is followed by a word beginning with the letter и, then k is pronounced, followed by the ɨ or ɩ allophone of the i-phoneme, depending on the location of the stress. Thus: ˈk ɨgər̩u к Игорю (to Igor), k ɩˈvanu к Ивану (to Ivan). The sequence kɩ also occurs when the word following the preposition к begins with the letter э and the stress does not fall on the first syllable, as in k ɩkskʌˈvatəru к экскаватору (towards the excavator). If the stress falls on the first syllable of a word beginning with э after the preposition к then the sequences kɛ and ke occur, as in ˈk ɛtəmu к этому (to this), ˈk eȶ ɩm к этим (to these). Very occasionally the sequence kɩ may occur where a word ending with k is followed by another word beginning with the phoneme i in unstressed position, as in ˈrak ɩ ˈrɨbə рак и рыба (crayfish and fish).

17.114   The phoneme k also occurs before j, again at the juncture of preposition and following word, as in ˈk jolkȶɩ к ёлке (towards the fir-tree), ˈk jugu к югу (to the south).

17.115   The phoneme k is represented in spelling by the letter к and at the end of a word or before a voiceless consonant, also by the letter г.

17.116   *Words illustrating the phoneme* k

kak	как	(how)
zʌˈkas	заказ	(order)
kəȶ ˈso	колесо	(wheel)
ˈkuklə	кукла	(doll)
pʌˈkupkə	покупка	(purchase)

---

[1] The occurrence of k before the phoneme i within a word (i.e. the sequence kɨ or kɩ, spelt кы) is found in some *dialect* words. The exclamation kʃ (*shoo!*) is sometimes written кш, sometimes кыш. The latter spelling is merely a graphic device to represent a suggestion of an indeterminate vowel between k and ʃ and/or to avoid having a word written without a vowel-letter.

'ʃkurə	шкура	(hide)
koɲ	конь	(horse)
'skorə	скоро	(soon)
prʌ'kol	прокол	(puncture)
ļok	лег	(lay down)
rok	рок	(fate)
rok	рог	(horn)
klaşţ	класть	(to put)
'kraskə	краска	(paint)
akt	акт	(act)
pakt	пакт	(pact)
kvas	квас	(kvass)
'kyɛrxu	кверху	(upwards)
'k‿m̥ɛstu	к месту	(pertinent)
ʌ'kno	окно	(window)
'kɲigə	книга	(book)
'moknuţ	мокнуть	(to become wet)
tknuţ	ткнуть	(to prod)
'k‿i̥gəʀu	к Игорю	(towards Igor)
k‿t'vanu	к Ивану	(towards Ivan)
'k‿ɛtəmu	к этому	(to this)
'k‿eţ̥m	к этим	(to these)
'k‿jolķɩ	к елке	(towards the fir-tree)
'k‿jugu	к югу	(to the south)
'k‿jalţɩ	к Ялте	(towards Yalta)

ķ

17.117 For most practical purposes it is not necessary to distinguish more than one allophone of the phoneme ķ. It is formed as follows:

(1) *articulating organs:* back of tongue against central and forward parts of soft palate, front of tongue raised towards hard palate, middle of tongue usually touching rear part of hard palate (see Fig. 16);

(2) *state of air passage:* completely closed at place of articulation; when closure is released, air escapes suddenly, producing plosion;

(3) *position of soft palate:* raised, so that air cannot issue through the nose;

(4) *state of larynx:* vocal cords apart, in the position for breath.

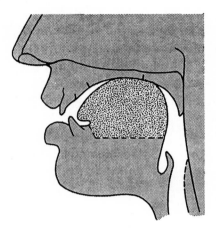

Fig. 16. Tongue-position of Russian and ķ and g̦

17.118 Russian ķ is a voiceless palatalized (soft) velar consonant.[1]

17.119 The principal difference between ķ and k lies, of course, in the fact that in the pronunciation of ķ the front of the tongue is raised towards the hard palate. At the same time, because of this raising of the front of the tongue, the back of the tongue makes contact with the soft palate at a point in front of the place where contact is made in the pronunciation of k.

17.120 Russian ķ has a slightly more forward place of articulation and a greater part of the back of the tongue in contact with the soft palate than does the fronted k in English *key* (kiː). The student may find it helpful to start from the k in English *key* and, by moving the point of articulation slightly forward and raising the front of the tongue nearer to the hard palate, arrive at Russian ķ.

[1] Alternatively, it may be described as a voiceless, pre-velar plosive consonant.

17.121 It is also possible to approach ǩ by taking the sequence of sounds kj in English *cube* (kjuːb) and trying, so to speak, to merge the j into the k. Care must be taken, however, not to arrive at an affricate like that represented by *ch* in English *chew* (tʃuː) or that which occurs in sub-standard pronunciations of *tube* (tʃuːb). The student should bear in mind that Russian ǩ is still clearly a sound of the *k*-type.

17.122 Russian ǩ occurs before j and the vowel phonemes i, e *only within one and the same word*. Since Russian k *and* Russian ǩ both occur before the phonemes a, o and u within the same word they are considered, in terms of the theory underlying the present description, to be separate phonemes.[1]

17.123 The phoneme ǩ is represented in spelling by the letter к, followed by one of the vowel letters и, е, ю or я, or the soft sign, ь.

17.124 *Words illustrating the phoneme* ǩ

ǩit	кит	(whale)
ǩiʂt	кисть	(bunch)
ruˈǩi	руки	(hand, *gen. sing.*)
ˈruǩι	руки	(hands)
ǩιrʌˈʂιι	керосин	(kerosene)
ǩɛm	кем	(whom, *instr.*)
v̬ ruˈǩɛ	в руке	(in the hand)
rʌˈǩɛtə	ракета	(rocket)
ˈǩaxtə	Кяхта	(Kyakhta)
tǩot	ткет	(weaves)
ǩιʌsˈǩor	киоскер	(kiosk-attendant)
məɲιˈǩur	маникюр	(manicure)
ǩüˈɣɛtkə	кюветка	(developing dish)
ǩüˈɣi	кюри	(curie)
luˈǩjanəf	Лукьянов	(Lukyanov)

---

[1] It must be pointed out, however, that ǩ occurs before a, o and u in very few words and that nearly all of these are of foreign origin. Foreign proper names are not considered.

g

17.125 For practical purposes, three allophones of the phoneme g may be distinguished. All three allophones of the phoneme g are produced with the vocal cords close together and vibrating throughout the duration of the consonant. Otherwise the allophones of g correspond in place and manner of articulation to the allophones of k and the single allophone of ķ. Thus there is a principal allophone corresponding to the principal allophone of k (see § 17.107 and Fig. 15), a labialized allophone corresponding to the labialized allophone of k (§ 17.109) and a palatalized allophone corresponding to ķ (see § 17.117 and Fig. 16).

17.126 Russian g is a voiced velar plosive consonant, with two subsidiary allophones, one labialized, one palatalized.

17.127 The principal allophone presents no difficulty to English-speaking students, but it is to be noted that all the allophones of g are voiced throughout the duration of the closure (see § 17.12). The labialized allophone can be acquired by adding lip-rounding to English g, though care must be taken not to allow got год (year), for example, to sound like gwot.

17.128 The palatalized allophone of g, which may when necessary be represented by the phonetic symbol g, may be acquired by adding voice to Russian ķ, or by approaching it from English sounds.

17.129 Russian g has a slightly more forward place of articulation and a greater part of the back of the tongue in contact with the hard palate than does the fronted g in English *geese* (giːs). The student may find it helpful to start from the g in English *geese* and, by moving the point of articulation slightly forward and raising the front of the tongue to the hard palate, arrive at Russian g.

17.130 It is also possible to approach g by taking the sequence of sounds gj in English *argue* (ˈɑːgju) and trying, so to speak, to merge the j into the g. Care must be taken, however, not to arrive at an affricate like that represented by j in English *Jew* (dʒuː) or that which occurs in sub-standard pronunciations of *dew* (dʒuː).

17.131 The labialized allophone of ɡ occurs only before u and o, the palatalized allophone only before i and e,[1] the principal allophone elsewhere, i.e. before a and voiced consonants. Before heterorganic plosives ɡ has its own release (see § 17.27). This is also the case when ɡ occurs before v, ɣ, m, m̦, n and ŋ.

17.132 The phoneme ɡ does not occur before voiceless consonants. It occurs at the end of a word when the word is the preposition written к and the next word begins with a voiced consonant other than v, ɣ, j or a sonant. It is also usual at the end of any other word where г or к is written and the next word is a particle beginning with a voiced consonant other than v, ɣ, j or a sonant or is the unstressed past tense of the verb 'to be', and may occasionally occur before other words.

17.133 The phoneme ɡ is represented in spelling by the letter г and also by к before voiced consonants other than v, ɣ or a sonant and in those cases described in the preceding paragraph where ɡ occurs at the end of a word.

17.134 *Words illustrating the phoneme* ɡ

ɡʌˈra	гора	(mountain)
zʌˈgatkə	загадка	(riddle)
ɡas	газ	(gas)
ˈɡubɪ	губы	(lips)
prʌˈɡulkə	прогулка	(stroll)
ɡuˈdok	гудок	(hooter)

[1] In a very few loan-words, not in common use, ɡ̦ occurs before other vowel phonemes, e.g. ɡ̦üjs гюйс (jack). Moreover, the forms kəbʌrˈɡ̦onək кабаргенок (young musk-deer) and ɣɪlərʌˈɡ̦onək вилорогенок (young prong-horn) occur, though kəbʌrˈʒonək кабаржонок and ɣɪlərʌˈʒonek вилорожонок are nearly four times commoner (see *Русский язык и советское общество — Словообразование современного русского литературного языка*, ed. M. V. Panov, Moscow, 1968). Thus there are grounds for considering ɡ̦ to be a separate phoneme but for our present purposes we shall consider it to be an allophone of ɡ. The sequence ɡɪ may sometimes occur but only at the junction of two closely bound words, as in ʌˈlɛɡ‿ɪ ˈpaɣɪl Олег и Павел (Oleg and Paul). Within a word only the sequences ɡ̦i and ɡ̦ɪ occur.

got	год	(year)
'gorət	город	(town)
goʂʈ	гость	(guest)
kʌg'da	когда	(when)
tʌg'da	тогда	(then)
ʌɲɪg'dot	анекдот	(anecdote)
gvalɪ	гвалт	(hubbub)
gnuʈ	гнуть	(to bend)
gnaʈ	гнать	(to chase)
'ɟ̑ipҟɪ(j)	гибкий	(supple)
nʌ'ɟ̑i	ноги	(foot, *gen. sing.*)
ɟ̑ɪɲɪ'ral	генерал	(general)
'nogɪ	ноги	(feet)
'ɟ̑eɲɪ(j)	гений	(genius)
nə nʌ'ɟ̑ɛ	на ноге	(on the foot)
ʌ vrʌ'ɟ̑ɛ	о враге	(about the enemy)
'mog bɪ	мог бы	(could)
'ʂɲɛg bɪ	снег бы	(if only it would snow)
'ʈog bɪ	тек бы	(would flow)
g dɪɾeɣɲɪ	к деревне	(towards the village)

18

THE RUSSIAN FRICATIVE CONSONANTS

Voiced fricatives

18.1 Before describing the Russian fricative consonants in detail, it is desirable to make a few general remarks regarding voiced fricatives.

18.2 In pronouncing a normal voiced fricative consonant the vocal cords are made to vibrate throughout the whole duration of the sound. The Russian voiced fricatives (v, z, etc.) are as a rule pronounced in this way.

18.3 Other varieties of voiced fricatives exist, in which the voicing is only partial. In English the voiced fricatives are generally so pronounced, and more particularly when they occur initially or finally. Thus in the word *vote* (voʊt), said in isolation, the first part of the v is voiceless, and voice is only put on towards the end; in the word *leave* (liːv), said in isolation, the first part of the v is voiced, but the latter part is voiceless.

18.4 Some English speakers are unable, without special practice, to make voiced v, z, ʒ, etc., at all. In speaking English they substitute the sounds known as 'voiceless v, z, ʒ' (phonetically ʋ, ᶎ, ᶽ). These sounds differ from f, s, ʃ, in being pronounced with weak force of the breath.

18.5 Those who only partially voice v, z and ʒ in English, and still more those who do not voice these sounds at all, generally have some difficulty in learning to make the fully voiced Russian v, z, etc.

18.6 The best way of learning to voice such sounds properly is to try to sing them, sustaining them on various notes.

18.7 If any difficulty is experienced in doing this, the student should try to make his English v and əː (the vowel in *bird*) *simultaneously* (not consecutively); he must be able to sustain the v for ten seconds and have the impression of hearing əː the whole time. Yet another method is to say əː, and while this sound is being sustained, gradually to bring the lower lip towards the upper teeth, until a fully voiced v results. The other fully voiced fricatives may be practised similarly.

18.8 It is worthy of note that voiced fricative consonants do not occur finally in Russian, except in the few circumstances described below.

The Russian fricative consonants in detail

18.9 There are from 11 to 13 fricative consonant phonemes in standard Russian. All speakers of standard Russian have the eleven fricative phonemes: f, ſ, v, ɣ, s, ş, z, ʐ, ʃ, ʒ and x. Some also have the phoneme ʝ and others have yet a further phoneme ʒ.

18. RUSSIAN FRICATIVE CONSONANTS

Formation of the Russian fricative consonants

f

18.10   The principal allophone of the Russian f-phoneme is formed as follows:

(1) *articulating organs:* inside of lower lip against upper front teeth;

(2) *state of air-passage:* narrowed at place of articulation;

(3) *position of soft palate:* raised, so that air cannot issue through the nose;

(4) *state of larynx:* vocal cords apart, in position for breath.

18.11   The principal allophone of Russian f is a voiceless labio-dental fricative consonant.

18.12   During the formation of the principal allophone of f the incisors, or at least the two central incisors, may actually be in contact with the inside of the lower lip. The closure, however, is so weak that the stream of air is not stopped. It passes between the teeth and the lower lip, producing the friction characteristic of f.

18.13   Before o and u labio-velarized allophones of f occur and before i a velarized allophone occurs (see chapter 15). In the labiovelarized allophones the place of articulation is slightly further down on the inside of the lower lip and there is no appreciable contact between lip and incisors.

18.14   The principal members of the Russian f and v phonemes (see below, §§ 18.18, 19) are almost indistinguishable from the normal English f and v as in *far* (fɑ:) and *vine* (vain). The Russian sounds may however be slightly more weakly articulated than the English sounds, as a result of which the friction of Russian f, for example, is not quite as great as that of English f. This is particularly noticeable in initial position before s or ş, as in fşɩg'da всегда (always), where the presence of f may escape the English speaker's ear.

18.15   The phoneme f does not occur before voiced consonants other than the sonants. Nor does f occur before the vowel phoneme e.

18. RUSSIAN FRICATIVE CONSONANTS

18.16 The phoneme f is represented in spelling by the letter ф and before voiceless consonants and at the end of a word also by в.

18.17 *Words illustrating the phoneme f*

'fabrɨkə	фабрика	(factory)
fəkuʃ'tɛt	факультет	(faculty)
'formə	форма	(form)
fon	фон	(background)
tɨʃɨ'fon	телефон	(telephone)
funt	фунт	(pound)
'fɨrkət	фыркать	(to snort)
fsɨg'da	всегда	(always)
'fskorɨ	вскоре	(soon)
'fpriskɨvət	впрыскивать	(to inject)
ftɨ'nut	втянуть	(to pull in)
rof	ров	(ditch)
ru'kaf	рукав	(sleeve)

v

18.18 The allophones of the phoneme v differ from the allophones of the phoneme f (§§ 18.10–13) in that the vocal cords are close together and vibrating throughout the duration of the consonant.

18.19 Thus the principal allophone of v is a voiced labio-dental fricative consonant.

18.20 The subsidiary allophones occurring before u and o are labio-velarized and that occurring before ɨ is velarized.

18.21 For a comparison of Russian v with English v see §§ 18.14.

18.22 The phoneme v does not occur before voiceless consonants or the phoneme e. It occurs at the end of a word when the word is the preposition written в (in) and the next word does not begin with a voiceless consonant. It is also usual at the end of other words when the next word is a particle beginning with a voiced consonant other than j or a sonant or is the unstressed past tense of the verb 'to be', and may occasionally occur at the end of a word in other circumstances. Otherwise v does not occur at the end of a word.

18.23 The phoneme v is represented in spelling by the letter в and, in a few instances, by the letter ф before a voiced consonant. Both в and ф represent v at the end of words in the circumstances described in the preceding paragraph.

18.24 *Words illustrating the phoneme* v

vas	вас	(you, *gen. & acc.*)
dʌ'vaɾ	давать	(to give)
'povər	повар	(cook)
vus	вуз	(higher educational establishment)
ʒɩ'vut	живут	(they live)
vot	вот	(here is)
volk	волк	(wolf)
'vɨstəfkə	выставка	(exhibition)
'vɨnul	вынул	(took out)
vnuk	внук	(grandson)
vzgʃat	взгляд	(glance)
ʌvgəɲɩs'tan	Афганистан	(Afghanistan)
'rov ʒɩ	ров же	(the ditch)
ru'kav bɩ	рукав бы	(sleeve would)
'ʃkav ʒɩ	шкаф же	(the cupboard)

ʃ

18.25 For practical purposes only one allophone of the phoneme ʃ need be distinguished. It differs from the principal allophone of f in that the tongue is in the j-position throughout the articulation of the consonant.

18.26 Russian ʃ is a voiceless palatalized (soft) labio-dental fricative consonant.

18.27 The constriction of the lower lip against the upper teeth is released slightly before the tongue descends from the j-position, thus producing a j-glide before a following vowel. This glide must not be exaggerated. When ʃ occurs at the end of a word the same effects are to be observed as after ɓ at the end of a word (see §§ 17.51, 52).

18.28   English speakers do not usually experience difficulty in producing ʃ and ɣ (see below, §§ 18.34–6), since they consist of the articulation of, respectively, f and v, with simultaneous articulation of ʝ. They should, however, be wary of so exaggerating the ʝ-glide before vowels that, for example, ʃo sounds like ʃʝo and ɣo sounds like ɣʝo.

18.29   The nearest English sounds to Russian ʃ and ɣ are the sequences of consonants fʝ and vʝ, as in *few* (fjuː) and *view* (vjuː). It must be clearly understood, however, that these *are* sequences of phonemes in English whereas Russian ʃ and ɣ are single phonemes (followed in certain positions, as described in §§ 18.27, 36, by a slight ʝ-glide).

18.30   English speakers who find difficulty in achieving ʃ and ɣ from the descriptions given in §§ 18.25, 34 may try to approach ʃ and ɣ from English fʝ and vʝ by shortening the ʝ and also making the articulation of ʝ throughout the duration of the fricative. The student will be able to verify whether he is making the ʝ articulation throughout the duration of ʃ and ɣ by prolonging these sounds and comparing them with prolonged f and v respectively. He will find that ʃ has a higher pitch than f, that in the prolonged ɣ this higher pitch produces the effect of an 'indistinct' i-sound throughout the duration of ɣ and that this 'indistinct' i-sound is not present in the prolonged v.

18.31   The phoneme ʃ occurs before vowels and at the end of words. Its occurrence before consonants is nowadays usually restricted to cases where the preposition в is followed by a word beginning with ʃ, when ʃʃ (i.e. an uninterrupted ʃ of twice the normal length) is pronounced. It may also occasionally be heard before the palatalized labial consonants ɓ and m̡, and in some words before ʈ and ʂ, though the pronunciation of f here is equally correct and in fact commoner, especially among younger speakers.

18.32   The phoneme ʃ is represented in spelling by the letter ф followed by one of the vowel letters е, и, ю, я, or the soft sign, ь.

18. RUSSIAN FRICATIVE CONSONANTS

At the end of a word it is also represented by the letter в followed by ь, and the letter в may also represent ʃ when the next phoneme is ʃ (see preceding paragraph).

18.33 *Words illustrating the phoneme* ʃ

'ʃirmə	фирма	(firm)
ʃiḷm	фильм	(film)
'ʃinιk	финик	(date)
'ʃɛrmə	ферма	(farm)
bu'ʃɛt	буфет	(sideboard)
pʌr'tʃeḷ	портфель	(briefcase)
ʃʌ'ʃor	шофер	(driver)
ʃüʒι'ḷaʃ	фюзеляж	(fuselage)
yɛrʃ	верфь	(dockyard)
broʃ	бровь	(eye-brow)
kroʃ	кровь	(blood)
'obuʃ	обувь	(footwear)
'tsɛrkəʃ	церковь	(church)
'ʃ ʃiḷmι	в фильме	(in a film)
ʃ ʃιvrʌ'ḷɛ	в феврале	(in February)

ɣ

18.34 For practical purposes only one allophone of the phoneme ɣ need be distinguished. It differs from the Russian ʃ in that the vocal cords are close together and vibrating throughout the duration of the consonant.

18.35 Russian ɣ is a voiced palatalized (soft) labio-dental fricative consonant.

18.36 The constriction of the lower lip against the upper teeth is released slightly before the tongue descends from the j-position, thus producing a j-glide before a following vowel. This glide must not be so exaggerated that ɣo for instance sounds like the sequence ɣjo, which does occur in Russian (see next paragraph).

18.37 When ɣ is followed by j, some speakers have a glide between the ɣ and the j which is the voiced equivalent of the ç-glide described in § 17.52. Other speakers do not produce audible friction between ɣ and j. They have instead a glide like a very short i-sound. Such speakers nevertheless distinguish between for example ɣo and ɣjo, which testifies to the fact that the glide between ɣ and o in ɣo must not be exaggerated so that ɣjo is produced.

18.38 Remarks on the nearest English correspondent to Russian ɣ and the difficulties of English-speaking students are to be found in §§ 18.29, 30.

18.39 Russian ɣ does not occur before voiceless consonants nor at the end of a word, unless the next word is the unstressed past tense of the verb 'to be' or a particle beginning with a voiced consonant other than j or a sonant. The phoneme ɣ also occurs before ɣ within one word or at the junction of two words when the first word is the preposition written в. It also occurs before m̦ within one word and may occur at the junction of two words when the second word begins with m̦ and the first word is the preposition written в. From § 18.37 it is apparent that ɣ also occurs before the consonant j.[1] The sequence ɣj can often be distinguished from the sequence vj occurring at the junction of two words, of which the first is the preposition written в, by the presence in the sequence ɣj of the glide described in § 18.37 and its absence in the sequence vj (as in 'v jamu в яму (into the pit)).

18.40 The phoneme ɣ is represented in spelling by the letter в followed by one of the vowel letters e, и, ю, я, or the soft sign, ь. It may also be represented, in the circumstances described above, by the letter в not followed immediately by one of these letters. At the junction of two words the letters фь may also represent ɣ.

18.41 *Words illustrating the phoneme* ɣ

'ɣilkə	вилка	(fork)
ɣit	вид	(view)
ɣɪ'no	вино	(wine)
ɣeş	весь	(all)

---

[1] In a few words some people pronounce ɣ before l̦ and n̦, e.g., dɪ'ʃeɣl̦ɪ (or dɪ'ʃevl̦ɪ) дешевле (cheaper), dɪ'reɣn̦ə (or dɪ'revn̦ə) деревня (village).

18. RUSSIAN FRICATIVE CONSONANTS

prʌ'yerɪʐ	проверить	(to verify)
syɛt	свет	(light)
'yanuʈ	вянуть	(to wither)
'yaskə	вязка	(bundle)
yol	вел	(led)
'zyozdɪ	звезды	(stars)
kʌ'yor	ковер	(carpet)
səlʌ'yja	соловья	(nightingale, *gen. sing.*)
yjot	вьет	(weaves)
yjut	вьют	(they weave)
'kroy bɪ	кровь бы	(blood would)
'broy ʒɪ	бровь же	(the eyebrow)
yyɛrx	вверх	(upwards)
yyol	ввел	(led in)
'ymeʂʈɪ	вместе	(together)
'yɛry ʒɪ	верфь же	(the dockyard)

s

18.42 The principal allophone of the Russian s-phoneme is formed as follows:

(1) *articulating organs:* blade of tongue near back part of teeth-ridge, without making complete contact; the tip of the tongue is either pointing towards the upper front teeth, lying under the middle part of the teeth-ridge, or is lowered to the base of the lower front teeth[1] (Fig. 17);

(2) *state of air-passage:* narrowed at place of primary articulation, i.e. between blade of tongue and teeth-ridge so that friction is produced by the air-stream as it passes through this gap;

(3) *position of soft palate:* raised, so that air cannot issue through the nose;

(4) *state of larynx:* vocal cords apart in position for breath.

18.43 The principal allophone of Russian s is a voiceless alveolar fricative consonant.

---

[1] There is a slight hollowing along the central line of the tongue but this will probably arise naturally.

18. RUSSIAN FRICATIVE CONSONANTS

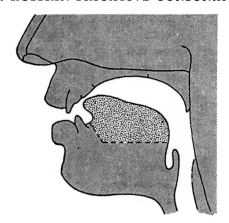

Fig. 17. Tongue-position of Russian s and z with tip of tongue in raised position

18.44 Before u and o occur labio-velarized allophones of the phoneme s and before ɨ a velarized allophone occurs (see §§ 15.1, 2).

18.45 English s and z are formed by some speakers in much the same way as are the principal allophones of Russian s and z (see below, §§ 18.50, 51). The majority of English speakers however form s and z in a different way, namely with the tongue-tip against the back part of the teeth-ridge: their s and z are apical, not laminal, as are Russian s and z (cf. §§ 17.70, 79 on English and Russian t and d). Moreover, in this type of English s and z the blade of the tongue is raised slightly towards the hard palate. English s and z formed in this way have a slightly higher pitch than Russian s and z, and this may be easily detected by uttering first a prolonged Russian s and then a prolonged English s.

18.46 In order to overcome any tendency to pronounce apical s and z in Russian the student should best adopt the variety with the tongue-tip behind the lower front teeth and make sure that it stays there throughout the pronunciation of Russian s and z, which may be prolonged for this purpose. In this way s and z inevitably have to be laminal sounds.

18. RUSSIAN FRICATIVE CONSONANTS

18.47 The phoneme s does not occur before ʂ, ʈ or voiced consonants other than v, ɣ and the sonants. The sequence s + tʃ does not occur either: in place of this some pronounce ʄtʃ, in which ʃ is a member of the phoneme ʃ, others pronounce ʄʃ (see §§ 18.87–91). Finally, s does not occur before the vowel phoneme e.[1]

18.48 The phoneme s is represented in spelling by the letter с and in front of voiceless consonants and at the end of a word also by з.

18.49 *Words illustrating the phoneme* s

sat	сад	(garden)
sam	сам	(self)
rʌ'sa	роса	(dew)
səlʌ'yej	соловей	(nightingale)
pʌ'sudə	посуда	(crockery)
'sunuʈ	сунуть	(to thrust)
son	сон	(sleep)
soḷ	соль	(salt)
sɨn	сын	(son)
pʌ'sɨlkə	посылка	(parcel)
prʌs'tor	простор	(space)
'spravə	справа	(on the right)
'srazu	сразу	(at once)
'svaɖbə	свадьба	(wedding)
ḷɛs	лес	(wood)
gas	газ	(gas)

[1] Some speakers do not pronounce s before p, m, f and v. Instead they pronounce ʂ here, as in

'ʂpitʃkə	спичка	(match)
'ʂmɛnə	смена	(shift)
'ʂfɛrə	сфера	(sphere)
ʂyɛt	свет	(light)

The general tendency among younger speakers, however, is to pronounce s in such words.

18. RUSSIAN FRICATIVE CONSONANTS

z

18.50 The allophones of the Russian z-phoneme differ from the allophones of the s-phoneme (see §§ 18.42–4 and Fig. 17) in that the vocal cords are close together and vibrating throughout the duration of the consonant.

18.51 Thus the principal allophone of z is a voiced alveolar fricative consonant.

18.52 Before u and o occur labio-velarized allophones of the phoneme z and before ɨ a velarized allophone occurs (see §§ 15.1, 2).

18.53 For a comparison of Russian z with English z see §§ 18.45, 46.

18.54 The phoneme z does not occur before voiceless consonants nor before the phonemes ʒ, ḍ, ḷ, ṇ, e or ʒ. It occurs at the end of a word when the word is one of the simple prepositions без (without), из (out of) or через/чрез (across) and the next word does not begin with a voiceless consonant or one of the phonemes ʒ, ḍ, ḷ, ṇ or ʒ. The preposition written с (with; from) is also pronounced z when the next word begins with a voiced consonant other than ʒ, ḍ, j, v, ɣ, ʒ and the sonants. It is also usual at the end of other words where з or с is written and the next word is the unstressed past tense of the verb 'to be' or a particle beginning with a voiced consonant other than ʒ, ḍ, j, v, ɣ, ʒ and the sonants, and may occasionally occur before other words beginning with a voiced consonant other than those just enumerated.

18.55 The phoneme z is represented in spelling by the letter з and also, before voiced consonants other than ʒ, ḍ, ʒ, j, v, ɣ and the sonants, by the letter с.

18.56 *Words illustrating the phoneme z*

'zaftrə	завтра	(tomorrow)
nʌ'zat	назад	(back)
zʌ'bɨl	забыл	(forgot)
'rɛzəṭ	резать	(to cut)

zup	зуб	(tooth)
vzor	взор	(gaze)
zof	зов	(call)
zɨɓ	зыбь	(swell)
znak	знак	(sign)
zloj	злой	(evil)
zrʌ'tʃok	зрачок	(pupil of the eye)
'z goşṭɪm	с гостем	(with a guest)
'z ɓɛlɪm	с белым	(with white)
'ɣoz bɪ	вез бы	(would convey)
'roz bɪ	рос бы	(would grow)
'ŋoz bɪ	нес бы	(would be carrying)

ş

18.57 For practical purposes only one allophone of the phoneme ş need be distinguished. It is formed as follows:

(1) *articulating organs:* blade of tongue near back part of teeth-ridge, without making complete closure; front of tongue simultaneously raised towards the hard palate;[1] tip of tongue lowered to a position behind the base of the lower front teeth (Fig. 18) or pointing towards the gap between upper and lower teeth;

(2) *state of air-passage:* narrowed at place of primary articulation (i.e. between blade of tongue and teeth-ridge), fairly narrow at place of secondary articulation (i.e. between front of tongue and hard palate);

(3) *position of soft palate:* raised, so that air cannot issue through the nose;

(4) *state of larynx:* vocal cords apart, in position for breath.

18.58 Russian ş is a voiceless, palatalized (soft) alveolar fricative consonant.

18.59 When ş and ʒ (§§ 18.65, 66) occur before vowels, the constriction of the blade of the tongue against the teeth-ridge is released very slightly before that of the front of the tongue against the hard palate. The result is a slight j-glide between ş

---

[1] In the pronunciation of ş and ʒ the front of the tongue is not usually raised as high as in the pronunciation of ṭ and ḍ (§§ 17.84, 98).

18. RUSSIAN FRICATIVE CONSONANTS

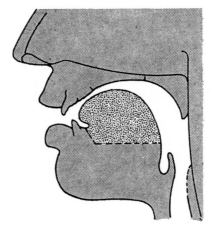

Fig. 18. Tongue-position of Russian ʂ and ʐ with tongue-tip lowered

or ʐ and a following vowel. This glide must not be exaggerated. Before the i-phoneme, in any case, the glide is only faintly audible or is not heard at all, since the front of the tongue remains in more or less the same position as for ʂ or ʐ. In other positions ʂ and ʐ are usually clearly distinct from s and z by virtue of their higher pitch and 'sharper' effect on the ear.

18.60 Sounds similar to Russian ʂ and ʐ occur in the pronunciation of some English speakers in such words as *assume* (ə'sjuːm), *presume* (prɪ'zjuːm), though the English s and z here do not have quite as high a pitch as Russian ʂ and ʐ and, moreover, are articulated with the tongue-tip raised, near the teeth-ridge, by most speakers.[1] In pronouncing such an English word as *associate* some speakers say (very precisely) ə'sousɪeit, others ə'sousjeit, and yet others ə'souʃeit.

18.61 It may help English-speaking students to acquire Russian ʂ by aiming at a sound midway between the s of ə'sousjeit and the ʃ of ə'souʃeit, without however producing a sound of the ʃ-type for Russian ʂ.

18.62 The phoneme ʂ occurs before all the vowel phonemes, at the end of words and before the consonants ʂ, ʈ, l̩, ŋ and j,

[1] Cf. § 18.45 on Russian and English s and z.

130

and occasionally before other (voiceless) consonants. Some speakers also pronounce ş before m̩ and ɣ, at least in some words, such as şm̩ɛx смех (laughter), şɣɛt свет (light).

18.63 The phoneme ş is represented in spelling by the letter с followed by one of the vowel letters е, и, ю or я; before t̩, l̩, n̩ and ş simply by the letter с, before other consonants by the letters сь; at the end of a word by the letters сь or зь; and before j by сь or съ. In the last instance some speakers pronounce съел (ate), for example, as şjɛl, others as sjɛl. Both groups pronounce such a word as колосья (ears of corn) with ş, thus kʌˈloşjə.

18.64 *Words illustrating the phoneme* ş

'şilə	сила	(strength)
spʌ'şibə	спасибо	(thank you)
fşɪg'da	всегда	(always)
şɪs'tra	сестра	(sister)
şem̩	семь	(seven)
fşɛ	все	(everybody)
'şadu	сяду	(I shall sit)
'fşæk̩ɪ(j)	всякий	(each, every)
fşo	все	(everything)
ʌ'şol	осел	(ass)
'fşudu	всюду	(everywhere)
şu'da	сюда	(hither)
şt̩ɪ'ɾet̩	стереть	(to wipe off)
şl̩ɛt	след	(trace)
şn̩ɛk	снег	(snow)
ɪş'şaknut̩	иссякнуть	(to dry up)
p̩ɪ'şmo	письмо	(letter)
vʌ'şm̩i	восьми	(eight, *gen., dat., prep.*)
oş	ось	(axle)
guş	гусь	(goose)
maş	мазь	(grease)
kʌ'loşjə	колосья	(ears of corn)
şjɛl	съел	(ate)

18. RUSSIAN FRICATIVE CONSONANTS

ʑ

18.65 For practical purposes only one allophone of ʑ need be distinguished. It differs from ɕ (§ 18.57) in that the vocal cords are close together and vibrating throughout the duration of the consonant.

18.66 Russian ʑ is a voiced, palatalized (soft) alveolar fricative consonant (Fig. 18).

18.67 Remarks on the glide after ʑ are to be found in § 18.59 and a comparison of ʑ with a similar sound in English in § 18.60.

18.68 The phoneme ʑ occurs before all the vowel phonemes, before the consonants ɖ, ļ, ņ, ʑ and j, and occasionally before other voiced consonants. Other than before words beginning with a voiceless consonant or ʒ, the prepositions written сквозь (through) and близ[1] (near) are usually pronounced with a final ʑ. The prepositions written без (without), из (out of) and через/чрез (across) are pronounced with final ʑ before words beginning with ʑ, ɖ, ļ and ņ, and the preposition written с (with; from) is pronounced ʑ before words beginning with ʑ or ɖ. Words with the final letter sequences зь or сь are usually pronounced with final ʑ before the unstressed past tense of the verb 'to be' and before particles beginning with a voiced consonant other than v, ɣ, j, ʒ or a sonant, and may occasionally be so pronounced before other words beginning with a voiced consonant other than v, ɣ, j, ʒ or a sonant. Otherwise ʑ does not occur at the end of a word.

18.69 The phoneme ʑ is represented in spelling by the letter з followed by one of the vowel letters е, и, ю or я, or the soft sign, ь. It is also represented by сь and by з or с alone in the circumstances described in the preceding two paragraphs.

18.70 *Words illustrating the phoneme ʑ*

vʌˈʑiʦ̡	возите	(convey!)
ʑ̡ˈma	зима	(winter)
ˈʑeļ̡ņ	зелень	(verdure)

[1] Note the spelling—no soft sign, in spite of the pronunciation.

vʒæʈ	взять	(to take)
ŋ̩ʲ'ʒa	нельзя	(one cannot)
kʌ'ʒol	козел	(goat)
ɣɩ'ʒot	везет	(is taking)
ɩ'ʒum	изюм	(raisins)
'ʒlitsə	злиться	(to be vexed)
'raʒŋɩtsə	разница	(difference)
b̩ɩʒ‿ʲü'dej	без людей	(unpeopled)
ɩʒ'ʒabnuʈ	иззябпуть	(to be chilled)
b̩ɩʒ‿ʒɩm'ʲli	без земли	(landless)
ʒ‿ʒɩm'ʲöj	с землей	(with land)
rəʒd̩ɩ'vatsə	раздеваться	(to undress)
'ʒdɛləʈ	сделать	(to do)
b̩ɩʒ‿d̩ɩ'ʈej	без детей	(childless)
'ʒ‿d̩evuʃkəj	с девушкой	(with a girl)
dru'ʒja	друзья	(friends)
ʌb̩ɩ'ʒjanə	обезьяна	(ape)
ɩ'ʒjæʈ	изъять	(to take out)
vʌ'ʒmu	возьму	(I shall take)
'proʒbə	просьба	(request)

ʃ

18.71 In one style of pronunciation the phoneme ʃ has
two allophones, the principal allophone being formed as
follows:

(1) *articulating organs:* tip of tongue near back part of teeth-
ridge, back of tongue raised, front of tongue being as far
as possible flattened, so as not to approach the hard
palate (Fig. 19); the lower jaw is raised so that the lower
teeth are almost or quite in contact with the upper teeth;
the lips are somewhat protruded;

(2) *state of air-passage:* narrowed at place of primary articulation (i.e. between tip of tongue and back part of teeth-
ridge); the space between the back of the tongue and the
soft palate being about the same as in the case of the
cardinal vowel o or the unstressed allophone of the
phoneme u (§ 12.187);

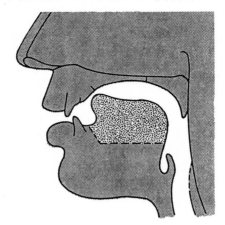

Fig. 19. Tongue-position of Russian ʃ and ʒ

(3) *position of soft palate:* raised, so that air cannot issue through the nose;

(4) *state of larynx:* vocal cords apart, in position for breath.

18.72 This allophone of the phoneme ʃ is a voiceless, post-alveolar, labio-velarized fricative consonant.

18.73 The subsidiary allophone of the phoneme ʃ is described and discussed below (§§ 18.87 ff.). The remainder of this section is concerned only with the principal allophone.

18.74 English ʃ (as in *ship* (ʃʟp), *shop* (ʃɒp)) differs from Russian ʃ in some important particulars. The tip of the tongue is slightly further forward, or is lowered to a position behind the lower front teeth, and the front of the tongue is raised towards the hard palate (though not so high as in the pronunciation of Russian ʃ; see § 18.87). English ʃ therefore is a somewhat palatalized sound (cf. Fig. 20), in comparison with Russian ʃ, and does not have the characteristic 'dark' or 'hollow' quality of the latter. Some English speakers, moreover, pronounce ʃ with slightly protruded lips, others with spread lips. In the pronunciation of the latter therefore there is one more point of difference between English ʃ and Russian ʃ.

18.75 English-speaking students may try to acquire Russian ʃ

18. RUSSIAN FRICATIVE CONSONANTS

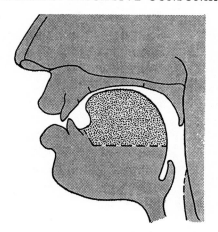

Fig. 20. Tongue-position of Russian ʃ and ʒ

by starting from English ʃ and drawing the front of the tongue away from the hard palate. Alternatively, having tested for themselves that in pronouncing English ʃ the tongue forms in lateral profile a somewhat 'humped' shape, they may try to pronounce ʃ by deliberately making the tongue into a 'saddle' shape, i.e. with the tip and back raised, but the middle depressed. Either of these methods will usually result in the tip automatically being drawn back slightly from its position for English ʃ. Another method is to devoice the ʒ reached by the method described in § 18.83.

18.76 Russian ʃ does not occur before voiced consonants other than j, v, ɣ and the sonants.

18.77 It is represented in spelling by the letter ш and also, before voiceless consonants and at the end of a word, by the letter ж. It should be noted that the soft sign has no effect on the phonetic value of the letters ш and ж. Final шь and жь therefore represent ʃ and within a word шь indicates that ʃ is followed by j.

18.78 The sequence ʃʃ, i.e. a ʃ of twice the normal length, is represented by the letters сш or зш, which also represent ʃʃ at the junction of preposition and following word.

18.79 *Words illustrating the phoneme ʃ*

ʌ'ʃtpkə	ошибка	(mistake)
ʃɨt̬	шить	(to sew)
'ʃɨnə	шина	(tyre)
ʃes̩t̬	шесть	(six)
ʃɛst	шест	(pole)
ʃak	шаг	(step)
dɨ'ʃat̬	дышать	(to breathe)
ʃolk	шелк	(silk)
pʌ'ʃol	пошел	(went)
'ʃubə	шуба	(fur coat)
pɨ'ʃu	пишу	(I write)
kʌ'ʃmar	кошмар	(nightmare)
ʃnur	шнур	(cord)
ʃram	шрам	(scar)
ʃγɛt	швед	(Swede)
naʃ	наш	(our)
noʃ	нож	(knife)
'loʃkə	ложка	(spoon)
mɨʃ	мышь	(mouse)
loʃ	ложь	(lie)
ʃju	шью	(I sew)
ʃjot	шьет	(sews)
bɨʃ'ʃumnə	бесшумно	(noiselessly)
ʃʃɨt̬	сшить	(to sew, *pfv.*)
pɾɨ'γoʃʃt(j)	привезший	(having brought)
'ʃ‿ʃuməm	с шумом	(noisily)
ɨʃ‿'ʃolkə	из шелка	(of silk)
bɨʃ‿'ʃapkɨ	без шапки	(hatless)
sumʌ'ʃɛt-ʃt(j)[1]	сумасшедший[2]	(mad)
mʌʃ'tap	масштаб[2]	(scale)
ʌt-ʃʌ'gat̬[1]	отшагать	(to stride)
pət-ʃt'vat̬[1]	подшивать	(to line)

[1] Because of the notation adopted in this book to register the consonant similar to that represented by *ch* in English spelling (e.g. *china*), namely tʃ (see § 19.20), it is necessary to insert a hyphen here to show that t followed by ʃ is to be pronounced.

[2] Note that in these words сш is pronounced as ʃ, *not* as ʃʃ.

18. RUSSIAN FRICATIVE CONSONANTS

ʒ

18.80 In the widespread, contemporary style of pronunciation the phoneme ʒ may have a subsidiary allophone (see below, § 18.97), but it is extremely restricted in occurrence. Otherwise there is only one allophone, which differs from the principal allophone of ʃ (§§ 18.71, 72 and Fig. 19) in that the vocal cords are close together and vibrating throughout the duration of the consonant.

18.81 Russian ʒ is a voiced, post-alveolar labio-velarized fricative consonant.

18.82 English ʒ (as in *measure* ('meʒə), *leisure* ('leʒə)), differs from Russian ʒ in exactly the same way that English ʃ differs from Russian ʃ (§ 18.74).

18.83 To acquire Russian ʒ, English-speaking students may try methods similar to those described in § 18.75, starting of course from English ʒ. Another method is to start from the fricative r which is typical of most pronunciations of English in such words as *raw*. In pronouncing English fricative r the tip of the tongue is just behind the teeth-ridge. If, while continuing to pronounce r, the student pushes the tip of the tongue nearer to the teeth-ridge, he will find that friction arises. It will be of help to raise the lower jaw so that upper and lower teeth meet or nearly meet and to round the lips slightly (see also §§ 22.8, 9). The resultant sound will be very like Russian ʒ. Russian ʃ can then be acquired from this by devoicing, i.e. articulating ʒ without the vibration of the vocal cords.

18.84 Russian ʒ does not occur before voiceless consonants. The occasions when it occurs at the end of a word are as follows. The prepositions written без (without), из (out of), через/чрез (across), с (with; from), сквозь (through) and близ (near) are usually pronounced with final ʒ before words beginning with ʒ. Words ending with the letters ш, ж, шь or жь are usually pronounced with final ʒ before the unstressed past tense of the verb 'to be' or before a particle beginning with a voiced consonant other than v, ɣ, j or a sonant. Words ending with the letters с, з, сь or зь are usually pronounced with final ʒ before the particle written же. Final ʒ may also occur occasionally in other circumstances, as for example when the usually unstressed possessive pronouns written наш (our) and ваш (your) are followed by a word beginning with a voiced consonant other than v, γ, j or a sonant.

18.85 Russian ʒ is represented in spelling by the letter ж and also, in the circumstances described in the preceding paragraph, by ш, шь and жь.[1] The sequence ʒʒ, i.e. a ʒ of twice the normal length, is represented by зж, сж and, less commonly, by жж;[2] and, at the junction of two words, by сь + ж, зь + ж, ш + ж, шь + ж, жь + ж, as well as з + ж, с + ж, and ж + ж.

18.86 *Words illustrating the phoneme ʒ*

ʒɨt̬	жить	(to live)
slu'ʒɨt̬	служить	(to serve)
ʒestʲ	жесть	(tin)
ʒɛst	жест	(gesture)
ʒaļ	жаль	(it's a pity)
nʌ'ʒa	ножа	(knife, *gen. sing.*)
'ʒonɨ	жены	(wives)
tʃu'ʒoj	чужой	(alien)
'rɛʒu	режу	(I cut)
xʌ'ʒu	хожу	(I go)
ʒdat̬	ждать	(to wait)
ʒd̬ot	ждет	(waits)
'druʒbə	дружба	(friendship)
'ʒmurkɩ	жмурки	(blind man's buff)
'vaʒnɨ(j)	важный	(important)
'noʒ̮ bɨ	нож бы	(knife would)
'mɨʒ̮ bɨ	мышь бы	(mouse would)
ʒʒat̬	сжать	(to compress)
ɩʒ'ʒogə	изжога	(heartburn)
u(j)ɩʒ'ʒat̬	уезжать	(to ride away)

---

[1] A rare word, волшба vʌlʒ'ba (witchcraft), shows the phoneme ʒ represented by ш within a word.

[2] For an older mode of pronouncing жж and, in certain words, зж, see § 18.96.

ʒuʒ'ʒatɕ жужжать (to buzz)
ɪʒ ʒtʲ'tomɪrə из Житомира (from Zhitomir)
ʒ ʒtʲ'noj с женой (with one's wife)
'toʈtʃəʒ ʒt тотжас же (at once)
'oʒ ʒt ось же (the axle)

The sound ʃ and the complex ʃtʃ

18.87 In all types of educated pronunciation the sound ʃ occurs. It is similar to the English ʃ (see § 18.74) but differs from it in that a greater area of the front of the tongue is raised close to the hard palate (Fig. 20). The sound ʃ is a voiceless palato-alveolar fricative consonant and is one of the palatalized (soft) consonants of Russian. The back of the tongue is not raised nor are the lips rounded as in the pronunciation of ʃ (§ 18.71).

18.88 The sound ʃ occurs in pronunciation where the letter щ occurs in spelling. Where this letter occurs some speakers pronounce ʃʃ, i.e. a long, palatalized (soft) 'ʃ'. In the pronunciation of such speakers the sound ʃ must constitute a phoneme distinct from ʃ, since the latter also occurs as a double consonant, cf. ʃʃit щит (screen, shield) and ʃʃit сшит (sewn). Moreover, the sound ʃ (i.e. a single ʃ, not a double ʃʃ) is common at the end of words and in contiguity with other consonants, as in tʌ'varɪʃ товарищ (comrade), 'suʃnəʂtɕ сущность (essence), gərdɪ'ropʃɪk гардеробщик (cloak-room attendant), where a rather careful pronunciation could have ʃʃ.

18.89 Other speakers pronounce, where the letter щ occurs, a complex of sounds which may be described as a long ʃ 'interrupted' in the middle by a very slight stop element, very like the Russian tɕ, thus ʃtʃ. It must be emphasized that the tɕ element is very brief and weakly articulated. The Russian affricate consonant tʃ (similar to the *ch* in English *cheese*, see §§ 19.29) is similar to the tʃ part of the complex ʃtʃ and, since in the pronunciation of these speakers the sequence of consonants s+tʃ, which would arise in the process of word-formation, is replaced by ʃtʃ, it is appropriate to consider the complex ʃtʃ as being ʃ+tʃ. Moreover, the principal allophone

139

of ʃ (§ 18.71) does not occur before tʃ; ʃ occurs instead. Pho-
nemically, therefore, the complex ɟtɟ in the pronunciation of
these speakers, whether it is written щ or сч, is ʃ + tʃ. Hence-
forth, we shall write in fact ʃtʃ for this complex, it being understood that the complex is palato-alveolar and that ʃ does not
stand for the principal allophone of the phoneme ʃ.

18.90 Those who pronounce ʃtʃ where the letter щ and the
sequence of letters сч is written, also pronounce ʃtʃ where the
sequence of letters зч is written. Those who pronounce ɟɟ
where the letter щ is written usually pronounce ɟɟ (a) where
the letters сч and зч are written at the junction of a root and
the suffix -чик, as in pɪrɪ'pɪɟɟɪk переписчик (copyist), 'smaɟɟɪk
смазчик (greaser); and (b) in 'ɟɟæʂtjɪ счастье (happiness)
and in some other words where сч is written but where the
original junction of prefix and root is no longer appreciated,
as in ɟɟot счет (bill), ɪʃ'ʃɛznuʈ исчезнуть (to disappear). In
both (a) and (b) however, 'ɟɟ-speakers' may occasionally be
heard pronouncing ʃtʃ.

18.91 Moreover, where suffixes other than -чик are concerned,
where the junction of prefix and root is still clearly appreciated,
and where с ч, з ч are written at the junction of preposition and
following word, 'ɟɟ-speakers' usually pronounce ʃtʃ. (Words
exemplifying these combinations are given below, § 18.95.)

18.92 By and large, at least the younger generation seems to
prefer the pronunciation ʃtʃ, rather than ɟɟ, and it is appropriate therefore to take this as 'basic' for the purposes of this
book. It should be borne in mind, however, that because of the
weakness of the stop-element in ʃtʃ, the complex may merge
with ɟɟ, especially at rapid speeds. This is particularly the case
with certain words which are frequently spoken at high speed.
Thus the word сейчас (now) is pronounced ʂɪj'tʃas but when
it is used, as it often is, in the sense of (*I'm doing it*/*I'm coming*)
now it is habitually pronounced ʃtʃas or ɟɟas. Moreover, at the
end of words and in contiguity with other consonants a single ʃ
is frequently heard in the speech of those who otherwise
pronounce ʃtʃ.

18. RUSSIAN FRICATIVE CONSONANTS

18.93 Other less common spellings of the complex ʃtʃ are здч, as in бороздчатый bʌ'roʃtʃətɨ(j) (furrowed), шч, as in веснушчатый ɣɨ'snuʃtʃətɨ(j) (freckled), жч, as in мужчина muʃ'tʃinə (man), and стч, as in жестче 'ʒoʃtʃɪ (harder) and хлестче 'xⱡöʃtʃɪ (more trenchantly). One should also note the word тысяча (thousand) which in very careful pronunciation or when it is necessary to specify particularly 'one thousand' is pronounced 'tɨşətʃə but otherwise is pronounced 'tɨʃtʃə (or 'tɨʃʃə), particularly in dates and long numbers.

18.94 Finally the word дождь (rain) must be commented on. It is commonly pronounced doʃtʃ (or doʃʃ) but, with the spread of spelling pronunciation, doʃt̞ is also heard. The word вождь (leader), being a more bookish word, seems less liable to be pronounced voʃtʃ.

18.95 *Words illustrating the complex* ʃtʃ

ʃtʃit	щит	(screen)
tʌʃ'tʃit̞	тащить	(to drag)
prʌʃ'tʃeɲ(ɪ)jɪ	прощение	(forgiveness)
'ʃtʃɛdrɪ(j)	щедрый	(generous)
prʌʃ'tʃæɲ(ɪ)jɪ	прощание	(leave-taking)
pʌʃ'tʃadə	пощада	(mercy)
'ʃtʃotkə	щетка	(brush)
ɪʃ'tʃu	ищу	(I seek)
ʌʃtʃuʃ'tʃæt̞	ощущать	(to feel)
tʌ'varɪʃtʃ (tʌ'varɪʃ)	товарищ	(comrade)
borʃtʃ (borʃ)	борщ	(beetroot soup)
'suʃtʃnəşt̞ ('suʃnəşt̞)	сущность	(essence)
gərdɪ'ropʃtʃɪk (gərdɪ'ropʃɪk)	гардеробщик	(cloak-room attendant)
'tʃtʃɛtnə[1]	тщетно	(in vain)
'tʃtʃæt̞ɪⱡnə[1]	тщательно	(thoroughly)
pɪrɪ'piʃtʃɪk	переписчик	(copyist)
'smaʃtʃɪk	смазчик	(greaser)
'ʃtʃæşt̞jɪ	счастье	(happiness)

[1] Some phoneticians transcribe the sequence tʃtʃ as a 'double tʃ', thus tʃtʃɛtnə.

ʃtʃot	счет	(bill)
ɪʃ'tʃɛznuʈ	исчезнуть	(to disappear)
rʌʃ'tʃiʂʈɪʈ	расчистить	(to clear)
ɪʃtʃɪr'paʈ	исчерпать	(to exhaust)
bɪʃtʃɪlʌ'yetʃnɪ(j)	бесчеловечный	(inhuman)
ʃ tʃɛm	с чем	(with what)
ɪʃ tʃɪ'vo	из чего	(from what)
rʌʃ'tʃeɪɪnə	расщелина[1]	(crevice)
rʌʃ'tʃitɪvəʈ	рассчитывать[1]	(to calculate)
bʌ'roʃtʃətɪ(j)	бороздчатый	(furrowed)
yɪ'snuʃtʃətɪ(j)	веснушчатый	(freckled)
muʃ'tʃinə	мужчина	(man)
'ʒoʃtʃɪ	жестче	(harder)
'xɭöʃtʃɪ	хлестче	(more trenchantly)

The sound ʒ

18.96 In the old Moscow pronunciation a voiced consonant corresponding to the voiceless ʃ (§ 18.87 and Fig. 20) was used, always of double length (i.e. ʒʒ), where зж or жж are written *within* a root (i.e. not at the junction of prefix and root or root and suffix, where ʒʒ were pronounced). Thus such words as езжу (I ride), уезжать (to ride away), позже (later), визжать (to squeal), жужжать (to buzz), вожжи (reins) were pronounced respectively 'jeʒʒu, u(j)ɪʒ'ʒæʈ, 'poʒʒɪ, yɪʒ'ʒæʈ, ʒuʒ'ʒæʈ, 'voʒʒɪ. This pronunciation may still be heard, but the modern pronunciation is thus: 'jeʒʒu, u(j)ɪʒ'ʒaʈ, 'poʒʒɪ, yɪʒ'ʒaʈ, ʒuʒ'ʒaʈ, 'voʒʒɪ.

18.97 Similarly, the oblique cases of the word дождь (cf. § 18.94), were pronounced with ʒʒ—dʌʒ'ʒa дождя (*gen. sing.*), dʌʒ'ʒom дождем (*instr. sing.*), etc., as also such derivatives as дождик 'doʒʒɪk (a spot of rain), дождевой dəʒʒɪ'voj (of rain). These pronunciations are still used, but many speakers pronounce in these words ʒd, in which the ʒ may be slightly palatalized or even quite palatalized and is a subsidiary allophone of the phoneme ʒ.

---

[1] Where сщ occurs the c is not pronounced. Similarly the first c in ссч is not pronounced.

18. RUSSIAN FRICATIVE CONSONANTS

x

18.98 The principal allophone of the Russian phoneme x is formed as follows:

(1) *articulating organs:* back of tongue near soft palate (Fig. 21);
(2) *state of air-passage:* somewhat narrowed at place of articulation;
(3) *position of soft palate:* raised, so that air cannot issue through the nose;
(4) *state of larynx:* vocal cords apart, in position for breath.

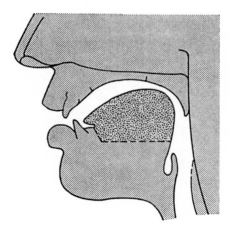

Fig. 21. Tongue-position of Russian x and ɣ

18.99 This allophone of Russian x is a voiceless velar fricative consonant.

18.100 There is very little friction in the Russian x, much less than in the German x, as in *ach* (ax), less even than in the Scots x, as in *loch* (lox). At times the friction is barely audible. The German or Scots x may be taken as a starting-point for the production of Russian x. Alternatively the sound may be reached by starting from k and then releasing the closure slightly so that air passes between the tongue and the palate in a continuous stream. In either case the friction must then be reduced until it is very slight.

18.101 Before u and o occur allophones of x which are labio-velarized (see § 15.4).

18.102 Before i, ɪ, e and ɛ there occurs a fronted or palatalized allophone of x, in which the place of articulation is slightly further forward than for the non-palatalized allophones, a greater area of the back of the tongue approaches the soft palate and the front of the tongue is raised slightly towards the hard palate (Fig. 22). This allophone is written in this book as x̟. The sound x̟ is about half-way, in place of articulation, between cardinal x and cardinal ç, the sound heard in German *ich* (iç). (See Figs. 21 and 23.)

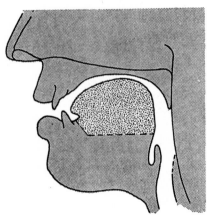

Fig. 22. Tongue-position of Russian x̟

18.103 The occurrence of the phoneme x before voiced consonants, other than v, ɣ, j or the sonants, is restricted to the juncture of closely bound words, where a voiced allophone ɣ occurs.[1]

---

[1] The sound ɣ is pronounced in the loan-words бухгалтер (accountant) and its derivatives—buˈɣalţɪr, etc.—and бюстгальтер (brassière)—bˌuzˈɣalţɪr. The words благо (good) and господь (Lord) are pronounced with g—ˈblagə, gʌsˈpoţ—not with ɣ, as formerly. The modern pronunciation of господи (heavens!) is ˈgospədɪ, though ˈɣospədɪ may also be heard.

18. RUSSIAN FRICATIVE CONSONANTS

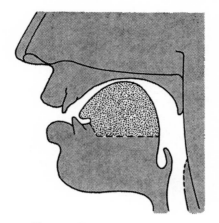

Fig. 23. Tongue-position of ç

18.104 The phoneme x is represented by the letter х. In those forms and derivatives of лёгкий (light) and мягкий (soft) where г and к occur together, it is also represented by г. In the modern pronunciation of бог (god) the letter г represents k, not x, as formerly, and in the oblique cases g, not ɣ. Thus, *nom.* bok бог, *gen.* 'bogə бога, etc. The preposition written к is now pronounced k before k, and g before g, not x and ɣ respectively, as used to be the case. Thus, k kʌ'mu к кому (to whom), etc., 'g gorədu к городу (towards the town), etc.

18.105 *Words illustrating the phoneme x*

'xatə	хата	(hut)
uxʌ'dit̪	уходить	(to go away)
xərʌ'ʃo	хорошо	(good)
'xolət	холод	(cold)
pʌ'xot	поход	(campaign)
'xuʒt̪	хуже	(worse)
xu'doj	худой	(thin)
'xitrt̪(j)	хитрый	(cunning)
pɪtu'xi	петухи	(cocks)
st̪ɪ'xi	стихи	(verses)
'xerɪs	херес	(sherry)

18. RUSSIAN FRICATIVE CONSONANTS

v̯ u'χɛ	в ухе	(in the fish-soup)
'ţíxɩ(j)	тихий[1]	(quiet)
mox	мох	(moss)
gʌ'rox	горох	(peas)
xvost	хвост	(tail)
krʌ'xmal	крахмал	(starch)
mxa	мха	(moss, *gen. sing.*)
sxʌ'dịţ	сходить	(to come down)
'ʃaxtə	шахта	(mine)
xrʌ'p̦eţ	храпеть	(to snore)
'ḷoxkɩ(j)	легкий	(light)
'm̦axkɩ(j)	мягкий	(soft)
gʌ'roɣ‿ʒt	горох же	(the peas)

19

THE RUSSIAN AFFRICATE CONSONANTS

19.1 All the plosive consonants hitherto mentioned are pronounced with rapid or fairly rapid separation of the articulating
organs. It is possible, however, to pronounce plosive consonants
with relatively slow separation of the articulating organs. When
they are so pronounced, the fricative consonant corresponding
most nearly to the plosive is distinctly audible as the organs
separate.

19.2 Thus the group ba is pronounced both in English and in
normal Russian with rapid separation of the lips. Consequently
no fricative sound is audible before the commencement of the
vowel a. It is, however, not difficult to perform the separation
slowly in such a way that the voiced bi-labial fricative β[2] is
heard before the vowel begins, the effect being roughly bβa. It

---

[1] In an older mode of pronunciation, which may still be heard, the nom.
sing. masc. of adjectives ending in -хий was pronounced -xəj, thus 'ţíxəj.

[2] The sound β does not occur either in English or in Russian. It may be
heard in many parts of Germany as a pronunciation of *w*.

19. RUSSIAN AFFRICATE CONSONANTS

is not difficult to pronounce in a similar way a dental d followed by a; the result may be written dða.[1]

19.3 Plosive consonants pronounced with slow separation of the articulating organs, so that the corresponding fricative is audible as the separation takes place, are called affricates.

19.4 It is convenient, as a rule, to represent affricates by means of the symbol for a plosive consonant immediately followed by the symbol for a corresponding fricative. An affricate may also be represented by a ligature, i.e. a single symbol composed of the appropriate plosive and fricative symbols (e.g. ʦ for ts), or by a single, specially designed symbol.

19.5 In this book affricates are represented digraphically, i.e. by a succession of two separate symbols, thus ts, tʃ. In cases where t is followed by s or ʃ as separate phonemes a hyphen is inserted between t and the following s or ʃ. Thus t-s, as in ʌt-stˈlaȶ отсылать (to send away), represents two phonemes, whereas ts, as in ʌtstˈɳiȶ оценить (to evaluate), represents one phoneme.

19.6 The Russian language has two affricate phonemes, namely ts and tʃ.

ts

19.7 In forming the stop of the affricate ts the tongue-tip is placed further back than for the position for Russian t (§ 17.68) and on the release of the stop the blade adopts a position slightly more advanced than that for Russian s (§ 18.42).

The formation of this affricate is therefore as follows:

(1) *articulating organs:* tip of tongue and blade against teeth-ridge so that tip is slightly behind upper front teeth (Fig. 24), then tip and blade very slightly lowered and withdrawn from this position;

(2) *state of air passage:* completely closed and then slightly opened so that the breath, passing through the aperture so formed, produces friction;

(3) *position of soft palate:* raised, so that air cannot issue through the nose;

---

[1] ð is the English sound of *th* in *then*.

19. RUSSIAN AFFRICATE CONSONANTS

(4) *state of larynx:* vocal cords apart, in position for breath.

19.8 Russian ts is a voiceless alveolar[1] affricate consonant.

19.9 Russian ts must always be finished off by separating the articulating organs. It can never be reduced to 'stop' only,[2] neither can it be exploded nasally or laterally like the Russian plosive consonants t, d, etc. (see §§ 17.73, 78).

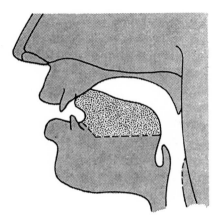

Fig. 24. Tongue-position for closure of Russian ts and dz

19.10 Russian ts appears to be unaspirated, i.e. no perceptible h is inserted between it and a following vowel.

19.11 In Russian the sequence t+s (written here t-s if occurring within one word) occurs as well as the affricate ts. The stop and fricative elements of the affricate ts are not produced in quite the same places as t and s respectively, as is evident from the foregoing description and §§ 17.68 and 18.42. Roughly speaking, each of the sounds t and s in t-s occupies the same length of time as the whole of the affricate ts. Conversely, this means that ts occupies roughly the same length of time as t or s and neither the plosive nor the fricative element in the affricate must be unduly prolonged.

[1] If greater precision of terminology were required one could say that ts is 'pre- and mid-alveolar' or 'post-dental and alveolar'.

[2] But see footnote 1, p. 149.

19. RUSSIAN AFFRICATE CONSONANTS

19.12 The sequence tts also occurs in Russian, as in ʌt'tsa отца (father, *gen. sing.*). This sequence in effect consists of the affricate ts *with the t-element prolonged*[1] and the whole sequence tts occupies roughly the same length of time as the sequence t-s.

19.13 When the affricate phoneme ts occurs before a voiced consonant other than v, ɣ, j and the sonants, a subsidiary allophone dz ('voiced ts') is pronounced. Thus plʌdz'darm плацдарм (bridge-head). Similarly, when the phoneme ts occurs at the end of a word and the next word begins with a voiced consonant, other than v, ɣ, j and the sonants the voiced allophone dz may be used by some speakers, usually when the second word is enclitic, thus ʌ'tsɛdz bɪ отец бы (father would). The sequence d + z, as distinct from the voiced allophone of ts (dz), occurs quite commonly in Russian, as in nʌ'd-zor надзор (supervision). The remarks above (§ 19.11) concerning the respective lengths of ts and t + s apply equally to dz and d + z.

19.14 The sequence of sounds t + s occurs in English as in *bits* bɪts, *eats* iːts, but one must note that the English sounds t and s are both apical in many accents of England and that t and s in, for example, *bits* are each as long, approximately, as the Russian affricate ts.

19.15 In the early stages of learning Russian, speakers of English may confuse Russian ts and Russian tɕ (which, as described above, § 17.86, is slightly affricated). The affrication of tɕ, however, is very slight. Furthermore, tɕ is a palatalized consonant, having the front of the tongue raised towards the hard palate, and thus has a higher inherent pitch than ts.

19.16 The phoneme ts occurs before consonants and vowels and at the end of words. Since ts is always hard,[2] only the ɨ and ɪ allophones of the i-phoneme can follow it.

---

[1] In this book we choose to regard ts with a prolonged t-element as a sequence of t + ts, in which the t is an allophone of the phoneme t occurring only before ts, but some phoneticians consider this sequence to be a geminate ('double') ts with only one release of closure.

[2] In foreign proper names ts is still pronounced hard, even though it may be followed by the vowel letter ю, as in 'tsjürɪx Цюрих (Zurich), tsju'rupɪnsk Цюрупинск (Tsiurupinsk, a Ukrainian place-name).

19. RUSSIAN AFFRICATE CONSONANTS

19.17   The phoneme ts is represented in spelling by the letter ц and also by various letter-combinations in certain positions. At the junction of prefix and root the letter-combinations тс and дс normally represent the sequence of consonants t-s (or ţş), as in ʌt-st'laţ отсылать (to send away), pət-sʌ'znaţɪ|nt(j) подсознательный (subconscious). In rapid pronunciation the affricate ts may occasionally be heard in such words. In adjectives formed with the suffix -ский/-ской after a root ending in т or д, thus having the letter combinations тс or дс, it is usual to pronounce the affricate ts, as in sʌ'yɛtskɪ(j) советский (Soviet), gərʌts'koj городской (urban). The sequence t-s is heard in such words only in a precise pronunciation. Similarly тс and дс in such words as детство (childhood), садоводство (horticulture), ответственный (responsible), непосредственный (immediate), usually represent ts, thus, respectively, 'dɛtstvə, sədʌ'votstvə, ʌ'tyɛtstyɪnt(j), ɲɪpʌ'srɛtstyɪnt(j). The words двадцать (twenty) and тридцать (thirty) are often pronounced 'dvatsəţ, 'tɾitsəţ though the more precise 'dvattsəţ, 'tɾittsəţ are also heard.

19.18   In reflexive infinitives ending in -ться the soft sign has no *phonetic* function. Such infinitives and the third persons singular and plural of reflexive verbs are pronounced, at normal conversational speed, with ts, and the letter я does not have the significance of 'preceding palatalized consonant' which it would normally have after a consonant letter. Thus ku'patsə купаться (to bathe), ku'pa(j)ɪtsə купается (bathes), ku-'pajutsə купаются (they bathe). As the speed of pronunciation decreases, the stop element of ts in such words is prolonged, until, in a slow, precise manner of speaking, such words are pronounced with the sequence t-s.

19.19   *Words illustrating the phoneme* ts

tsɨkl	цикл	(cycle)
ʌgur'tsɨ	огурцы	(gherkins)
tst'na	цена	(price)
tsɛx	цех	(workshop)
tsep	цепь	(chain)

tsʌ'rapəʦ	царапать	(to scratch)
ʟɪ'tsa	лица	(face, *gen. sing.*)
tsokəʟ	цоколь	(socle)
ʟɪ'tso	лицо	(face)
tsu'kat	цукат	(candied peel)
ʟɪ'tsu	лицу	(face, *dat. sing.*)
ʌ'ʦets	отец	(father)
pʦits	птиц	(birds, *gen. pl.*)
'braʦɪts	братец	(little brother)
tsyɛt	цвет	(colour)
rʌs'tsyɛt	расцвет	(blossoming)
plʌts'kartə	плацкарта	(seat-ticket)
rəstsʌ'rapəʦ	расцарапать	(to scratch, *pfv.*)
ʌt'tsa	отца	(father, *gen. sing.*)
'brattsə	братца	(little brother, *gen. sing.*)
ʌttsɪ'pʲiʦ	отцепить	(to uncouple)
ʌttsyɪʂ'ʨi	отцвести	(to wither)
ɲɪ'mʲɛtskɪ(j)	немецкий	(German)
gərʌts'koj	городской	(urban)
sʌ'yɛtskɪ(j)	советский	(Soviet)
'dʲɛtstvə	детство	(childhood)
ɲɪpʌ'srʲɛtstyɪnt(j)	непосредственный	(immediate)
'dvatsəʦ	двадцать	(twenty)
'trʲitsəʦ	тридцать	(thirty)
ku'patsə	купаться	(to bathe)
ku'pajutsə	купаются	(they bathe)
bʌ'(j)itsə	боится	(fears)
plʌdz'darm	плацдарм	(bridge-head)
kənf ɪ͜ ,rɛndz'zal	конференц-зал	(conference-room)
ʌ'ʦedz bɪ	отец бы	(father would)

tʃ

19.20 In forming the stop of the affricate tʃ[1] the tongue is placed as for a variety of alveolar t. The formation of this sound is therefore as follows:

---

[1] Note that the symbols t and ʃ in tʃ do not have the same value as when they are not part of the digraph tʃ. (See below, § 19.24.)

19. RUSSIAN AFFRICATE CONSONANTS

(1) *articulating organs:* tip of tongue at a point slightly behind the mid-point of the teeth-ridge, blade of tongue against teeth-ridge and fore part of hard palate, front of tongue being at the same time raised towards the hard palate (Fig. 25); there is probably slight lateral contraction of the tongue; the lower jaw is raised so that the lower teeth are almost or quite in contact with the upper teeth; the lips are spread; the tip and blade of the tongue are then slightly lowered from the position of closure just described;

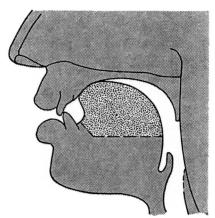

Fig. 25. Tongue-position for closure of Russian tʃ and dʒ

(2) *state of air-passage:* completely closed by tip and blade of tongue against teeth-ridge and fore part of hard palate, then opened slightly so that the breath, passing through the aperture so formed, produces friction;

(3) *position of soft palate:* raised so that air cannot issue through the nose;

(4) *state of larynx:* vocal cords apart, in position for breath.

19.21 Russian tʃ is a voiceless palatalized (soft) alveolar affricate consonant.

19.22 The sound tʃ must always be finished off by separating the articulating organs. It can never be reduced to 'stop' only, neither can it be exploded nasally or laterally. In this respect it differs from the Russian plosive consonants t, d, etc. (see §§ 17.73, 78).

19.23 The Russian tʃ appears to be unaspirated, i.e. no perceptible h is inserted between it and a following vowel.

19.24 The sequence of sounds t+ʃ occurs in Russian as well as the affricate tʃ. The sequence t+ʃ is easily distinguishable from the affricate tʃ since each sound of the sequence t+ʃ is roughly as long as the whole of the affricate tʃ and the sounds themselves are articulated in a different way from the elements of the affricate tʃ. The sounds t and ʃ in the sequence t+ʃ are *hard* (non-palatalized), whereas the affricate tʃ is *soft* (palatalized). In a narrow notation the affricate tʃ may be indicated by a special symbol, or by a ligature of t and ʃ. In a digraphic transcription the two elements of the affricate tʃ may be shown as palatalized, thus ţ ʃ̡, but in this book the ordinary symbols t and ʃ are used. When a hyphen is inserted between them they are to be understood to represent the sequence t+ʃ, as in ʌt-ʃʌˈgaţ отшагать (to step away), cf. ʌˈtʃak очаг (hearth).

19.25 The sequence ţ+tʃ also occurs, as in ʌţtʃɩˈvo отчего (why). The ţ is then formed in the same place as the t-element of tʃ. This sequence consists, in effect, of the affricate tʃ with the t-element prolonged and the whole sequence occupying roughly the same length of time as the sequence t+ʃ (see § 17.92).

19.26 The reduction or weakening of the stop element in the sequence ʃtʃ and the pronunciation of this sequence are described in §§ 18.88, 89.

19.27 A voiced allophone of tʃ, which may be written dʒ, is pronounced before a voiced consonant other than v, ɣ, j or a sonant. Similarly, when the phoneme tʃ occurs at the end of a word and the next word begins with a voiced consonant other than v, ɣ, j or a sonant, the voiced allophone dʒ may be used by some speakers, though usually only when the second word is enclitic, as in ˈdodʒ bɩ дочь бы (daughter would).

19.28 The sequence hard d plus hard ʒ occurs in compounds and loan-words and differs from the affricate dʒ in the same way that t + ʃ differs from the affricate tʃ (§ 19.24). Thus d-ʒas джаз (jazz), ʌd-ʒt'vaʈ отживать (to die out).

19.29 Speakers of English should have little or no difficulty in pronouncing Russian tʃ since it is very similar to the English tʃ in, for example, *cheese* tʃiːz. The Russian tʃ is slightly softer (more palatalized), having more of the front of the tongue raised nearer the hard palate and having more of the blade of the tongue in contact with the fore part of the hard palate. The voiced allophone dʒ differs in a similar way from the sound often written *j* or *g* in English (e.g. *Jean* dʒiːn).

19.30 The phoneme tʃ occurs before vowels and consonants and at the end of words.

19.31 It is represented in spelling by the letter ч.

19.32 *Words illustrating the phoneme* tʃ

u'tʃiʈɪl	учитель	(teacher)
tʃɪlʌ'ɣɛk	человек	(man)
tʃeʂʈ	честь	(honour)
tʃɛk	чек	(cheque)
tʃas	час	(hour)
'tʃastə	часто	(often)
plɪ'tʃo	плечо	(shoulder)
'tʃornɪ(j)	черный	(black)
xʌ'tʃu	хочу	(I want)
'tʃulķɪ	чулки	(stockings)
ɲetʃ	печь	(to bake)
lutʃ	луч	(beam)
'totʃkə	точка	(point)
tʃlɛn	член	(member)
prʌ'tʃla	прочла	(read, *past tense fem.*)
kʌp'tʃonɪ(j)	копченый	(smoked)
ptʃɪ'la	пчела	(bee)
'tʃʈeɲ(ɪ)ɪʊ	чтение	(reading)
tʃrɪ'zmɛrnə	чрезмерно	(excessively)
ʌʈtʃɪ'vo	отчего	(why)
ʌʈtʃɪkʌ'ɲiʈ	отчеканить	(to mint)

ʌldʒ'ba	алчба	(greed)
nʌdʒ'ɟif	начдив	(divisional commander)
'dodʒ‿bɪ	дочь бы	(daughter would)

20

THE RUSSIAN NASAL CONSONANTS

20.1 The Russian language has four nasal consonants; they are represented in this book by the symbols m, m̜, n and ŋ.

Formation of the Russian nasal consonants

m

20.2 The principal allophone of the Russian m-phoneme is formed as follows:

(1) *articulating organs:* the two lips;

(2) *state of air-passage:* mouth-passage completely closed at point of primary articulation (but nose-passage open, see (3));

(3) *position of soft palate:* lowered, so as to allow air to pass through the nose;

(4) *state of larynx:* vocal cords close together and vibrating throughout the duration of the consonant.

20.3 The principal allophone of Russian m is a voiced bi-labial nasal consonant.

20.4 Before u and o there occur labio-velarized allophones of m and before ɨ a velarized allophone (§§ 15.3–8). A rare voiceless allophone, which if necessary may be symbolized by m̥, may occur at the end of a word after a voiceless fricative consonant.[1]

20.5 The principal allophone of Russian m presents no difficulty to English-speaking learners, being identical with the normal English m in *man*. The velarized allophones are obtained by raising the back of the tongue and the labio-velarized allophones by raising the back of the tongue and rounding the lips

---

[1] Less commonly, also after a voiceless plosive.

during the labial closure. The voiceless allophone ɱ is obtained by articulating m without accompanying vibration of the vocal cords. The relationship of ɱ to m is the same as that of f to v, or s to z.

20.6 The phoneme m occurs before vowels[1] and consonants and at the end of words. When m occurs initially before another consonant no vowel must be inserted between the two consonants nor before the m. Thus mgla мгла (haze) must not sound like mə'gla or ə'mgla, and mnoj мной (me, *instr.*) must not sound like mə'noj or ə'mnoj. Similarly, when m occurs at the end of a word after another consonant (other than a plosive—see below) there must be no intervening ə. Thus məţɪɾɪʌ'ļizm материализм (materialism), not məţɪɾɪʌ'ļizəm. Since plosives in Russian usually have nasal plosion only when followed by homorganic nasal consonants (see § 17.33), such phonemes as t, d have independent plosion or release before m. In such a word as ɾitm ритм (rhythm) therefore the t is released before the m is articulated. As a result there is a faint glide like an ə-vowel between the t and the m, but this must not be so exaggerated that ɾitm for example sounds like 'ɾitəm.

20.7 The phoneme m is represented in spelling by the letter м.

20.8 *Words illustrating the phoneme* m

maţ	мать	(mother)
'malə	мало	(little)
'domə	дома	(at home)
məlʌ'doj	молодой	(young)
muʃ	муж	(husband)
jɪ'mu	ему	(him, *dat.*)
mox	мох	(moss)
mok	мог	(could)
dʌ'moj	домой	(homewards)
'molədəsţ	молодость	(youth)
mɨ	мы	(we)
mɨţ	мыть	(to wash)

[1] Being a hard consonant, m cannot occur before the phoneme e, nor before the front allophones (i and ɪ) of the phoneme i.

'smɨtʃkə	смычка	(closure)
ʌ'tmɨtʃkə	отмычка	(picklock)
ţɪļɪ'grammə	телеграмма	(telegram)
'summə	сумма	(sum)
ţma	тьма	(darkness)
mgla	мгла	(haze)
mnoj	мной	(me, *instr.*)
mxa	мха	(moss, *gen. sing.*)
'mlat-ʃt(j)	младший	(younger)
'mŋeŋ(ɪ)jɪ	мнение	(opinion)
'mramər	мрамор	(marble)
'mʃtʃeŋ(ɪ)jɪ	мщение	(revenge)
'mtʃatsə	мчаться	(to rush)
ʌt'korm	откорм	(fattening up)
norm	норм	(norm, *gen. pl.*)
ɾɪʌ'ļizm	реализм	(realism)
məţɪɾɪʌ'ļizm	материализм	(materialism)
bəļʃɪ'ɣizm	большевизм	(bolshevism)
spazm	спазм	(spasm, *gen. pl.*)
ɾitm[1]	ритм	(rhythm)
dɪʌ'fragm	диафрагм	(diaphragm, *gen. pl.*)
ɣedm	ведьм	(witch, *gen. pl.*)
draxm̩	драхм	(drachma, *gen. pl.*)
ɾifm̩	рифм	(rhyme, *gen. pl.*)
m̩ɪkrʌ'kosm̩	микрокосм	(microcosm)

m̩

20.9 For most practical purposes only one allophone of m̩ need be distinguished. It is formed, as is the principal allophone of m, by a closure of the lips while the breath-stream issues through the nose; in addition, the tongue is in the j-position through the duration of the consonant.[2]

20.10 Russian m̩ is a voiced palatalized (soft) bilabial nasal consonant.

---

[1] Or ɾitm̩.

[2] The remarks in § 17.50 on the height of the tongue in the articulation of ɲ apply also to m̩.

20. RUSSIAN NASAL CONSONANTS

20.11 When m̩ is followed by i or ι there is, at the most, only a faintly detectable j-glide between the consonant and the following vowel. The glide becomes more obvious before the more open front vowels and before the back vowels (cf. § 17.50). It must not however be so exaggerated that the sequence m̩ + vowel sounds like m̩ + j + vowel, since this sequence occurs in Russian and is distinct from m̩ + vowel. When m̩ occurs at the end of a word the j-glide is usually absent and the softness of m̩ is revealed in the allophone of the preceding vowel or by an i-glide between the vowel and m̩, thus: ѕem̩ семь (seven), but sʌf'ѕɛm совсем (entirely).

20.12 English speakers should experience no difficulty in pronouncing m̩, since it is easily acquired by articulating j simultaneously with the normal English articulation of m. Exaggerated pronunciation of the glide between m̩ and a following vowel must, however, be rigorously avoided.

20.13 The phoneme m̩ occurs before vowels[1] and at the end of words. It also occurs before another m̩ (i.e. a m̩ of twice the normal length is pronounced) and before the consonant j (see § 20.11 above). The only other consonants before which it occurs are the soft labial plosives p̡ and b̡ and even here its occurrence is largely optional. Thus, words such as лампе (lamp, *dat.*, *prep. sing.*), бомбе (bomb, *dat.*, *prep. sing.*), which have other forms with hard p and b, may be pronounced respectively 'lamp̡ι, 'bomb̡ι or, in an older style of pronunciation, 'lam̩p̡ι, 'bom̩b̡ι, whereas in words such as имбирь (ginger), амбиция (ambition), in all forms of which there is soft b̡, soft m̩ is likely to occur in various styles of pronunciation—ιm̩'b̡iɾ, ʌm̩'b̡itsιjə.

20.14 The phoneme m̩ is represented in spelling by the letter м followed by one of the letters е, и, ю or я, or the soft sign, ь. In cases such as those mentioned in the preceding paragraphs it is represented simply by the letter м.

20.15 *Words illustrating the phoneme* m̩

m̩ik	миг	(moment)

---

[1] Not, of course, before the non-front allophones (ɨ, ι) of the i-phoneme.

m̟ir	мир	(world)
vʌ'zm̟iʈʟ	возьмите	(take!)
'm̟eʂəts	месяц	(month)
'vm̟eʂʈʟ	вместе	(together)
'm̟ɛstə	место	(place)
'm̟ɛtət	метод	(method)
kʌ'm̟ɛtə	комета	(comet)
'm̟asə	мясо	(meat)
ʂʟ'm̟an	семян	(seeds, *gen. pl.*)
m̟æʈ	мять	(to crumple)
m̟ot	мед	(honey)
'm̟orznuʈ	мерзнуть	(to freeze)
zʌ'm̟orznuʈ	замерзнуть	(to freeze, *pfv.*)
'm̟ülʃtʃʟk	мюльщик	(mule-operator)
ʂem̟	семь	(seven)
fpræm̟	впрямь	(indeed)
'voʂʟm̟	восемь	(eight)
ʈʟˌlʟ'gram̟m̟ʟ	телеграмме	(telegram, *dat., prep. sing.*)
'sum̟m̟ʟ	сумме	(sum, *dat., prep. sing.*)
skʌ'm̟ji	скамьи	(bench, *gen. sing.*)
ʂʟ'm̟jɛ	семье	(family, *dat., prep. sing.*)
ʂʟ'm̟ja	семья	(family)
ʂʟ'm̟jöj	семьей	(family, *instr. sing.*)
skʌ'm̟ju	скамью	(bench, *acc. sing.*)
ʟm̟'b̟ir	имбирь	(ginger)
ʌm̟'b̟itsʟ(j)ə	амбиция	(ambition)

n

20.16 The principal allophone of the Russian n-phoneme is formed as follows:

(1) *articulating organs:* tip of tongue touching front teeth in angle formed by upper incisors and teeth-ridge; blade of tongue against front part of teeth-ridge (Fig. 26);

(2) *state of air-passage:* mouth-passage completely closed at point of articulation (but nose-passage open, see (3));

(3) *position of soft palate:* lowered, so as to allow air to issue through the nose;

20. RUSSIAN NASAL CONSONANTS

(4) *state of larynx:* vocal cords close together and vibrating throughout the duration of the consonant.

20.17 The principal allophone of the Russian n-phoneme is a voiced, denti-alveolar nasal consonant.[1]

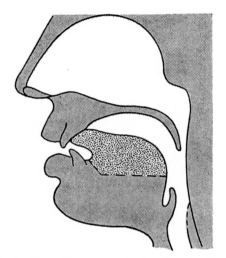

Fig. 26. Position of tongue and soft palate for Russian n

20.18 Before u and o occur labio-velarized allophones of n and before ɨ a velarized allophone (see chapter 15).

20.19 In the principal allophone of English n the tip of the tongue is placed at or slightly in front of the angle where the teeth-ridge begins to turn up towards the roof of the mouth (cf. English and Russian t and d, §§ 17.70, 79). It is not difficult for the English speaker to learn to form the Russian n correctly, but it may be necessary for him to remind himself of the difference between Russian and English n by marking every n in the phonetic transcriptions of Russian passages which he is practising. Note that Russian does not have the '-ing' sound (phonetic symbol ŋ, as in English *thing* θɪŋ) before the velar plosives k, ḳ, g and g̣. Thus the n is still denti-alveolar in such words as bank банк (bank), ʌn'glijskɪ(j) английский (English).

---

[1] The note on t, p. 98, applies, *mutatis mutandis,* to n also.

20. RUSSIAN NASAL CONSONANTS

20.20 The phoneme n occurs before vowels[1] and consonants (other than ʈ, ɖ, ʂ, ʐ, ɳ, tʃ and ʃtʃ)[2] and at the end of words. In a few words it occurs finally after another consonant, when no vowel should be allowed to intrude between the two consonants.

20.21 The phoneme n is represented in spelling by the letter н.

20.22 *Words illustrating the phoneme* n

nas	нас	(us, *gen., acc., prep.*)
nam	нам	(us, *dat.*)
ʌ'na	она	(she)
tsʈ'na	цена	(price)
vnuk	внук	(grandson)
nuʒ'da	нужда	(need)
nos	нос	(nose)
pʌ'dnos	поднос	(tray)
u'noʂʈt	уносит	(takes away)
niʈ	ныть	(to mope)
'strannʈ(j)	странный	(strange)
nraf	нрав	(temperament)
kʌn'tsɛrt	концерт	(concert)
kʌn'tsa	конца	(end, *gen. sing.*)
ʞɪn'ʒal	кинжал	(dagger)
kʌn'va	канва	(canvas)
'bronzə	бронза	(bronze)
bank	банк	(bank)
'tonʞɪ(j)	тонкий	(thin)
kʌr'ʈinkə	картинка	(little picture)
ʌn'glijskɪ(j)	английский	(English)
'jungə	юнга	(cabin-boy)
g̩imn	гимн	(hymn)
sʌ'blazn	соблазн	(temptation)

---

[1] n occurs before the front allophones of the i-phoneme (i and ɪ) and before the e-phoneme only in some loan-words and such native acronyms as нэп (New Economic Policy), pronounced nɛp.

[2] Before ļ some speakers pronounce n, others pronounce ɳ.

20. RUSSIAN NASAL CONSONANTS

ɲ

20.23 The principal allophone of the Russian ɲ phoneme is formed as follows:

(1) *articulating organs:* blade of tongue against teeth-ridge and front of tongue close to front part of hard palate[1] (the tip of the tongue is usually lowered, making contact or near contact with the base of the lower front teeth; see Fig. 27);[2]

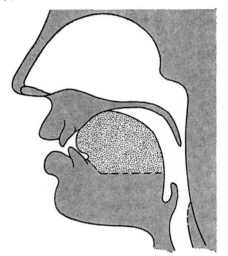

Fig. 27. Position of tongue and soft palate for Russian ɲ

(2) *state of air-passage:* mouth-passage completely closed at point of articulation (but nose-passage open, see (3));

(3) *position of soft palate:* lowered, so as to allow air to issue through the nose;

(4) *state of larynx:* vocal cords close together and vibrating throughout the duration of the consonant.

---

[1] Contact of the foremost part of the front of the tongue and even a considerable part of the front of the tongue with the hard palate is not uncommon in the articulation of ɲ.

[2] Less commonly, the tip of the tongue is in a position slightly behind the upper front teeth but there is usually no contact with the upper front teeth.

20. RUSSIAN NASAL CONSONANTS

20.24 The principal allophone of Russian ɲ is a voiced, palatalized (soft) alveolar nasal consonant.

20.25 The subsidiary allophone of ɲ is voiceless and may, when necessary, be transcribed as ɲ̥.

20.26 When ɲ is followed by i or ɩ there is, at the most, only a faintly detectable j-glide between the consonant and the following vowel. The glide becomes more obvious before the more open front vowels and before the back vowels. It must not, however, be so exaggerated that the sequence ɲ + vowel sounds like the sequence ɲ + j + vowel, since this sequence occurs in Russian and is distinct from ɲ + vowel. When ɲ occurs before other consonants there is no appreciable glide, whereas when ɲ occurs finally (i.e. before a pause) a slight j-glide is heard after the consonant which may strike English speakers as a short i-sound. It must on no account be exaggerated so that koɲ конь (horse) for example sounds like two syllables—'koɲɩ.

20.27 The nearest English equivalent to the Russian ɲ is the nj in *new* njuː or *union* (pronounced as two syllables, i.e. 'juːnjən). There are, however, considerable differences and the substitution of the English sequence of phonemes nj for Russian ɲ is not satisfactory. English n in nj is apical, i.e. has the tip of the tongue against the teeth-ridge while Russian ɲ is laminal, i.e. has the blade of the tongue against the teeth-ridge; the front of the tongue is in the raised position throughout the whole of the Russian ɲ, while in the English n in nj, though there may be a certain raising of the front of the tongue anticipating the j, such raising is not essential.

20.28 English speakers who find difficulty in achieving ɲ from the description given in § 20.23 may find it easier to approach the sound from the English combination of phonemes nj, as in *new* njuː or *union* 'juːnjən. They must then try to make the closure further forward, with the blade of the tongue against the teeth-ridge, trying at the same time to combine the j-element as closely as possible with the n-element.

20.29 The phoneme ɲ occurs before vowels[1] and consonants

[1] Not, however, before the non-front allophones ɨ and ɩ of the i-phoneme.

20. RUSSIAN NASAL CONSONANTS

(other than t, d, s, z and n) and at the end of words. The subsidiary allophone ŋ̥ occurs, rarely, at the end of a word after a voiceless consonant.

20.30 The phoneme ɲ is represented in spelling by the letter н followed by one of the vowel letters e, и, ю or я, or the soft sign, ь. Before ţ, d̦, ş, z̦, ɲ, tʃ and ʃtʃ the phoneme ɲ is represented by the letter н alone.[1]

20.31 *Words illustrating the phoneme ɲ*

ɲiţ	нить	(thread)
xrʌ'ɲiţ	хранить	(to keep)
pəɲɪ'delɲ̩k	понедельник	(Monday)
şɪ'ɲeţ	синеть	(to become blue)
'ɲɛbə	небо	(sky)
pʌ'ɲæţ	понять	(to understand, *pfv.*)
kʌ'ɲa	коня	(horse, *gen. sing.*)
'ɲobə	нёбо	(palate)
kʌ'ɲok	конек	(little horse)
pɪɾɪ'ɲos	перенес	(took across)
'ɲuxəţ	нюхать	(to sniff)
ko'ɲu	коню	(horse, *dat. sing.*)
tsɪ'ɲu	ценю	(I value)
kʌɲ'ķi	коньки	(skates)
'malɪɲķɪ(j)	маленький	(small)
'deɲg̦ɪ	деньги	(money)
'ranʃɪ	раньше	(earlier)
ɭɪɲ'ţæj	лентяй	(lazybones)
kʌ'maɲd̦ɪ	команде	(team, *dat., prep. sing.*)
'peɲşɪjə	пенсия	(pension)
b̦ɪɲ'z̦in	бензин	(petrol)
'vaɲɲɪ	ванне	(bath, *dat., prep. sing.*)
gʌɲ'tʃar	гончар	(potter)
bərʌ'baɲʃtʃɪk	барабанщик	(drummer)
vrʌ'ɲjo	вранье	(lies)
sɪ'ɲja	свинья	(pig)

[1] And before ɭ in the case of speakers who pronounce ɲ and not n before this consonant.

20. RUSSIAN NASAL CONSONANTS

sprʌˈsoɲjə	спросонья	(half-awake)
koɲ	конь	(horse)
daɲ	дань	(tribute)
dɽæɲ	дрянь	(rubbish)
ʎeɲ	лень	(laziness)
ʒⁱʒɲ	жизнь	(life)
kaʒɲ	казнь	(execution)
ȵeʂɳ̥	песнь	(song)

21

THE RUSSIAN LATERAL CONSONANTS

21.1 There are many varieties of l-sounds. While the tongue-tip is touching the upper teeth or teeth-ridge, the main part of the tongue may be made to assume various positions. Thus the usual English l in *people* ˈpiːpl has, besides the tongue-tip articulation, a certain raising of the back of the tongue something like that shown in Fig. 28. The Russian ʎ has, besides the tongue-tip articulation, considerable raising of the front of the tongue as shown in Fig. 29. In fact each possible position of the main part of the tongue (within certain limits) gives rise, when combined with the tongue-tip articulation, to a special variety of l-sound.

21.2 These possible positions are similar to the positions required for producing different vowels. And, in fact, the different varieties of l-sounds have a certain acoustic resemblance to vowels; every l-sound has a definite vowel-resonance depending on the position occupied by the main part of the tongue.

21.3 Thus the most usual type of Russian l has an acoustic resemblance to cardinal o or even u (cf. Figs. 7 and 28), and the Russian ʎ has an acoustic resemblance to cardinal i (cf. Figs. 6 and 29).

21.4 l-sounds which have front vowel resonance are often termed 'clear' varieties of l. Those which have back vowel resonance are often termed 'dark' varieties of l.

21. RUSSIAN LATERAL CONSONANTS

21.5 The Russian ļ is a particularly 'clear' variety of l; the Russian ł is a particularly 'dark' variety of l. The most usual English l in *law* has a medium resonance (about that of ə). The l in the English group lj (as in *million*) has a somewhat 'clearer' resonance than this, but it is less 'clear' than the Russian ļ.

21.6 The precise degree of 'clearness' or 'darkness' of any particular variety of l-sound is best described by stating what the vowel resonance is. It is worthy of note that lip-rounding does not greatly affect the quality of 'dark' l-sounds.

21.7 The vowel-resonance of any particular kind of l may be shown in writing, when desired, by placing the vowel-letter as an index to the letter l. Thus an l with i-resonance may, when required, be written lⁱ; l with u-resonance may be written lᵘ and so on.

21.8 The best way of learning to make any particular variety of l is to place the tongue-tip as for any l-sound, and, keeping it firmly there, to try to say the required vowel. Thus to learn to make a very 'clear' lⁱ, place the tongue-tip as for any kind of l, and then try to say simultaneously a cardinal i. If this exercise is found difficult, it is a good plan to perform it with the tip of the tongue held firmly between the teeth.

21.9 Another useful exercise is to hold the tongue-tip firmly in an l-position and, while doing so, to pronounce a series of vowels, say u, o, a, ɛ, i. Students often find it easier to make such a series of l-sounds than to make a single isolated variety. Any desired variety such as lⁱ can subsequently be isolated from the series.

21.10 Any of these varieties may be 'sulcalized' (§ 21.12). It seems impossible to describe in writing the acoustic effect of sulcalization, but the effect is produced by endeavouring to apply considerable lateral contraction to the back of the tongue.

21.11 The Russian language has two lateral consonants. They are represented in this book by l and ļ. In some works the symbol ł is used for the sound here written l.

The Russian lateral consonants in detail

l

21.12 The principal allophone of the Russian l-phoneme is formed as follows:

(1) *articulating organs:* tip of tongue in angle formed by upper teeth and teeth-ridge; front of tongue hollowed and back of tongue somewhat raised in the direction of the soft palate (see Fig. 28); the sound is also somewhat 'sulcal', i.e. a furrow is made down the centre of the back of the tongue, or the tongue is laterally contracted.

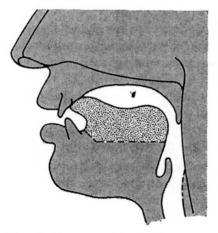

Fig. 28. Tongue-position for Russian l

(2) *state of air-passage:* closed in the centre (by tip of tongue), but one or both sides of front of tongue lowered, so as to allow continuous escape of air laterally, without friction;

(3) *position of soft palate:* raised, so that air cannot issue through the nose;

(4) *state of larynx:* vocal cords close together and vibrating throughout the duration of the consonant.

21.13 The principal allophone of Russian l is a voiced,

velarized dental lateral consonant. This type of l is sometimes called 'dark'.

21.14   The degree of raising of the back of the tongue is such as to give Russian l a resonance approaching that of o, though the back of the tongue may be raised slightly higher or even not quite so high.

21.15   The subsidiary allophone of Russian l differs from the principal allophone only in that it is voiceless, i.e. the vocal cords are apart, in the position for breath. It may be represented, when necessary, by the symbol ḷ.

21.16   It is not very difficult for most English people to produce a dark l at the end of a word or in isolation. All they have to do is to isolate the l of *people*, and try to pronounce the sound with the tip of the tongue somewhat further forward and with some lateral contraction of the back of the tongue. They have likewise no difficulty in pronouncing such words as bal бал (ball), 'palkə палка (stick). Again, the English l-sounds of *ball* and *pall* may be used as starting-points and made somewhat 'darker' by moving the tip of the tongue slightly further forward and making sure that the tongue is laterally contracted and, in particular, that the back of the tongue is well raised.

21.17   However, English speakers have as a rule some difficulty in using the sound in other positions. In the most usual English pronunciation the dark l is never used when a vowel follows; it is only used finally (as in *people*) or before consonants (as in *fold*). In such words as *leave, left, like, law, look*, a much 'clearer' variety of l is employed.[1] Consequently it is not easy for some English speakers to pronounce a dark l when immediately followed by a vowel, as is necessary in such Russian words as 'loʃkə ложка (spoon), plit плыть (to swim).

21.18   To acquire the correct pronunciation of such words the learner should begin by saying the dark Russian l he has learnt according to the preceding paragraphs, followed by oʃkə,

---

[1] The various l's of English are all members of one phoneme. In Russian, however, the dark l and the very clear ḷ (§ 21.29 below) are members of different phonemes.

21. RUSSIAN LATERAL CONSONANTS

thus: ɫ oʃkə, making a complete break between the ɫ and the vowel o and then gradually shortening the interval until it finally disappears. The exercise might be shown graphically thus: ɫ———oʃkə, ɫ———oʃkə, ɫ—oʃkə, 'loʃkə. Carry out the same exercise with plit, thus: pl———it, pl———it, pl—it, plit.

21.19 Alternatively, instead of making a pause before the vowel, the student should prolong the dark ɫ and, without a break, continue the rest of the word. Then gradually shorten the ɫ until it is of normal length, thus: ɫɫɫɫɫloʃkə, ɫɫɫloʃkə, ɫloʃkə, 'loʃkə, and likewise for plit.

21.20 It is helpful to practise syllables with dark ɫ in front of various vowels (la, lo, li, lu), if necessary going first through either or both of the two exercises just described.

21.21 Many Scots use a dark ɫ in all positions in English (i.e. before vowels as well as before consonants) and consequently will not experience in learning to pronounce Russian ɫ the difficulty just dealt with. However, they must ensure that they acquire a sufficiently dark ɫ for correct Russian. The same applies to many Americans.

21.22 On the other hand some people from the North of England and most Irish people do not possess a dark ɫ at all, but use a 'clear' variety in such words as *people, field*, as well as before vowels. They often have very great difficulty in learning to form the Russian ɫ.

21.23 The best way for them to proceed is to notice that every ɫ-sound has a definite 'vowel-resonance' (see §§ 21.1, 2 above). The vowel-resonance of the Russian ɫ is that of a back vowel; it is best to aim for cardinal o, though a slightly closer or even more open vowel may be adequate (cf. § 21.14). The Russian ɫ may therefore be acquired by placing the tongue-tip as for any ɫ-sound and endeavouring simultaneously to pronounce a vowel of the o-type or of the ɔ-type.[1] This exercise should be

---

[1] We do not suggest aiming at a vowel-resonance of the u-type. Irish people who have no dark ɫ generally do not possess any vowel in the neighbourhood of cardinal u. Their vowel in *food* is generally a very advanced variety of u (about the Russian ü), which would not give at all the right effect when given as a resonance to ɫ.

practised at first with lip-rounding and then in the normal Russian way without lip-rounding. These learners must also endeavour to get the 'sulcal' effect by lateral contraction of the back of the tongue.

21.24 If any difficulty is experienced in performing the exercise, the student should try first to make a series of l-sounds with different vowel-resonances (say those of i, ɛ, a, o and u).

21.25 The subsidiary allophone ɬ does not occur in normal English. It may easily be acquired once l has been learnt by placing the tongue in the l-position and then simply blowing out a stream of air. ɬ differs from l in the same way that t does from d, or s from z. In making ɬ, one should not expel the air with such force that considerable friction is heard. Such a sound would be a voiceless lateral fricative.

21.26 The subsidiary allophone of l occurs at the end of words after voiceless consonants. The principal allophone occurs elsewhere: at the end of words when not preceded by a voiceless consonant, before vowels,[1] before consonants and, occasionally between consonants. When l occurs initially before another consonant, care must be taken not to insert a vowel of the ə-type either before or after the l. Thus: lba лба (forehead, *gen. sing.*) *not* əl'ba or lə'ba. If necessary, such words should be practised at first by prolonging the l, subsequently shortening it until it becomes of normal length. Similarly no vowel must be allowed to intrude when l occurs (as it does in a very few words) between two consonants, thus: ˌobl'sut облсуд (district court), *not* ˌobəl'sut or ˌoblə'sut. Nor must a vowel be inserted where final l occurs after a voiced consonant, as in igl игл (needles, *gen. pl.*), *not* 'igəl.

21.27 Russian l is represented in spelling by the letter л.

21.28 *Words illustrating the phoneme* l

'lɨʒt	лыжи	(skis)
'slɨʃət	слышать	(to hear)
skʌ'lɨ	скалы	(crag, *gen. sing.*)

[1] Excluding the phoneme e and the front allophones (i and ɩ) of the phoneme i.

21. RUSSIAN LATERAL CONSONANTS

dʌ'la	дала	(gave, *fem.*)
'lampə	лампа	(lamp)
'voləst	волосы	(hair)
'loʃkə	ложка	(spoon)
'slovə	слово	(word)
luk	лук	(onion)
lu'na	луна	(moon)
jɛl	ел	(ate)
dul	дул	(blew)
ʂŋal	снял	(took)
dolk	долг	(duty)
kəlbʌ'sa	колбаса	(sausage)
sʌl'dat	солдат	(soldier)
kʌl'xos	колхоз	(collective farm)
lba	лба	(forehead, *gen. sing.*)
lgaṭ	лгать	(to lie)
igl	игл	(needle, *gen. pl.*)
smɨsḷ	смысл	(sense)
tuxḷ	тухл	(rotten, *sh. fm. masc.*)
tuskḷ	тускл	(dim, *sh. fm. masc.*)
rɨxḷ	рыхл	(friable, *sh. fm. masc.*)

ḷ

21.29 The principal allophone of the Russian ḷ phoneme is formed as follows:

(1) *articulating organs:* tip of tongue against fore part of teeth-ridge; blade of tongue against mid and back of teeth-ridge; front of tongue raised towards hard palate (Fig. 29);[1]

(2) *state of air passage:* closed in the centre (by tip and blade of tongue against teeth-ridge), but one or both sides of tongue lowered so as to allow continuous escape of air laterally, without friction;

(3) *position of soft palate:* raised, so that air cannot pass through the nose;

---

[1] Some speakers pronounce ḷ with the tongue-tip depressed behind the lower teeth.

(4) *state of larynx:* vocal cords close together and vibrating throughout the duration of the consonant.

21.30 The principal allophone of Russian ǀ is a voiced palatalized (soft) alveolar lateral consonant.

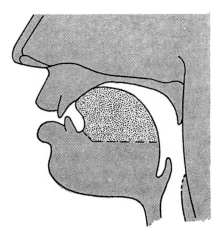

Fig. 29. Tongue-position for Russian ǀ

21.31 The remarks made in § 17.86 as to the manner of making and releasing contact in the articulation of ʈ, apply also to ǀ. A slight j-glide is heard on the release of contact of ǀ when a vowel follows, but not usually in other cases. The glide must not be exaggerated so that ǀ sounds like ǀj. This sequence occurs in Russian but is always distinct from ǀ alone—cf. ǀjot льет (pours) and ǀot лед (ice). Before the phoneme i there is no appreciable glide.

21.32 The subsidiary allophone of the Russian ǀ phoneme differs from the principal allophone only in that it is voiceless, i.e. the vocal cords are apart, in the position for breath. Voiceless ǀ may be represented when necessary by the symbol ǀ̥.

21.33 The Russian ǀ presents some difficulty for most English speakers, especially in certain positions, noted in § 21.36.

21.34 The nearest English equivalent to the Russian sound ǀ is the sequence lj in *million* 'mɪljən. There are, however, differences of three kinds.

(1) In the Russian ļ the tip of the tongue is a little more forward than in the English l in *million*. The English learner must take care to put the tip of the tongue slightly nearer the upper front teeth when pronouncing the Russian ļ.

(2) The front of the tongue is in raised position throughout the whole of the Russian ļ; as a result there is a notable difference of quality between the Russian and English sounds (apart from accompanying glides); in the English l in *million* there may be a certain raising of the front of the tongue anticipating the j, but it is not sufficient to give to this English l such a 'clear' quality as the Russian ļ has.

(3) Russian ļ is a single sound, whereas lj in *million* is a sequence of sounds; care must be taken that ļ, in Russian words, does not sound like a sequence l + j or ļ + j. Note that the area of contact of the articulating organs extends further back in the Russian ļ than in the English lj in *million*.

21.35 From what has been said it will be seen that a means of learning to make the Russian ļ is as follows. First learn, by the methods described in §§ 21.8, 9, to make a very 'clear' l-sound, i.e. an l-sound having a resonance of cardinal i. Practise prolonging the sound, without adding any other sound after it. Then practise it with following vowels: ļi, ļɛ, ļa, ļo, ļu.

21.36 The sound ļ requires special practice on the part of English learners when it has to be said in connected speech before another consonant or at the end of a word, since in most varieties of English a dark l occurs in these positions. Examples of words with ļ in these positions are:

'toļkə	только	(only)
'paļmə	пальма	(palm)
soļ	соль	(salt)
ʒaļ	жаль	(it's a pity)

21.37 The subsidiary allophone ļ does not occur in normal English. Once Russian ļ has been learnt, however, it is easy to form ļ by placing the tongue in the position for ļ and then simply blowing out a stream of air. ļ differs from ļ in the same way that f differs from v, or s from z. In making ļ one should not expel the air with such force that considerable friction is heard.

21.38 The subsidiary allophone of ļ occurs at the end of words after voiceless consonants. The principal allophone occurs elsewhere: at the end of words when not preceded by a voiceless consonant, before vowels[1] and before other consonants. When ļ occurs initially before another consonant or finally after a voiced consonant, care must be taken not to insert a vowel of the ɪ-type or i-type. Thus: ļda льда (ice, *gen. sing.*), not ɪļ'da or ļɪ'da, and kʌ'rabļ корабль (ship), not kʌ'raļɪ.

21.39 Russian ļ is represented in spelling by the letter л followed by one of the vowel letters и, е, ю or я, or the soft sign, ь.[2]

21.40 *Words illustrating the phoneme* ļ

ļiţ	лить	(to pour)
'ļitsə	лица	(faces)
ļɪx'ko	легко	(easily)
bʌ'ļeţ	болеть	(to be ill)
'ļebɪţ	лебедь	(swan)
ļɛs	лес	(wood)
'bļɛdnɪ(j)	бледный	(pale)
gu'ļæţ	гулять	(to stroll)
'ļaʃkə	ляжка	(thigh)
'ʃļapə	шляпа	(hat)
ļot	лед	(ice)
pʌ'ļot	полет	(flight)
ļon	лен	(flax)

[1] ļ, unlike l, does occur before the phoneme e and the front allophones (i, ɪ), not the retracted allophones (ɨ, ɪ), of the i-phoneme.

[2] Note that in the one or two loan-words with the sequence ļjo the spelling is льо, not лье (examples in § 21.40). It is a rule of Russian spelling that the sequence jo in loan-words is indicated by ьо or йо (as in mʌ'jor майор major), not by ье (ьё) or е (ё).

ļuˈboʃ	любовь	(love)
ˈļüdι	люди	(people)
ˈtoļkə	только	(only)
ˈpaļmə	пальма	(palm)
ˈboļnə	больно	(it hurts)
ˈboļʃι	больше	(more)
jeļ	ель	(fir-tree)
soļ	соль	(salt)
ʃιˈvraļ	февраль	(February)
uˈtʃiţιļ	учитель	(teacher)
ļda	льда	(ice, *gen. sing.*)
ļna	льна	(flax, *gen. sing.*)
ļva	льва	(lion, *gen. sing.*)
ˈļgotə	льгота	(privilege)
rubļ	рубль	(rouble)
kʌˈrabļ	корабль	(ship)
ʒuˈravļ	журавль	(crane)
ļjot	льет	(pours)
pʌˈļjot	польет	(will pour)
buˈļjon	бульон	(broth)
pətʃtʌˈļjon	почтальон	(postman)
ļju	лью	(I pour)
ļjut	льют	(they pour)
ˈuļjι	ульи	(beehives)
miʂļ̩	мысль	(thought)
ɦιˈnokļ̩	бинокль	(binoculars)
ˌpolˈļitrə	пол-литра	(half-a-litre)
ˌpolιsˈta	пол-листа	(folio)

22

THE RUSSIAN ROLLED CONSONANTS

22.1 The Russian language has two rolled consonants. They
are represented in this book by r and ɾ.

r

22.2 Some allophones of Russian r are formed as follows:

(1) *articulating organs:* tip of tongue against middle of teeth-ridge (Fig. 30);

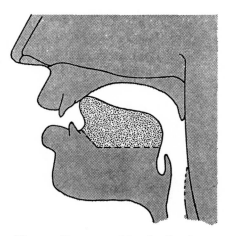

Fig. 30. Tongue-position for Russian r

(2) *state of air-passage:* alternately closed and opened a number of times at point of articulation with such rapidity that the whole process strikes the ear as forming a single sound; in other words, the tip of the tongue makes a very rapid succession of taps against the middle of the teeth-ridge;[1]

(3) *position of soft palate:* raised, so that air cannot issue through the nose;

(4) *state of larynx:* vocal cords close together and vibrating throughout the duration of the consonant.

22.3 Such allophones of r are voiced alveolar rolled consonants.

[1] The speaker does not make each tap consciously. All he does is to hold the tongue loosely against the teeth-ridge in such a position that when air-pressure is applied, the tongue vibrates without conscious effort. The action is similar to that of a musical reed.

22. RUSSIAN ROLLED CONSONANTS

22.4 Such allophones of Russian r are used at the end of words, when not preceded by a voiceless consonant. The number of taps is three or four normally. At the beginning of a word and before a consonant there are usually two taps. Between vowels there is usually only one tap of the tip of the tongue against the teeth-ridge. Such a tap against the teeth-ridge does not produce a sound of the d-type:[1] there is no appreciable length of closure. The tongue simply 'flaps' up to the teeth-ridge and makes a very brief contact with it. Sounds formed in this way are known as 'flapped' sounds. Hence one allophone of Russian r should, strictly speaking be described as a voiced alveolar flapped consonant.

22.5 It must be added, however, that in all positions the number of taps may be increased beyond the number stated in the preceding paragraph, for special 'affective' purposes. Thus the r in rat рад (glad) might have five or six taps if pronounced with particularly heavy emphasis. In such instances it would probably be desirable to write two or even more r-symbols in the phonetic transcription.[2]

22.6 A voiceless r, with about three taps, occurs as a subsidiary allophone of r and may, if necessary, be symbolized by ʀ.

22.7 The sound r as described in § 22.2 exists in some kinds of English pronunciation. In particular, it is commonly used in Scotland as the pronunciation of the letter r, and it is the form of r-sound generally recommended in England for use in elocution and in singing.

---

[1] Though it may strike some listeners as being more like a d than an r if their own r is not of the rolled type. For instance, many speakers of American English pronounce r as a retroflex fricative (formed with the tip of the tongue curled up towards the roof of the mouth) and the flapped (single-tap) r that often occurs in the British pronunciation of *very* (see § 22.21) strikes them as being like a d. Hence, the occasional spelling in literature of the word *very* as *veddy* to indicate a British pronunciation of this word.

[2] B. V. Bratus, of Leningrad University, has pointed out to D. Ward that there is theoretically no limit to the length of Russian *vowels* in emphatic or other types of affective pronunciation. The same seems to be true of certain Russian consonants (i.e. the ones which do not include a stop-element), at least in some positions.

22. RUSSIAN ROLLED CONSONANTS

22.8 The majority of English people are, however, quite unable to pronounce a rolled r without special practice. The sound used almost universally in England in such a word as *raw* is a fricative consonant and not a rolled one. If it is necessary to distinguish this sound from other r-sounds, it may be symbolized by ɹ.

22.9 Moreover, the most usual English fricative ɹ is formed with the tip of the tongue against the back part of the teethridge (about in the same place as for Russian з, see §§ 18.80, 83, and Fig. 19); whereas Russian rolled r is formed with the tip of the tongue further forward. There is also lateral contraction of the tongue, the lateral contraction being greater than in the case of Russian з, and still greater than in the case of English з.

22.10 English people who do not normally use a rolled r fall into three classes:

(1) there are some who can make a perfectly good and sustained rolled r with little or no practice and without effort;

(2) others can without practice make a kind of feeble rolled r, but they only manage it with difficulty and, generally, after preparation; moreover they are unable to prolong it;

(3) others are totally unable to make any kind of rolled r without long practice.

22.11 Learners of class (1) have only to remember to use the sound r properly in speaking Russian. They must particularly bear in mind to pronounce r before consonants and at the end of words where the spelling has p and the phonetic notation has r.

22.12 No learner should consider himself to be in class (1) unless he can without difficulty hold on a continuous rolled r for at least five seconds.

22.13 Certain sound-groups containing r may present difficulty to learners of class (1); they must be mastered by continued repetition of words or syllables containing those groups. Examples for such practice will be found below (§ 22.29).

22. RUSSIAN ROLLED CONSONANTS

22.14 Learners of class (2) should perfect their rolled r before attempting to use it in Russian words. There is nothing to do but to repeat their rolled r again and again, hundreds of times if necessary, endeavouring to sustain it as long as possible. It may be found in the first instance that a great deal of force of the breath has to be used in order to make the sound; if so, practice must be continued until the sound can be produced with normal force of the breath.

22.15 Many learners of class (2) will also find that they can make a rolled r of sorts in certain sound-combinations, but not in others. Thus it is not uncommon to meet with people who can make a rolled r when the sound is immediately preceded by t or d, but not in any other connexion. Such learners must continually practise the combinations with r which they can make, endeavouring to eliminate by degrees the adjoining sounds, until at last they can say the r in isolation. They must not be satisfied until they can start a rolled r without any perceptible preparation and can sustain it for five seconds without undue effort and without its becoming 'breathy'.

22.16 Learners of class (2) must moreover be able to join r on to any other sound without stumbling. In particular, they must learn to use the sound properly when final or followed by a consonant. Facility in the use of r in connected speech is attained by means of repetition exercises.

22.17 If they cannot isolate r from the combinations with r which they can make, they must proceed as learners of class (3) (see below).

22.18 To learners of class (3)—those who are unable to make the tongue-tip vibrate at all—the task of learning to make a good rolled r is generally a long and difficult one. It is, however, one which *must* be undertaken by those who wish to learn to speak Russian properly. Some people who claim to be unable to produce a rolled r will in fact produce a very good and prolonged rolled r if asked to make a noise like a motor-bike or a road-drill: brrrrr or drrrrr. They may also find that the noise indicating that they feel cold (usually written *brrrrr*) is a long, rolled r, or a voiceless rolled r (r̥).

22.19 Failing this, the best way to proceed is as follows. If the learner's English r-sound is the fricative ɹ described in § 22.8 he should pronounce this sound a number of times using strong sudden jerks of breath and trying to keep the tongue-tip as loose as possible. If he cannot manage by this means to make the tongue-tip vibrate, he should try the same exercise placing the tongue-tip against different points of the teeth-ridge. He may also try a similar exercise starting from ʒ or z instead of from ɹ. It is probable that after some trials he will hit upon the position which will cause the tongue-tip to vibrate a little.

22.20 When this stage has been reached, he becomes a learner of class (2) and must proceed as described above.

22.21 Some English people are able to acquire a rolled r by the following method. Pronounce slowly the exercise təda:təda:-təda:...[1] preferably with dental t's and alveolar d's; then gradually increase the speed. When said very fast indeed, the alveolar d has a tendency to turn into 'flapped' or 'semi-rolled' r-sound, i.e. a sound formed after the manner of rolled r but consisting of only one single tap of the tongue (see § 22.4 above). With r representing here the flapped r, the resulting sequence would be written təra:təra:təra:... or tra:tra:tra:... (according to the rate of saying it). It then remains to isolate this r and extend it into a fully rolled sound. Many speakers of (British) English pronounce a flapped r between vowels before an unstressed syllable, as in *very* 'vɛrɪ. This r may be isolated and extended into a fully rolled sound.

22.22 The phenomenon of English 'intrusive *r*' may be referred to here. Many, if not most English people who do not otherwise pronounce the *r* written at the end of a word do so if the next word begins with a vowel, as in *a pair of shoes, far away*.[2] The

---

[1] The : means that the vowel ɑ is to be pronounced long.
[2] Some people do this where no *r* is written, as in *the idea of it* ðɪ aidiər əv ɪt. In Russian the 'intrusive r' where no letter p is written is completely wrong.

22. RUSSIAN ROLLED CONSONANTS

'intrusive *r*' is not usually the normal English fricative ɹ but a flapped r. This too may be isolated and extended into a rolled r.

22.23 Many English people find the task of learning to make rolled r much facilitated by aiming in the first instance at the corresponding voiceless sound r̥. r̥ is a fairly easy sound to acquire by the method described in § 22.19 (starting from a voiceless ɹ̥,[1] or from ʃ, or from s). When r̥ has been acquired, it is not difficult to add voice, thus producing r.

22.24 When the learner can say r in isolation, he must practise the sound in combination with other sounds. To attain facility in the use of r in connected speech, he should practise repeatedly words such as those given below in § 22.29.

22.25 In the most usual form of educated Southern English the r-sound (ɹ) occurs in connected speech only before vowels; it is never heard finally or before consonants. Thus the English words *park*, *letter* are usually pronounced pɑːk, 'lɛtə. Consequently even when English people have learnt to pronounce rolled r, they are apt to omit it in such Russian words as u'dar удар (blow), 'saxər сахар (sugar), 'gorkə горка (hillock), tʃ ir'ta черта (line). The remedy is to practise such words repeatedly, exaggerating the r's in the first instance.

22.26 The sound r̥ does not exist in normal English.[2] Once r has been learnt, it is easy to achieve r̥ by pronouncing r with breath only, i.e. without vibrations of the vocal cords. The relationship of r̥ to r is the same as that of s to z, of f to v.

22.27 The phoneme r occurs before vowels[3] and consonants and at the end of words. In the last instance the voiceless allophone r̥ is used if there is a preceding voiceless consonant. Voiceless r̥ may also occasionally be heard at the end of a word after a vowel or a voiced consonant, usually however only when

---

[1] As in the English *tree* tɹiː.

[2] Do not confuse r̥ with the voiceless fricative r (ɹ̥) heard in Southern English *tree* tɹiː.

[3] Not, however, before the e-phoneme or the front allophones (i and ɪ) of the i-phoneme.

the word occurs before a pause. Its occurrence here is a personal idiosyncrasy and need not be imitated.[1] In a few words voiceless ̥r is pronounced medially (i.e. within the word) but only when there is a voiceless consonant on either side. When r occurs initially before a consonant or finally after a consonant there must be no intrusive vowel, thus: rta рта (mouth, *gen. sing.*) not ər'ta or rə'ta, bobr бобр (beaver), not 'bobər.

22.28 The phoneme r is represented in spelling by the letter p.

22.29 *Words illustrating the phoneme* r

'rɨnək	рынок	(market)
'rɨbə	рыба	(fish)
'm̜ɛrˌt	меры	(measures)
'ranə	рано	(early)
rat	рад	(glad)
pʌ'ra	пора	(it's time)
xərʌ'ʃo	хорошо	(good)
du'rak	дурак	(fool)
'gorət	город	(town)
rof	ров	(ditch)
rot	рот	(mouth)
pʌ'roj	порой	(at times)
gˌˌ'roj	герой	(hero)
'rukˌt	руки	(hands)
'm̜ɛru	меру	(measure, *acc. sing.*)
kuku'ruzə	кукуруза	(maize)
u'dar	удар	(blow)
ʒɨr	жир	(fat)
rʌs'tvor	раствор	(solution)
stʌ'l̜ar	столяр	(joiner)
park	парк	(park)
borʃtʃ	борщ	(borshch)
'gorlə	горло	(throat)
'gorkə	горка	(hillock)
kʌr'man	карман	(pocket)

[1] Final r before a pause not infrequently becomes voiceless towards the end, however; i.e. the vocal cords stop vibrating before the taps have finished.

'kartə	карта	(map)
kur'tʃavʟ(j)	курчавый	(curly)
ʌr'xif	архив	(archives)
dʟr'zaʐ	дерзать	(to dare)
kʌr'ʐinə	корзина	(basket)
dʟr'ʒaʐ	держать	(to hold)
brat	брат	(brother)
'nravʟ	нравы	(customs)
'trudnʟ(j)	трудный	(difficult)
'pravə	право	(right)
strʌ'ka	строка	(line)
grʌ'za	гроза	(storm)
rta	рта	(mouth, *gen. sing.*)
rʒɨ	ржи	(rye, *gen. sing.*)
'rʒavʟ(j)	ржавый	(rusty)
rtuʐ	ртуть	(mercury)
rtof	ртов	(mouths, *gen. pl.*)
'rɣeŋ(ʟ)jʟ	рвение	(zeal)
bobr	бобр	(beaver)
mudr	мудр	(wise, *sh. fm. masc.*)
mʌ'ŋovr	маневр	(manoeuvre)
ŋɛgr	негр	(negro)
ˌkontrnəstu'pleŋ(ʟ)jʟ	контрнаступление	(counter-attack)
ˌkontrrʌz'ɣɛtkə	контрразведка	(counter-intelligence)
tʟ'atr̥	театр	(theatre)
dŋɛpr̥	Днепр	(Dnieper)
ʌr'b̥itr̥	арбитр	(referee)
ķʟlʌ'm̥ɛtr̥	километр	(kilometre)
ʐʟr'mom̥ʟtr̥	термометр	(thermometer)
ʌ'smotr̥	осмотр	(inspection)
nʌt-'smotr̥ʃtʃʟk	надсмотрщик	(supervisor)
ˌkontr̥'fors	контрфорс	(buttress)

5

22.30 Some allophones of Russian ŗ are formed as follows:

(1) *articulating organs:* tip of tongue slightly in front of middle of teeth-ridge and front of tongue simultaneously raised in the direction of the hard palate (Fig. 31);[1]

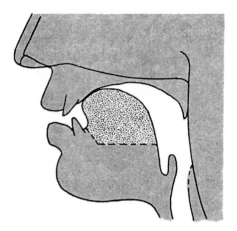

Fig. 31. Tongue-position for Russian ŗ

(2) *state of air-passage:* alternately closed and opened a number of times at point of primary articulation with such rapidity that the whole process strikes the ear as forming a single sound; in other words, the tip of the tongue makes a very rapid succession of taps against the middle of the teeth-ridge;[2]

(3) *position of soft palate:* raised, so that air cannot issue through the nose;

(4) *state of larynx:* vocal cords close together and vibrating throughout the duration of the consonant.

[1] The tip of the tongue is slightly more further forward in ŗ than in r. This seems to be caused by the raising of the front of the tongue and will occur automatically with such raising.

[2] See note 1, p. 176.

22. RUSSIAN ROLLED CONSONANTS

22.31 Such allophones of ɾ are voiced palatalized (soft) alveolar rolled consonants.

22.32 The remarks above (§ 22.4) on the number of taps which r has in various positions apply also to ɾ. The allophone of ɾ which occurs between vowels is therefore usually a voiced palatalized alveolar flapped consonant.

22.33 A slight j-glide is heard between ɾ and any member of the vowel phonemes a, o or u.[1] The glide must not on any account be exaggerated so that ɾ + vowel sounds like ɾ + j + vowel. The latter sequence does occur in Russian and is clearly distinct from ɾ + vowel. The glide is also present when ɾ occurs before a consonant or at the end of a word. In these positions it may strike the English-speaking student as being like a short vowel of the i-type. Again it must not be exaggerated. When ɾ is final the end if not all of the glide may be voiceless.

22.34 A voiceless ɾ, with two or three taps, occurs as a subsidiary allophone of ɾ and may, if necessary, be symbolized by ɾ̥. The glide following ɾ̥ is voiceless and some friction may be audible in the pronunciation of ɾ̥.

22.35 There is no English sound resembling the Russian consonant ɾ, which is not an easy sound to acquire. The best way of learning to make it, for whose who are unable to acquire it from the description in § 22.30, is to try to pronounce rolled r and the vowel i *simultaneously*. Long practice is often required even on the part of those who can make rolled r without difficulty.

22.36 The tendency of English people is to replace ɾ by the group ri, or, in certain positions, by the group ir. The learner must not be satisfied until he can hold on a uniform ɾ for several seconds;[2] the i-quality must be heard continuously throughout the duration of the sound.

---

[1] The j-glide is very slight before the e-phoneme and barely discernible before the i-phoneme.

[2] It is more difficult to prolong ɾ than to prolong r, since the raising of the front of the tongue restricts the vibrating of the tip, which is furthermore slightly more forward than in r (see note 1, p. 184).

22. RUSSIAN ROLLED CONSONANTS

22.37 Those who, in spite of long practice, cannot manage to make ɾ must content themselves with the nearest substitute—at best a very poor one—that is, the group rj when a vowel follows, and r followed by the shortest possible ɪ in other cases.

22.38 Once ɾ has been achieved it is easy to make ɾ̥ by pronouncing ɾ with breath only, i.e. without vibrations of the vocal cords. The relationship of ɾ̥ to ɾ is the same as that of f to v, or s to z.

22.39 The phoneme ɾ occurs before vowels[1] and consonants and at the end of words. In the last instance the voiceless allophone ɾ̥ occurs if there is a preceding voiceless consonant. Some speakers sometimes use ɾ̥ at the end of a word after a vowel or voiced consonant, more particularly before a pause. In the pronunciation of other speakers final ɾ in such positions may occasionally be partially voiceless, i.e. the vocal cords may stop vibrating before the taps have finished. In any case no vowel must be allowed to intrude between a consonant and final ɾ or ɾ̥.

22.40 The phoneme ɾ is represented in spelling by the letter p followed by one of the vowel letters e, и, ю or я, or the soft sign, ь.

22.41 *Words illustrating the phoneme* ɾ

ɾis	рис	(rice)
pɪ'ɾilə	перила	(banisters)
ɾɪ'ka	река	(river)
'bʲeɾɪk	берег	(bank)
pɪɾɪ'datʲ	передать	(to transmit)
ɾetʃ	речь	(speech)
'ɾezətʲ	резать	(to cut)
nə gʌ'ɾɛ	на горе	(on the mountain)
pətɪ'ɾætʲ	потерять	(to lose)
gʌ'ɾætʃɪ(j)	горячий	(hot)
ɾat	ряд	(row)
pʌ'ɾadək	порядок	(order)
ɾof	рев	(roar)

[1] Not, of course, before the non-front allophones (ɨ and ɤ) of the i-phoneme.

22. RUSSIAN ROLLED CONSONANTS

ʌˈɾol	орел	(eagle)
fʀʮˈɾot	вперед	(forward)
ˈɾumkə	рюмка	(wine-glass)
ˈɣeɾu	верю	(I believe)
gʌˈɾütʃʮ(j)	горючий	(combustible)
bʌɾˈba	борьба	(struggle)
ˈgoɾɋʮ(j)	горький	(bitter)
ˈzoɾkə	зорька	(dawn)
ˈtɾitsəʈ	тридцать	(thirty)
ˈtɾistə	триста	(three hundred)
ˈbɾitvə	бритва	(razor)
ˈbɾejus (ˈbɾejüş)	бреюсь	(I shave)
ˈbɾeᵯə	бремя	(burden)
ˈvɾeᵯə	время	(time)
ˈpɾamə	прямо	(straight)
ˈgɾaznʮ(j)	грязный	(dirty)
ʌˈtɾat	отряд	(detachment)
ˈpɾatəʈ	прятать	(to hide)
ˈgɾozə	греза	(daydream)
uˈpɾok	упрек	(rebuke)
ˈbɾüɋʮ	брюки	(trousers)
kɾuk	крюк	(hook)
ˈɾjanʮ(j)	рьяный	(zealous)
ˈɾjanəşʈ	рьяность	(zeal)
zyʮˈɾjo	зверье	(wild beasts)
ˈvzmoɾjʮ	взморье	(sea-shore)
pədmʌˈşʈəɾjʮ	подмастерье	(apprentice)
ɖyeɾ	дверь	(door)
zyeɾ	зверь	(wild beast)
ʈʮˈᵱeɾ	теперь	(now)
koɾ	корь	(measles)
ˈᵱɛkəɾ	пекарь	(baker)
ˈtokəɾ	токарь	(turner)
fʌˈnaɾ	фонарь	(torch)
şʮŋˈʈabɾ	сентябрь	(September)
ʌkˈʈabɾ	октябрь	(October)
nʌˈjabɾ	ноябрь	(November)

dɪ'kabr̥	декабрь	(December)
vnutr̥	внутрь	(inwards)
ɣixr̥	вихрь	(whirlwind)
ɣɛpr̥	вепрь	(wild boar)

23

SIMILITUDE AND ASSIMILATION

23.1 It often happens that a particular sequence of two phonemes involves the use of a certain subsidiary member of one of them which has a greater resemblance to the neighbouring sound than the principal member has. In this case there is said to be *similitude* between that subsidiary member and the neighbouring sound. Thus the ʈ-sound that occurs before tʃ is formed in a slightly different way from the ʈ used in other positions (see § 17.92) and we say that there is similitude between this ʈ-sound and the tʃ.

23.2 *Assimilation* is defined as the replacement of one phoneme by another phoneme under the influence of a third phoneme which is near to it in the word or sentence. In this case one phoneme is said to be assimilated to another. Thus, before most voiceless consonants in Russian the phoneme z is replaced by the phoneme s—it is assimilated to the voiceless consonant; before the phoneme ʃ, however, the phoneme z is replaced by the phoneme ʃ—it is assimilated not only to the voicelessness of ʃ but also to its tongue-position.

Similitudes

23.3 Similitudes in Russian affect both consonants and vowels and are of several kinds:

(1) resemblances in the matter of voice or breath;
(2) resemblances in tongue-position;
(3) resemblances of lip-position.

In the following paragraphs the similitudes which occur in

23. SIMILITUDE AND ASSIMILATION

Russian are described according to these categories, consonantal similitudes being described first, as a group, then vocalic similitudes.

Consonants

23.4 (1 *a*) The voiced allophones of those consonants whose principal allophones are voiceless are used before voiced consonant phonemes other than v, ɣ, j and the sonants.[1]

Examples

ʌ'ʧɛdz bɪ	отец бы	(father would), cf. ʌ'ʧɛts;
'dodʒ bɪ	дочь бы	(daughter would), cf. doʧʃ;
'doʒdʒ bɪ	дождь бы	(I wish it would rain), cf. doʃʧʃ;
ʌ'gloɣ bɪ	оглох бы	(would become deaf), cf. ʌ'glox.

Such similitudes, in which a feature of the second sound affects the pronunciation of the first consonant, are said to be *regressive*.

23.5 (1 *b*) When the sonants m, n, l, ļ, r, ɾ occur at the end of a word after certain voiceless consonants their voiceless allophones (m̥, n̥, l̥, ļ̥, r̥, ɾ̥) are used. This normally occurs either before a pause (as at the end of a sentence) or before a word beginning with a voiceless consonant. Since such similitudes are caused both by the following silence or the voicelessness of the following consonant *and* by the voicelessness of the preceding consonant, they are both regressive and *progressive* at the same time.

Examples

m̥ɪkrʌ'kosm̥	микрокосм	(microcosm)
ρɛsn̥	песнь	(song)
smɪsļ̥	смысл	(sense)
mɪsļ̥	мысль	(thought)
ʌ'smotɾ̥	осмотр	(inspection)
vnutɾ̥	внутрь	(inwards)

[1] The sonant phonemes of Russian are m, m̥, n, n̥, l, ļ, r and ɾ.

23. SIMILITUDE AND ASSIMILATION

Occasionally a sonant may occur between two voiceless consonants within a word; in that case regressive-progressive similitude also occurs, as in

| ˌkontr̥'fors | контрфорс | (buttress) |

When, as sometimes happens, such devoicing of a sonant *not* preceded by a voiceless consonant occurs before a pause or a voiceless consonant at the beginning of the next word, the similitude is simply regressive.

23.6 (2 *a*) The fronted (palatalized) allophones of the phonemes g and x are used before members of the vowel phonemes i and e.

Examples

nʌ'ɟ̟i	ноги	(foot, *gen. sing.*)
'noɟ̟ʟ	ноги	(foot, *nom. pl.*)
nʌ'ɟ̟ɛ	ноге	(foot, *dat. prep. sing.*)
du'χi	духи	(scent)
'duχʟ	духи	(spirits)
v dʌ'χɛ	в дохе	(in a fur coat)

23.7 (2 *b*) Before tʃ the palatalized allophone of the phoneme ʃ is used, as in

| 'proʃtʃʟ | проще | (simpler) |
| yeʃtʃ | вещь | (thing) |

23.8 (2 *c*) Velarized allophones of hard consonant phonemes are used before the non-front allophones, ɨ and ɪ, of the i-phoneme. This is most noticeable in the case of labial and labio-dental consonant phonemes.

Examples

biʈ	быть	(to be)
pɨl	пыл	(ardour)
'mɨlə	мыло	(soap)
'fɨrkəʈ	фыркать	(to snort)
vɨʈ	выть	(to howl)

The three foregoing types of similitude are regressive.

23. SIMILITUDE AND ASSIMILATION

23.9 (3) Labialized allophones of the velar consonant phonemes k, g and x are used before the vowel phonemes u and o.

Examples

kust	куст	(bush)
kot	кот	(tom-cat)
guş	гусь	(goose)
got	год	(year)
'xuʒ̵	хуже	(worse)
xot	ход	(move)

These similitudes are regressive.

23.10 (2 and 3) Labio-velarized allophones of other hard consonants are used before the vowel phonemes u and o. This is most noticeable in the case of labial and labio-dental consonants.

Examples

'bukvə	буква	(letter)
bop	боб	(beans)
puţ	путь	(path)
pot	пот	(sweat)
muʃ	муж	(husband)
mox	мох	(moss)
vus	вуз	(higher educational institution)
vot	вот	(here is)
funt	фунт	(pound)
fon	фон	(background)

These similitudes are regressive.

Vowels

23.11 (1) Voiceless allophones of the vowel phonemes occur not infrequently in weakly stressed position between two voiceless consonants. Such similitudes, being caused by both the following and preceding consonant together are both regressive and progressive.

23. SIMILITUDE AND ASSIMILATION

Examples

'vistəfkə	выставка	(exhibition)
pətʌ'mu ʃtə	потому что	(because)
'dɛvuʃ̩k	девушек	(girls, *gen. pl.*)

When such a similitude is brought about only by a following voiceless consonant, as in

'tʃer̩p	череп	(skull),

it is regressive only.

23.12 (2) Most of the allophonic variations of the vowel phonemes in Russian can be described in terms of similitudes.

23.13 (*a*) Thus a retracted allophone of the a-phoneme, namely aʳ (or ɑ⁺),[1] is used before l, as in znal (narrowly znaʳl or znɑ⁺l) знал (knew). This is a regressive similitude.

23.14 (*b*) Since the front allophones of the i-phoneme are less restricted in their occurrence than the non-front allophones (the latter occur only after hard consonants, whereas the former occur after soft consonants *and* in absolute initial positions), it is appropriate to consider i and ι as the 'basic' members of this phoneme and ɨ and ɬ as the respective counterparts of i and ι whose occurrence is an outcome of similitude to a preceding hard consonant. Thus:

	isk	иск	(law-suit)
	ιs'kaṭ	искать	(to seek)
	ʃist	лист	(leaf)
	ʃι'sa	лиса	(fox)
but	'lɨs̩ɬnə	лысина	(bald patch)
	lɬ'ṣeṭ	лысеть	(to become bald),

where the non-front allophones are occasioned by similitude to the preceding hard consonants.

---

[1] The symbol ʳ means 'retracted', the 'plus' symbol means 'advanced'. aʳ and ɑ⁺ are two ways of symbolizing a vowel which is further back than cardinal a but not as far back as cardinal ɑ.

23. SIMILITUDE AND ASSIMILATION

23.15 Explained in these terms, the allophonic variation of the i-phoneme provides examples of *progressive* similitude in Russian. Other examples of progressive similitude in Russian are provided by the allophones of the e-phoneme which occur after the hard consonants ʃ, ʒ and ts. These allophones are slightly retracted in this environment and may, when necessary, be symbolized by eₑ and ɛₑ respectively.

Examples

	ʃeₑʂt	шесть	(six),
cf.	ļeʂt	лесть	(flattery);
	ʒɛₑst	жест	(gesture),
cf.	'mɛstə	место	(place);
	'tsɛₑnt	цены	(prices),
cf.	'pɛnə	пена	(foam).

23.16 (c) All the other vocalic similitudes of Russian are brought about by adjacent soft consonants. In the neighbourhood of soft consonants, raised and/or fronted vowel allophones are used. Thus, before a soft consonant the closer allophone of the e-phoneme is used, as in

	yeʂ	весь	(all),
cf.	yɛs	вес	(weight).

Such a similitude is regressive.

23.17 The other vocalic similitudes are brought about by following and preceding soft consonants together and are thus both regressive and progressive. Thus, between two soft consonants, an allophone of i is used which is almost cardinal i (and may, when necessary, be symbolized by iₐ, to distinguish it from 'normal' Russian i), a raised allophone of a (phonetic symbol æ) is used, a raised and fronted (advanced) allophone of o (phonetic symbol ö) is used and a fronted (advanced) allophone of u (phonetic symbol ü) is used.

Examples

ŋiₐt	нить	(thread)
'dædə	дядя	(uncle)
'töʈə	тетя	(aunt)
ʈül	тюль	(tulle)

23. SIMILITUDE AND ASSIMILATION

Assimilations

Vowels

23.18 In unstressed position the phoneme e is replaced by the phoneme i (*sci.* by the ᴛ allophone after the hard consonants ʃ, ʒ and ts,[1] otherwise by the ι allophone). Thus:

	'mɛstə	место	(place),
but	mιs'ta	места	(places);
	ʃeʂ̧	шесть	(six),
but	ʃᴛʂ'ʈ̧i	шести	(six, *gen., dat., prep.*);
	v d̦ιkʌ'bɾɛ	в декабре	(in December),
but	'v marʈ̧ι	в марте	(in March).

23.19 The phonemes o and a are also replaced by the phoneme i, but only in pretonic positions and in the case of o only after soft consonants, j and the hard consonants ʃ and ʒ, and in the case of a only after soft consonants and j.[2] Thus:

	ŋos	нес	(was taking, *masc.*),
but	ŋι'sla	несла	(was taking, *fem.*);
	joʃ	еж	(hedgehog),
but	jι'ʒa	ежа	(hedgehog, *gen. sing.*);
	'ʃopət	шепот	(whisper),
but	ʃιp'taʈ̧	шептать	(to whisper);
	'ʒonι	жены	(wives),
but	ʒι'na	жена	(wife);
	'ʈ̧æŋιt	тянет	(pulls),
but	ʈ̧ι'nu	тяну	(I pull);
	tʃas	час	(hour),
but	dva tʃι'sa	два часа	(two o'clock);
	'jadrə	ядра	(nuclei),
but	jι'dro	ядро	(nucleus).

[1] And some other consonants in a relatively few loan-words and abbreviated compounds.

[2] In the style of pronunciation described in this book. In the older Moscow style this replacement also occurred *in a few words* after ʒ and ʃ. Thus (older Moscow style) ʒaɬ жаль (it's a pity), but ʒι'lɛʈ̧ жалеть (to pity); 'loʃəʈ̧ лошадь (horse), but ləʃι'd̦ej лошадей (horses, *gen. pl.*).

23. SIMILITUDE AND ASSIMILATION

23.20 In other positions the phonemes a and o are not replaced by the ɨ-phoneme. In unstressed absolute initial position and in immediate pretonic position after a hard consonant the allophone ʌ of the a-phoneme is used, for instance,[1] while in other pretonic positions after a hard consonant, as well as in post-tonic positions after a hard or a soft consonant,[2] the allophone ə is used (see § 12.113). In the same positions the phoneme o is replaced by the phoneme a (*sci.* the appropriate allophone of a according to the distribution described in the preceding sentence).

23.21 In view of the facts given in §§ 23.18, 19, it is possible to say that there occurs assimilation of the vowel phonemes e, o and a to the phoneme ɨ. The 'rule' for this assimilation, derived from the facts given above, would be:

The phoneme e is replaced by the phoneme ɨ in unstressed positions.

The phoneme o is replaced by the phoneme ɨ in pretonic positions after soft consonants, j, ʃ and ʒ.

The phoneme a is replaced by the phoneme ɨ in pretonic positions after soft consonants and j.

23.22 The rule as it stands, however, is not complete, since the replacement of a and o by ɨ occurs also in post-tonic positions *in certain grammatical forms*. The circumstances are as follows:

(1) When the perfectivizing prefix 'vɨ (вы-) is added to a verb form the replacement of a and o by ɨ after a soft consonant, etc., still occurs, as in

'vitʲɪɲɪt	вытянет	(he will pull out),
cf. 'tʲæɲɪt and tʲɪ'ɲu (§ 23.19);		
'yɨɲɪs	вынес	(took out),
'yɨɲɪsu	вынесу	(I shall take out),
cf. ɲos and ɲɪ'sla (§ 23.19).		

(2) The phoneme o is replaced by ɨ after soft consonants in post-tonic positions in the following grammatical forms:

[1] Also in other pre-tonic positions in a sequence of two vowels (see § 12.105)
[2] But see below, § 23.22.

23. SIMILITUDE AND ASSIMILATION

(*a*) nom. sing. ending of neuter nouns, adjectives and pronouns. Thus:

	ʒʏˈɾjo	зверье	(wild beasts),
but	ˈvzmoɾjʏ	взморье	(sea-shore);
	mʌˈjo	мое	(my),
	tvʌˈjo	твое	(thy),
	svʌˈjo	свое	(one's own)
but	ˈnaʃʏ	наше	(our),
	ˈvaʃʏ	ваше	(your),
and	ˈkrasnəjʏ	красное	(red),
	kruˈtojʏ	крутое	(steep), etc.[1]

(*b*) Instr. sing. ending of masculine and neuter nouns. Thus:

	kʌˈŋom	конем	(horse),
but	uˈtʃiʈʏlʏm	учителем	(teacher);
	ʒʏˈɾjom	зверьем	(wild beasts),
but	ˈvzmoɾjʏm	взморьем	(sea-shore).

(*c*) Gen., dat., and prep. sing. of masculine and neuter adjectives. Thus kruˈtovə крутого, kruˈtomu крутому, kruˈtom крутом (steep) and (unstressed after a hard consonant) ˈkrasnəvə красного, ˈkrasnəmu красному, ˈkrasnəm красном (red), but ˈşiŋʏvə синего, ˈşiŋʏmu синему, ˈşiŋʏm синем (blue).

(*d*) Instr. sing. of feminine nouns and adjectives. Thus:

	şʏˈmjöj	семьей	(family),
	ʒʏm̩ˈļöj	землей	(land);

and (after a hard consonant)

	gʌˈroj	горой	(mountain),
	kruˈtoj	крутой	(steep);

and (unstressed after a hard consonant)

	ˈkomnətəj	комнатой	(room),
	ˈkrasnəj	красной	(red);

[1] Many pronounce взморье, наше, ваше, красное, крутое, etc., as ˈvzmoɾjə, ˈnaʃə, ˈvaʃə, ˈkrasnəjə, kruˈtojə, etc. After hard consonants too ə may be heard in the pronunciation of the ending of the nom.-acc. sing. of neuter nouns—ˈsontsə солнце (sun).

but	'doʮj	долей	(portion),
	'kutʃɪj	кучей	(heap),
	'ʂiɳʲj	синей	(blue).

(*e*) Second and third person sing., first and second person pl., of first conjugation verbs. Thus:

	ɳʲ'ʂoʃ	несешь	(you carry),
	ɳʲ'ʂot	несет	(carries),
	ɳʲ'ʂom	несем	(we carry), etc.;
but	'ʦæɳʲʃ	тянешь	(you pull),
	'ʦæɳʲt	тянет	(pulls),
	'ʦæɳʲm	тянем	(we pull), etc.,
and	tʃʲ'ta(j)ʲʃ	читаешь	(you read), etc.,

and (after a hard consonant)

| | 'pʲiʃʲtʃ | пишешь | (you write), etc. |

Thus, in general, the phoneme **o** is replaced by the phoneme **i** after soft consonants and **j** in unstressed positions.

Consonants

23.23 All the consonant assimilations of Russian are regressive and are of three types:

(1) assimilations of voice to breath and vice versa;
(2) assimilations affecting the position of the tongue;
(3) combinations of (1) and (2).

23.24 (1 *a*) Any voiced consonant phoneme which forms a pair with a corresponding voiceless consonant phoneme is replaced by that corresponding voiceless consonant phoneme at the end of a word or before another voiceless consonant phoneme. The consonant phonemes paired in this way are:

Voiced	b, ḅ, v, ɣ, d, ḍ, z, ʑ, ʒ, g	
Voiceless	p, ṗ, f, f̣, t, ṭ, s, ṣ, ʃ, k	

Examples

| | gərʌ'da | города | (towns), |
| but | 'gorət | город | (town); |

	gərʌ'dok	городок	(little town),
but	gərʌt'ka	городка	(little town, *gen. sing.*) ;
	'zubt	зубы	(teeth),
but	zup	зуб	(tooth) ;
	zu'bok	зубок	(little tooth),
but	'zupkʲ	зубки	(little teeth).

Remarks on the occasions when 'devoicing' does not occur at the end of a word are to be found in the sections of this book dealing with the appropriate consonants. In brief, those occasions are when two words are closely bound; the second word is then usually[1] a particle beginning with a voiced consonant (other than a sonant), such as bt бы, or the unstressed past tense of the verb 'to be' btl был, etc.

23.25 (1 *b*) Conversely, any voiceless member of a pair is replaced by the corresponding voiced phoneme when the next phoneme is a voiced consonant other than v, ɣ, j or one of the sonants m, m̦, n, n̦, l, l̦, r and r̦. This 'voicing' always occurs within a word and may sometimes occur at the juncture of two closely bound words in the circumstances described at the end of the preceding paragraph.

Examples

	ʌtu'tʃiʈ	отучить	(to cure of, to wean),
but	ʌdgəvʌ'r̦iʈ	отговорить	(to dissuade) ;
	prʌ'şiʈ	просить	(to request),
but	'prozbə	просьба	(request).

23.26 (2 *a*) The hard consonants p, b, m, f, v, t, d, n, s, z, l, r and k do not occur before the vowel phoneme e.[2]

[1] Though not always.
[2] Except in some loan-words, such as:

konso'mɛ	консоме	(consommée)
stɛnt	стенд	(stand)
tɛmbr	тембр	(timbre)
mʌ'del̦	модель	(model)
'del̦tə	дельта	(delta)

23. SIMILITUDE AND ASSIMILATION

Where the processes of word-formation or accidence would lead to the occurrence of any of these consonants before e, the consonant is replaced by its soft counterpart.

Examples

	gu'ba	губа	(lip),
but	nə gu'b̦ɛ	на губе	(on the lip);
	kot	кот	(tom-cat),
but	ʌ kʌ'ţɛ	о коте	(about the tom-cat);
	gʌ'ra	гора	(mountain),
but	nə gʌ'ɾɛ	на горе	(up the mountain);
	ru'ka	рука	(hand),
but	v ru'k̦ɛ	в руке	(in the hand).

23.27 Where the phoneme e is replaced, because of the location of the stress, by the ɪ-allophone of the i-phoneme (see § 23.18) the same consonantal assimilation takes place, as in

	l̦ɛs	лес	(wood),
but	ʌ 'l̦eşɪ	о лесе	(about the wood);
	'komnətə	комната	(room),
but	'f komnəţɪ	в комнате	(in the room).

23.28 Furthermore, the phoneme k does not occur (except in the circumstances described below) before the i-phoneme. Here the phoneme k̦ occurs and then the allophones of i which follow it are necessarily the front ones i and ɪ. At word junction, however, the sequences ki and kɪ occur. Thus, on the one hand

	k̦it	кит	(whale),
	ru'k̦i	руки	(hand, *gen. sing.*);

	kʌ'ʃnə	кашне	(muffler)
	ʃo'sɛ	шоссе	(highway)
	zɛ'ro	зеро	(zero), etc.

In general, the more 'everyday' such loan-words become, the more likely is the pronunciation with a soft consonant, though some words are remarkably resistant to this 'Russification'.

In abbreviated compounds also hard consonants occur before the phoneme e, as in nɛp нэп (New Economic Policy), ɛ'sɛr эсер (Socialist Revolutionary). Those names of consonant letters which consist of the consonant sound plus the vowel ɛ are usually pronounced with a hard consonant—pɛ пе ('p'), bɛ бе ('b'), etc.

199

and on the other hand

'k i̯gə̯ru	к Игорю	(to Igor),
k t̯'vanu	к Ивану	(to Ivan).

23.29 (2 *b*) Some hard consonants are replaced by the corresponding soft consonants before certain soft consonants. There is some individual variation in this matter and also some difference between the older and younger generations. Broadly speaking, speakers of the younger generation carry out this replacement of hard by soft consonants in fewer positions than do speakers of the older generation. The following remarks reflect the most commonly occurring replacements among all speakers.

23.30 Before ɣ and m̥, the phoneme v is replaced by ɣ—

	vvʌ'd̥it̥	вводить	(to lead in, *impfv.*),
but	ɣɣɩʂ'ţi	ввести	(to lead in, *pfv.*);
	'vmazət̥	вмазать	(to putty in),
but	ɣm̥ɩ'tat̥	вметать	(to tack in).

23.31 Before t̥, ş, tʃ, ḷ, ɲ and the allophone ʃ of the ʃ-phoneme, the phoneme t is replaced by the phoneme t̥[1]—

	ʌt'kudə	откуда	(whence),
but	ʌ't̥şudə	отсюда	(from here);
	ʌtnʌ'şit̥	относить	(to take away, *impfv.*),
but	ʌt̥ɲɩʂ'ţi	отнести	(to take away, *pfv.*);

and the phoneme n by the phoneme ɲ—

	son	сон	(sleep),
but	sʌɲ'ḷivt(j)	сонливый	(sleepy);
	ʌ'bman	обман	(deception),
but	ʌ'bmanʃtʃɩk	обманщик	(deceiver);
	ɩ'ʒm̥ɛnə	измена	(treachery),
but	ɩ'ʒm̥entʃɩvt(j)	изменчивый	(inconstant).

[1] At the junction of prefix and root t is not replaced by t̥ before ş in the more modern style of pronunciation.

23. SIMILITUDE AND ASSIMILATION

23.32 Before d̦, z̦, ļ and ņ, the phoneme d is replaced by the phoneme d̦[1]—

	pʌd-zɪ'vaȶ	подзывать	(to call up),
but	pʌ'dʒɛmkə	подземка	(dug-out);[1]
	gədʌ'voj	годовой	(annual),
but	prəʃlʌ'godņɪ(j)	прошлогодний	(last year's).

23.33 Before ș, ȶ, ļ and ņ, the phoneme s is replaced by the phoneme ș—

	'massə	масса	(mass),
but	'v mașșɪ	в массе	(in a mass);
	slʌ'ʒiȶ	сложить	(to put together),
but	șļɪ'ȶɛtsə	слететься	(to fly together).

23.34 Before z̦, d̦, ļ and ņ, the phoneme z is replaced by the phoneme z̦—

	gņɪz'do	гнездо	(nest),
but	v gņɪz̦'dɛ	в гнезде	(in the nest);
	rəznʌ'șiȶ	разносить	(to distribute, *impfv.*),
but	rəz̦ņɪș'ȶi	разнести	(to distribute, *pfv.*).

23.35 (2 *c*) There is also some variation in the pronunciation of consonants at the end of a prefix before a root beginning with the consonant j, but as a general rule s is replaced here by ș, v by y and z by z̦.

Examples

	sɪ'graȶ	сыграть	(to play),
but	sjesȶ	съесть	(to eat up);
	vnʌ'șiȶ	вносить	(to carry in),
but	'yjɛxəȶ	въехать	(to drive in);
	ɪz'daȶ	издать	(to publish),
but	ɪ'z̦jæȶ	изъять	(to take out).

23.36 (2 *d*) The converse of the replacement of hard consonants by soft consonants, i.e. the replacement of soft consonants by hard consonants, is rarer, in the sense that the circumstances in which it occurs are very limited. Before

---

[1] At the junction of prefix and root d is not replaced by d̦ before z̦ in the more modern style of pronunciation.

23. SIMILITUDE AND ASSIMILATION

the suffix written -ец only the soft members of the paired hard and soft consonants occur. In most words with the suffix -ец the e is 'mobile', i.e. it lapses in cases other than the nominative (and nominative-accusative) and then any paired soft consonant (other than ļ) is replaced by its hard counterpart.[1] Thus:

	kʌˈŋɛts	конец	(end),
but	kʌnˈtsa	конца	(end, *gen. sing.*);
	ˈpɛrɪts	перец	(pepper),
but	ˈpɛrtsə	перца	(pepper, *gen. sing.*);
	ļɪtʌˈpiʂɪts	летописец	(chronicler),
but	ļɪtʌˈpistsə	летописца	(chronicler, *gen. sing.*).

23.37 The consonant ļ, however, does not undergo this assimilation—

kəmsʌˈmoļɪts	комсомолец	(comsomol member),
kəmsʌˈmoļtsə	комсомольца	(comsomol member, *gen. sing.*).

23.38 Similarly, when the vowel letter e lapses in the root of a word, soft labial and labio-dental consonants are replaced by their hard counterparts, as in

	pɛŋ	пень	(stump),
but	pŋa	пня	(stump, *gen. sing.*);

and, with simultaneous assimilation to breath:

[1] Note that the inserted vowel in the gen. pl. of fem. nouns ending in -ца and neuter nouns ending in -це or -цо is e, representing ɛ or ɪ, to which preceding paired hard consonants are assimilated:

ʌfˈtsa	овца	(sheep)
ʌˈyɛts	овец	(sheep, *gen. pl.*)
pəlʌˈtɛntsɪ	полотенце	(towel)
pəlʌˈtɛŋɪts	полотенец	(towels, *gen. pl.*)
slʌfˈtso	словцо	(word)
slʌˈyɛts	словец	(words, *gen. pl.*)

Similarly, where the inserted vowel in the short form masc. of adjectives is written e, a hard consonant at the end of a root is replaced by its soft counterpart:

ˈtomnɪ(j)	темный	(dark)
ˈtomɪn	темен	(dark, *sh. fm. masc.*)
ˈxitrɪ(j)	хитрый	(cunning)
xɪˈtɒr	хитер	(cunning, *sh. fm. masc.*)

202

| | yeʂ | весь | (all, *masc.*), |
| but | fʂa | вся | (all, *fem.*). |

23.39 (2 *e*) Before ʃ, the phoneme s is replaced by ʃ—

	u'ŋos	унес	(took away),
but	u'noʃʃt(j)	унесший	(having taken away);
	sɪ'graʈ	сыграть	(to play),
but	ʃʃɪʈ	сшить	(to sew);

and before tʃ by the soft allophone ʃ of the phoneme ʃ—

| | 'ʃtʃiʂʈɪʂ | счистить | (to clean). |

Before ʒ, the phoneme z is replaced by the phoneme ʒ—

	rəzvʌ'ḍiʈ	разводить	(to dilute),
but	rəʒʒt'ʒaʈ	разжижать	(to dilute);
	ḫɪ'zoblətʃnt(j)	безоблачный	(cloudless),
but	bɪʒ'ʒaləsnt(j)	безжалостный	(merciless).

23.40 (3) In certain positions, the phonemes t, d, s and z undergo assimilation both with respect to (i) voice and breath, and (ii) tongue-position. Thus:

23.41 (*a*) Before ḍ the phoneme t is replaced by ḍ—

| | ʌtku'ʂiʈ | откусить | (to bite off), |
| but | ʌḍ'dɛlət | отделать | (to finish off).[1] |

23.42 (*b*) Before ʈ the phoneme d is replaced by ʈ[2]—

| | pədmɪ'taʈ | подметать | (to sweep), |
| but | pəʈʈɪ'raʈ | подтирать | (to wipe). |

23.43 (*c*) Before ʐ the phoneme s is replaced by ʐ—

| | sɪ'graʈ | сыграть | (to play), |
| but | 'ʐdɛlət | сделать | (to do). |

23.44 (*d*) Before ʂ and ʈ the phoneme z is replaced by ʂ—

| | ḫɪzvʌ'lost(j) | безволосый | (hairless), |
| but | ḫɪʂ'ʂiḷnt(j) | бессильный | (powerless); |

[1] Also before ʐ in the older style of pronunciation.
[2] Also before ʂ in the older style of pronunciation.

23. SIMILITUDE AND ASSIMILATION

	rəzɡ̩ɪ'baʈ	разгибать	(to unbend),
but	rəsʈɪ'nuʈ	растянуть	(to stretch out).

23.45 (*e*) Before ʒ the phoneme s is replaced by ʒ—

	slʌ'ʒɨʈ	сложить	(to put together),
but	ʒʒaʈ	сжать	(to compress).

23.46 (*f*) Before ʃ the phoneme z is replaced by ʃ—

	bɪzvʌ'losʈ(j)	безволосый	(hairless),
but	bɪʃ'ʃumnʈ(j)	бесшумный	(noiseless),

while before tʃ it is replaced by the soft allophone ʃ of the ʃ-phoneme—

bɪʃtʃɪlʌ'yetʃnʈ(j) бесчеловечный (inhuman).

23.47 It is appropriate to mention here those cases where a consonant letter in the orthography has no phonetic value at all, where, so to speak, a consonant has been 'totally assimilated'. Thus the letters с and з are not pronounced before the sequence ʃtʃ, as in

	rəʃ'tʃeɪɪnə	расщелина	(crevice),
ɪ‿ʃ'tʃæʂtjə	из счастья	(out of happiness).

The second letter in all the following letter-sequences has no phonetic value:[1] стн, стч, здн, здч, стск, лвств, рдц, рдч, and лнц.

Examples

	'mɛsnʈ(j)	местный	(local),
cf.	mɛstə	место	(place);
	'ʒoʃtʃɪ	жестче	(harder),
cf.	'ʒostkɪ(j)	жесткий	(hard);
	'zyoznʈ(j)	звездный	(starry),
cf.	zyɪz'da	звезда	(star);
	bʌ'roʃtʃətt(j)	бороздчатый	(furrowed),
cf.	bərʌz'da	борозда	(furrow);

---

[1] In normal conversational pronunciation. In extremely meticulous or in 'hyper-correct' pronunciation the second letter in some of these sequences may be pronounced.

23. SIMILITUDE AND ASSIMILATION

	mʌrk'şisskι(j)	марксистский	(Marxist),
cf.	mʌrk'şist	марксист	(Marxist);
	ḫι'zmolstvəvəȿ	безмолвствовать	(to be silent),
cf.	mʌl'va	молва	(report, talk);
	'şertsι	сердце	(heart),
cf.	şιr'dets	сердец	(hearts, *gen. pl.*);
	şιr'tʃiʃkə	сердчишко	(heart, *diminutive*),
cf.	şιr'detʃnι(j)	сердечный	(cordial; cardiac);
	'sontsι	солнце	(sun),
cf.	'solnιtʃnι(j)	солнечный	(sunny; solar).

23.48 The т in стл is not pronounced in some words—

ʃtʃι'şļivι(j)	счастливый	(happy),
zʌ'yişļιvι(j)	завистливый	(envious),
'soyιşļιvι(j)	совестливый	(conscientious);

but is in others—

xvʌş'ţļivι(j)	хвастливый	(boastful),
kʌş'ţļavι(j)	костлявый	(bony).

23.49 Similarly the first в in вств is not pronounced in

'tʃustvə	чувство	(feeling)

and its derivatives, and

'zdrastvuj(ţι)[1]	здравствуй(те)	(how do you do);

but is in other words—

'defstyιnt(j)	девственный	(virgin),
kərʌ'ļεfstvə	королевство	(kingdom).

24

ACCENT, STRESS AND LENGTH

24.1 The examples given in previous chapters of this book to illustrate the sounds of Russian consist for the most part of single words, occasionally of two or three words. In these

---

[1] This is a fairly careful pronunciation. The plural or polite form 'zdrastvujţι is often 'reduced' to 'zdraşţι.

examples stress is marked by the symbol ' before the stressed syllable. Spoken language, however, consists of sentences and sentences may consist of one word (*Yes. No. Tomorrow. Who?*) but more often consist of more than one word. In a spoken Russian sentence, the length of sounds, the stress and the variations in the pitch of the voice (see chapter 25) are closely bound up together.

24.2 The length of many sounds depends on the surrounding sounds in the same syllable but it also depends on the position of that sound in relation to the accent (see below). The accent in Russian is usually said to be a stress-accent (i.e. is achieved by an increase in the force with which the breath-stream is emitted). In a sentence, however, a so-called accented syllable may not be pronounced with greater breath-force than surrounding unaccented syllables, yet it may be longer than the surrounding unaccented syllables. The accent is then marked by length. Furthermore, the structure of a sentence requires that a certain pitch or variation in the pitch of the voice, either within the syllable or in relation to surrounding syllables, shall fall on an accented syllable; the accented syllable is then stressed and is longer than surrounding unaccented syllables, while the presence of the stress on a particular syllable here may result in the absence of stress on accented syllables in other words in the sentence, though the length of those syllables may be greater than that of surrounding unaccented syllables (see below).

24.3 In spite of the complex interrelationship of these phenomena it is convenient to treat them separately, referring when necessary to the other phenomena, and this is the course followed below. There are moreover certain factors affecting vowel length which are independent of accent.

Accent and stress

24.4 When a word of more than one syllable is pronounced in isolation as an illustration (as in the preceding chapters of this book) the accent is realized as *stress*, i.e. the accented

24. ACCENT, STRESS AND LENGTH

syllable is spoken with greater force than the unaccented syllables in the same word.[1] It is for this reason that the accent of Russian is said to be a *stress*-accent.

24.5 It is possible to distinguish several degrees of stress. Thus the stress is different on each syllable of the word pəlʌ'ʒiʦɪｌnə положительно (positively). Using numbers to indicate the different degrees of stress (1 being the strongest), the stress of this word could be shown by the notation

$$3 \quad {}^2 1 5 \quad 4$$
$$\text{pəl ʌʒ iʦ ɪ|nə}$$

Such accuracy, however, is not required for most purposes. It is generally sufficient to distinguish two degrees of stress, strong and weak, and to speak of strongly stressed and weakly stressed syllables or simply stressed and unstressed syllables.

24.6 It is to be noted, however, that syllables immediately in front of the stress (pretonic syllables) in Russian are slightly more strongly stressed than other unstressed syllables. Such syllables may be said to have *secondary stress*.[2]

24.7 If a monosyllabic word constitutes a sentence in itself then it must be accented and its accent is actualized in the pitch.[3] Thus da Да (Yes) as a plain statement is spoken with a falling pitch, but as a question it is spoken with a high-rising pitch.

24.8 There is one feature that is always constant in a Russian accented syllable, whether or not there is stress or length present, and that is that it must contain one of the vowel allophones i, iᴸ, i, e, ɛ, ɛᴸ, æ, a, aᐟ,[4] o, ö, u or ü. The vowel allophones ɪ, ᵗ, ʌ, ə, ɷ and ö̈[5] do not occur in accented syllables.

---

[1] It is also common to pronounce illustrative words with a falling tone on the accented syllables. This is not essential for the realization of the accent.

[2] Strictly, they have secondary accent, which may be realized as secondary stress. If not, it may be realized as greater length (see § 24.46).

[3] It may also be that we intuitively perceive that the stress is (approximately) as great as that of stressed syllables in sentences of more than one syllable spoken by the same speaker.

[4] Transcribed throughout this book as a (see note 2, p. 49).

[5] ɷ and ö̈ are transcribed throughout this book as u and ü respectively (see note, p. 69 and § 12.199).

24. ACCENT, STRESS AND LENGTH

24.9 In some sentences the accent of all normally accentable words[1] is realized as stress. This general principle is exemplified in the following sentences:

u'tʃiʈɩl 'utʃɩt, utʃɩ'n̩ik 'utʃɩtsə
Учитель учит, ученик учится
(The teacher teaches, the pupil learns);

'rusʞɩ(j) u'tʃiʈɩl 'utʃɩt, ʌn'glijsʞɩ(j) utʃɩ'n̩ik 'utʃɩtsə
Русский учитель учит, английский ученик учится
(The Russian teacher teaches, the English pupil learns);

kəkʌ'va strʌ'na, təkʌ'va ʌ'bɨtʃəj
Какова страна, такова обычай
(As the country, so the custom).

24.10 It is mistaken, however, as it is in English, to give equal stress to all the stressed syllables in any one of these sentences. In one pronunciation of the first sentence, for example, the stressed syllable of u'tʃiʈɩl is slightly more strongly stressed than that of 'utʃɩt, and that of utʃɩ'n̩ik is slightly more strongly stressed than that of 'utʃɩtsə. Moreover, the stressed syllable of utʃɩ'n̩ik is slightly more stressed than that of u'tʃiʈɩl. This is because of the overtly contrastive meaning of this sentence.

24.11 When there is no overt contrast and no word is emphasized, then the last stressed syllable in the sentence usually bears the heaviest stress, as in

'maɭtʃɩk gu'ɭal pə ʃɩ'rokəmu 'poɭu ʌ'd̦in
Мальчик гулял по широкому полю один
(The boy was strolling through the open fields alone).

24.12 In this sentence the stressed syllable of ʌ'd̦in bears the heaviest stress. Moreover, the stressed syllable of 'poɭu may be slightly more heavily stressed than that of ʃɩ'rokəmu, since the

---

[1] I.e. all words except 'auxiliaries'—particles, conjunctions and most prepositions. It must be remembered, however, that *any* word can be pronounced with a stressed syllable for emphatic, contrastive, etc., purposes, just as a normally unaccented syllable can be stressed for such purposes (e.g. 'I said "*pre*tend" not "*in*tend"').

stressed syllable of a noun is usually more heavily stressed than that of its accompanying adjective, unless the adjective is emphasized.

24.13 The stressed syllable of a qualifying noun in the genitive, however, is usually more heavily stressed than that of the noun which it qualifies, if neither noun is emphasized, as in

> stʌ'kan vʌ'dɨ stʌ'jal nə̮stʌ'ʲɛ
> Стакан воды стоял на столе
> (The glass of water was standing on the table).

24.14 A steady increase of stress from stressed syllable to stressed syllable may be used when the same item is repeated, as in

> pʌ'ʲa, pʌ'ʲa, pʌ'ʲa
> Поля, поля, поля
> (Fields, fields and fields).

This may be a special instance of enumeration, where there also tends to be a steady increase of stress, as in

> nə̮pʌ'lu — mɪʃ'ḳi, 'jæʃtʃɪḳɪ, sundu'ḳi
> На полу — мешки, ящики, сундуки
> (On the floor—bags, boxes, trunks).

24.15 When it is desired to emphasize one word specially, the degree of stress on it may be increased and this increase is generally accompanied by a decrease in the stress of neighbouring words, to the extent of the accent of such words not being realized as stress at all. Thus the sentence ('I saw him yesterday') said without special emphasis would be pronounced ja 'ɣidɪl jɪvo ftʃɪ'ra (Я видел его вчера). But if ja were emphasized, 'ɣidɪl might lose its stress, thus 'ja ɣidɪl jɪvo ftʃɪ'ra. And if jɪ'vo were emphasized, both 'ɣidɪl and ftʃɪ'ra might lose their stress, thus ja ɣidɪl jɪ'vo ftʃɪra.

Further examples are:

rʌ'botəʈ xʌtʃu	Работать хочу	(I want to *work*)
'goşʈɪ prɪjɛxəlɪ	Гости приехали	(*Guests* have arrived)
'tʃort zna(j)ɪt	Черт знает!	(*Devil* knows!)
utʃɪŋik 'utʃɪt?	Ученик учит?	(A pupil *teaches*?)

24. ACCENT, STRESS AND LENGTH

24.16 When it is desired to give less than its natural prominence to a word, that word loses its stress. This often happens, for instance, when the word in question has just been used in the preceding sentence.

24.17 The following are examples:

'kto‿vəm skʌ'zal ʌb‿ɛtəm? — 'brat skʌzal

Кто вам сказал об этом? — Брат сказал

(Who told you about this?—My brother did).

'pɛrvɪ(j) 'dɛŋ bɪl 'doʃtʃ, i ftʌ'roj dɛŋ bɪl 'doʃtʃ

Первый день был дождь, и второй день был дождь

(It was raining the first day, and also the second).

24.18 In such sentences as the following, where the verb is almost devoid of meaning,[1] it is unstressed:

	'doʃtʃ ɪdot	Дождь идет	(It's raining),
	'ʂŋɛk pʌʃol	Снег пошел	(It's started to snow),
cf.	'doʃtʃ prɪkrʌ'tʂilsə	Дождь прекра-	(It's stopped raining).
		тился	

24.19 The shorter numerals followed by a noun are often not stressed, e.g.

	tri mɪ'dʲedə	три медведя	(three bears),
	f‿tʃɪtiɾɪ tʃɪ'sa	в четыре часа	(at four o'clock).

24.20 The short, common prepositions in Russian usually form an accentual unit with the following word. It is for this reason that such prepositions are linked by means of a ligature with the following word in the phonetic notations in this book. In some instances the stress is on the preposition and then the following word, being still part of the same accentual unit, not only has no stress but also no accent. This occurs only with some of the monosyllabic prepositions followed by some nouns and numerals which are monosyllabic or accented on the first syllable— 'na‿pəl на пол (on to the floor), 'na‿gəru на гору (up the mountain), 'za‿gərədəm за городом (out of town), rəzdɪ'lɪʦ 'na‿dvə

---

[1] The statement concerns the *rain*, which, in the Russian idiom, has to be said to be coming.

24. ACCENT, STRESS AND LENGTH

разделить на два (to divide by two). With numerals it is commonest in expressing multiplication, division and comparison.

24.21 Some compound words have two accents, which may be distinguished as the major and the subsidiary accent, and each part of the word forms an accentual unit in which the normal rules for the distribution of stress, length and vowel quality operate. If both accents are realized as stress, then the vowel in the position of the major accent receives the greater stress (the major stress), the vowel in the position of the subsidiary accent receives somewhat less stress (the subsidiary stress). When necessary the subsidiary stress may be marked by the symbol ˌ to distinguish it from the major stress, as in

səmʌˌɪotəstrʌˈjeŋ(ɪ)jɪ	самолетостроение	(aircraft-construction)
kʌrˌtoʃɪʃɪkʌˈpalkə	картофелекопалка	(potato-harvester)
ˌbortprəvʌˈdŋik	бортпроводник	(steward)
ˌsportkruˈʒok	спорткружок	(sports club)

In a sentence, however, the subsidiary accent is frequently not realized as stress, thus səmʌɪotəstrʌˈjeŋ(ɪ)jɪ, kʌrtoʃɪʃɪkʌˈpalkə, etc.

24.22 There are some words with more than two accents. In such words the last accent is the major one:

ɪˌɪɛktrəˌparəpədəgrɪˈvaʃɪɭ	электропароподогреватель	(electrical steam pre-heater)
ʌˌɛrəˌfotəˈsŋimək	аэрофотоснимок	(aerial photograph)[1]

24.23 The word-accent in Russian is 'free', as in English, not 'fixed', as in Polish and other languages. This is to say that the accent in Russian does not fall on the same syllable in every word (say, the first, as in Hungarian, the penultimate, as in

---

[1] It must be noted, however, that in such words the second accent is rarely actualized as stress.

14-2

24. ACCENT, STRESS AND LENGTH

Polish or, for the most part, Italian). The Russian word-accent is also 'mobile', i.e. it may move from syllable to syllable, as in the declension of gʌ'ra ropa (mountain)

acc. sing.	'goru	гору
gen. sing.	gʌ'rɨ	горы
nom. pl.	'gorɪ	горы, etc.,

or the present tense of pɪ'saṭ писать (to write)

1st pers. sing.	pɪ'ʃu	пишу
2nd pers. sing.	'piʃtʃ	пишешь
3rd pers. sing.	'piʃtt	пишет, etc.

24.24 The student must therefore learn not only the accent of every word as an integral part of the word, but also the patterns of accent-shifts and which words belong to each pattern.[1]

Length

24.25 Most speech-sounds can be held on for a longer or a shorter period. Thus a, z or the stop of p can be held on for a fraction of a second or for several seconds. When we speak of lengthening a plosive consonant, we mean prolonging the stop of that consonant.

24.26 In connected speech, sounds which are held on noticeably longer than most of the neighbouring sounds are called *long* sounds. The others are generally termed *short* sounds. It is sometimes convenient to distinguish an intermediate degree of length known as *half-long*.

24.27 Length is represented in the symbols of the International Phonetic Association by the mark : placed after the symbol of the sound which is long. Half-length is represented, when necessary, by ·.

24.28 It is possible to distinguish many more than three degrees of length, but no practical linguistic purpose is served by doing so.

---

[1] The student will find James Forsyth's *A Practical Guide to Russian Stress* very helpful in this matter.

24. ACCENT, STRESS AND LENGTH

Doubled sounds

24.29 By saying that a sound is *doubled* we mean that it is repeated without any pause in its continuity. The effect of repetition is obtained not by stopping the sound altogether, but by diminishing the force of the breath in the middle of it.

24.30 Thus a doubled a (written phonetically aa) is distinct from a long aː; also from two a's separated by a pause (a a), and from two a's separated by a glottal stop (aʔa), etc., etc.

24.31 The difference between long sounds and doubled sounds is only important in the case of vowels. Doubled vowels constitute two syllables, and may therefore be treated differently from long vowels in the matters of stress and intonation.

24.32 With most consonants the difference between lengthening and doubling is imperceptible to the ear in connected speech; in the case of voiceless plosive consonants the distinction is non-existent.

Consonant-length in Russian

24.33 Consonant-length plays a more important part than vowel-length in Russian. In some cases consonant-length serves to distinguish one word from another, but vowel-length never does so.

24.34 The lengthening of consonants in Russian is considered in this book to be a doubling rather than a mere prolongation (see §§ 24.32); accordingly the lengthened consonants are represented here in phonetic transcription by repeating the phonetic symbol, as in

ʃʃitɕ	сшить	(to sew, *pfv.*)
'dannɛ(j)ɪ	данные	(data)
sstʲ'latɕ	ссылать	(to exile)

24.35 The repetition of the symbol of a plosive consonant, as in

zʌ'buttɕɪ	забудьте	(forget!)
'ottɕɪpɪlʲ	оттепель	(thaw)

24. ACCENT, STRESS AND LENGTH

ʌd'deɪntˑ(j)	отдельный	(separate)
'oddɪx	отдых	(rest)

is to be understood to indicate a doubling or prolongation of the stop of that consonant.

24.36 The lengthening of the stop of an affricate is represented in this book by prefixing the symbol of the stop element of the affricate. Thus the lengthening of the stop of ts is represented by the notation tts, as in ʌt'tsɪ отцы (fathers).

24.37 The following are examples of words distinguished by consonant-length

pʌ'dɛrʒənt(j)	подержанный	(second-hand)
pʌd'dɛrzənt(j)	поддержанный	(supported)
ʃitɕ	шить	(to sew, *impfv.*)
ʃʃitɕ	сшить	(to sew, *pfv.*)

24.38 English people should as a rule have no particular difficulty in carrying out the distinctions between single and doubled consonants in Russian, since doubled consonants occur from time to time in English.

Compare

penny	and	pen-knife
bishop		fish-shop
poppy		hop-picker
looking		book-case
holy		solely

24.39 In practice, however, English people often fail to pronounce Russian doubled consonants with sufficient length. To pronounce the double consonants properly is in most cases not a matter requiring special practice; it is a matter of *remembering to do it*. If the phonetic transcription of the words is not a sufficient aid to the memory, the student should underline in his phonetic texts the letters representing the doubled consonants.

24.40 Two cases require special practice, viz. doubled r and doubled ɼ, since no doubled rolled r-sound occurs in Southern

24. ACCENT, STRESS AND LENGTH

English. In practising such phrases as stʌˈʃar ˈrad bʉl cтоляр рад был (the carpenter was glad), ʧɪˈp̡er ˈretkə тепеpь peдко (now rarely), it is best in the first instance to overdo the length of the r's and ɾ's.

Vowel-length

24.41 In the pronunciation of some varieties of English (notably RP[1]), some of the vowels are usually pronounced longer than the others, all other things being equal. Thus the vowels in *heed, hard, horde, food, herd,* are usually longer than those in *hid, head, had, hod, bud, hood.*[2] The vowels in the first set of words are customarily called the 'long' vowels of English, the others being called the 'short' vowels of English.

24.42 In Russian there is no such system of contrasting long and short vowels in accented syllables: all vowels in accented syllables are of roughly the same length, all other things being equal.

24.43 The length of any vowel in Russian however is affected by its position in relation to the accent (this is dealt with below, §§24.46–8) and by other factors, such as its occurrence in an open or a closed syllable,[3] the type of consonant(s) closing the syllable in which it occurs. These latter factors seem to operate in much the same way as similar factors in English, and therefore we shall say no more about them.

24.44 Certain other features of vowel-length in Russian may be noted. An unaccented vowel in a final open syllable may be lengthened, and is sometimes considerably longer than an unaccented vowel elsewhere. This may result in a length distribution between accented and unaccented vowel in a particular word which is strikingly different from the average length distribution described below. Stressed vowels, given special emphasis for certain purposes, are often lengthened, as

---

[1] 'Received Pronunciation'.

[2] Note, however, that some speakers of RP pronounce such words as *hid* and *had* with long vowels.

[3] An open syllable is one which ends in a vowel, a closed syllable one which ends in a consonant.

24. ACCENT, STRESS AND LENGTH

in 'tʃuːdnə чу-удно (ma-arvellous), yet for other purposes they may be shortened, as in i ʃʂo и все (and that's all), spoken abruptly, so as to convey the meaning of a brusque dismissal.[1]

Accent and vowel-length

24.45 In the preceding paragraphs we dealt with variations in vowel-length which are independent of accent and most of which will probably arise automatically in the pronunciation of the English-speaking student learning Russian.

24.46 The length of vowels in Russian, however, also varies according to whether the vowel is in an accented syllable, a syllable immediately before the accent (pretonic syllable) or an unaccented syllable. Thus, all other things being equal, and due allowance being made for variations from speaker to speaker, a vowel in a pretonic syllable is longer than a vowel in an unaccented syllable by a quarter to almost half (1·25 to 1·4 approx.), while a vowel in an accented syllable is from three-quarters to almost twice the length of an unaccented vowel (1·75 to 1·9 approx.).[2]

24.47 This is not to say that the student should pronounce Russian accented vowels as long as the long vowels of English. In relation to the latter, the Russian accented vowels in open syllables may be thought of as half-long. There is, however, no need for most purposes to mark the length of Russian accented vowels since their greater duration relative to unaccented vowels is due to the fact that they are accented. For practical learning purposes the student should not consciously aim at the greater length of accented vowels in Russian: their greater length will probably arise automatically if he aims at pronouncing the unaccented vowels, with the exception of those in pretonic position, very short.

---

[1] The relationship between vowel-length and emphasis of one kind or another still needs investigating in detail.

[2] It should be strictly borne in mind that the figures given represent *relative averaged* lengths and have been arrived at by establishing relative lengths of vowels in *one* word, then in another word, and so on, before calculating for all the words considered the average length of, say, pretonic syllables in relation to that of accented syllables.

24.48 Particular note should be made of the fact that vowels in pretonic syllables are somewhat longer (see §24.46) than vowels in unaccented syllables. This is because the pretonic syllable in Russian is the position of the secondary accent (see above, §24.6), and when the accent is realized as stress the pretonic syllable bears the next heaviest stress after the stressed vowel.[1]

24.49 In compound words with two accents, a major accent and a subsidiary, the major accent is the second in the word (see above, §24.21). The factors affecting length described in the preceding paragraphs operate on both the accents and, due allowance being made for these factors, the vowel occurring in the position of the major accent is slightly longer than that occurring in the position of the subsidiary accent (and, if both receive stress, receives slightly more stress than the latter).

25

INTONATION

25.1 When we speak normally, the voice does not remain at the same pitch all the time: there is variation in the pitch of the note produced by the vocal cords. Voiceless sounds are produced without vibration of the vocal cords and therefore there can be no variation of pitch in their pronunciation. The number of such sounds occurring in connected speech is small in comparison with the number of voiced sounds and therefore, for most practical purposes, we can say that an uninterrupted stretch of speech has a practically continuous contour of pitch-variations. This contour may be called the 'melodic contour'.

25.2 In the preceding chapter we dealt with stress and vowel-length. Those variations in stress and its location peculiar to a particular language produce the characteristic rhythm of that language.

[1] In English, pretonic syllables are particularly short and weakly stressed.

25. INTONATION

25.3 Melodic contour and rhythm together constitute the *intonation*[1] of a language. Each language has its own characteristic intonation, which must therefore be learnt if one wishes to speak the language as efficiently as possible.

25.4 There are several ways of showing intonation by means of notation. In this chapter we adopt the method of giving the phonetic transcriptions of sentences with parallel diagrams of melodic contours. The location of stressed syllables in the sentence is shown in the phonetic transcriptions, giving a rough indication of the rhythm of the sentence. The melodic contour diagram consists of lines and dots on a 'stave'.

25.5 Although we have said (§25.1) that the melodic contour may be regarded as practically continuous, we find it convenient, for purposes of notation and for purposes of teaching and learning the pronunciation of a language, to think of and represent each syllable as having its own pitch.[2] A dot on the stave represents the pitch of an unstressed syllable, a line the pitch or shift in pitch of a stressed syllable. These dots and lines are placed on the stave immediately above the syllable they refer to in the phonetic transcription.

25.6 The stave itself consists of three parallel lines, of which the upper one indicates the top of the compass of the voice used in normal speech by any one person, the lower one indicates the bottom of the compass and the middle one indicates the middle of the compass. The vertical position of a dot or line on this stave indicates the approximate pitch of the syllable to which it refers, thus:

[1] The term 'intonation' is also widely used in the meaning to which we have given the name 'melodic contour'.
[2] Experimental evidence shows in fact that many of the significant variations in pitch occur largely over a stretch of one syllable.

25. INTONATION

25.7 A line falling from left to right indicates that the pitch falls through the syllable, while a line rising from left to right indicates that the pitch rises, thus:

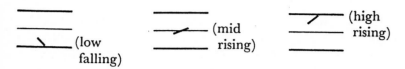

25.8 Combinations of these two indicate respectively a pitch which rises and then falls over one syllable (∧) and one which falls and then rises (∨). Occasionally, a horizontal line (—) may be needed to indicate no appreciable change in pitch.

25.9 The examples are therefore shown like this:

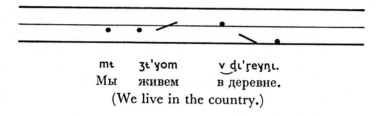

mɪ ʒɪ'yom v dɪ'reɣnɪ.
Мы живем в деревне.
(We live in the country.)

25.10 In using such a notation we have in fact indicated the salient points of the intonation of this sentence. A detailed contour of this sentence, in which all the consonants are voiced, would show a more or less steady rise through the first three syllables, reaching the highest point (just above the middle of the compass) towards the end of the syllable yom, the pitch then remaining at the high pitch for the next unaccented syllable v dɪ and then descending through the syllable rey to the lowest point, at which point it remains for the final unstressed syllable ɲɪ.

25.11 There will be slight variations in this contour from speaker to speaker and, in the pronunciation of the same speaker, from occasion to occasion. It is quite common, for example, for the pitch to begin to descend in the unstressed syllable v dɪ and even at the end of the syllable yom. Experience

25. INTONATION

has shown, however, that contours showing such detail tend to confuse the learner and that he achieves a good performance more rapidly if he works from the 'salient-feature' contours like those used in this book.

25.12 Although a fairly considerable amount of work has been done in recent years on Russian intonation, there is still much that remains to be settled. In what follows therefore we give no more than the basic and broad essentials of Russian intonation. It is, moreover, presented in an order suitable for easy acquirement by the learner.

Simple sentences

1. (a) *Plain statement*

25.13 The general characteristics of the melodic contour of this kind of sentence are as follows:

(1) the last stressed syllable has a falling pitch and the fall is from the mid-point of the compass to the bottom;[1] any following unstressed syllables remain at the low pitch;

(2) preceding stressed syllables have a slightly rising pitch, about the mid-point, and each of these rising pitches after the first is slightly lower than the preceding one;[2]

(3) unstressed syllables between the last rising pitch and the falling pitch remain at the level reached by the rising pitch.

25.14 *Examples*

'pravdə
Правда.
(That's true.)

on 'bil tam
Он был там,
(He has been there.)

---

[1] It is to be understood that throughout this chapter the indications of place in the compass are approximate.

[2] They thus form a descending scale of slightly rising pitches. The last such pitch may however be higher than the others for special purposes or if the speaker utters the sentence as if it were in two parts.

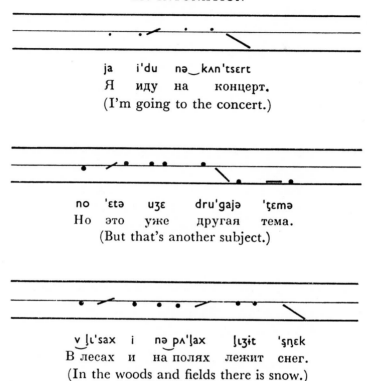

ja i'du nə‿kʌn'tsɛrt
Я иду на концерт.
(I'm going to the concert.)

no 'ɛtə uʒɛ dru'gajə 'tɕɛmə
Но это уже другая тема.
(But that's another subject.)

v ʟɪ'sax i nə pʌ'ʟax ʟɪʒɪt 'ʂnɛk
В лесах и на полях лежит снег.
(In the woods and fields there is snow.)

25.15 Note that the place of the falling pitch changes according to where the logical 'weight' falls:[1]

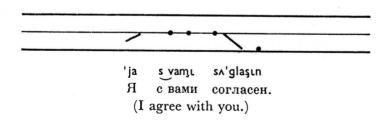

'ja s vam̩ɪ sʌ'glaʂɪn
Я с вами согласен.
(I agree with you.)

---

[1] The falling pitch is then usually the place of the last stressed syllable. If
later syllables *are* stressed, then the pitch remains low.

cf.

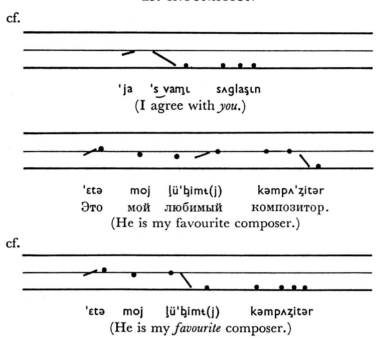

'ja 's‿vaɱʟ sʌglaşʟn
(I agree with *you*.)

'ɛtə moj ʟü'ḫimʟ(j) kəmpʌ'ʑitər
Это мой любимый композитор.
(He is my favourite composer.)

cf.

'ɛtə moj ʟü'ḫimʟ(j) kəmpʌʑitər
(He is my *favourite* composer.)

(b) Specific question

25.16 By 'specific' question we mean a question containing one of the question-words kto кто (who), kʌg'da когда (when), 'skoʟkə сколько (how much), etc., i.e. one which asks for specific information and not simply the answer 'yes' or 'no' or 'maybe', etc. (The latter kind of question is dealt with below.)

25.17 The characteristics of the melodic contour of this kind of sentence are the same as those of the plain statement.

25.18 *Examples*

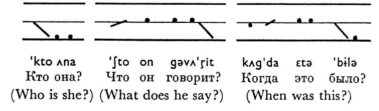

'kto ʌna   'ʃto on gəvʌ'ɾit   kʌg'da ɛtə 'bɨlə
Кто она?   Что он говорит?   Когда это было?
(Who is she?) (What does he say?)   (When was this?)

222

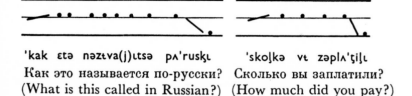

'kak ɛtə nəzɪva(j)ɪtsə pʌ'ruskɪ   'skoɭkə vɪ zəplʌ'ʨiɭɪ
Как это называется по-русски?   Сколько вы заплатили?
(What is this called in Russian?)   (How much did you pay?)

25.19 Here too the location of the final stress and falling pitch varies (cf. § 25.15) as the logical weight varies.

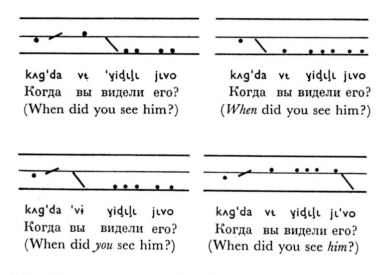

kʌg'da vɪ 'yidɪɭɪ jɪvo   kʌg'da vɪ yidɪɭɪ jɪvo
Когда вы видели его?   Когда вы видели его?
(When did you see him?)   (*When* did you see him?)

kʌg'da 'vɨ yidɪɭɪ jɪvo   kʌg'da vɪ yidɪɭɪ jɪ'vo
Когда вы видели его?   Когда вы видели его?
(When did *you* see him?)   (When did you see *him*?)

25.20 Note that in each of the last four examples the word kʌg'da когда could be replaced by tʌg'da тогда (then), leaving the melodic contour the same, each question then becoming a statement. This underlines the fact that the contours of plain statements and specific questions have the same characteristics.

(c) Commands

25.21 Commands have the same general characteristics as plain statements. Commands, however, are usually short (often consisting of one word) and, if they are simple sentences, often have few stressed syllables before the falling pitch. The stressed syllable therefore starts at the mid-point and falls to the bottom, any preceding unstressed syllables usually being slightly below the starting-point of the falling pitch.

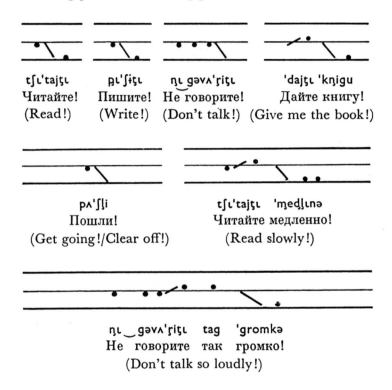

tʃɪ'tajʈɪ   ᵱɪ'ʃɨʈɪ   ŋɪ gəvʌ'ɾiʈɪ   'dajʈɪ 'kŋigu
Читайте!   Пишите!   Не говорите!   Дайте книгу!
(Read!)   (Write!)   (Don't talk!)   (Give me the book!)

pʌ'ʃli
Пошли!
(Get going!/Clear off!)

tʃɪ'tajʈɪ 'ᵯedɭɪnə
Читайте медленно!
(Read slowly!)

ŋɪ gəvʌ'ɾiʈɪ tag 'gromkə
Не говорите так громко!
(Don't talk so loudly!)

2. *Non-specific question*

25.22 By 'non-specific' question we mean the type of question to which, in English for example, the answer can be 'yes' or 'no' or 'maybe' or 'probably', etc., i.e. one which does not ask for specific information (cf. § 25.16).

25.23 The general characteristics of the melodic contour of this kind of question are:

(1) the last stressed syllable has a high pitch; this pitch may be more or less level but is often rising, starting above the

mid-point and rising to the top or near to the top of the compass (we shall mark it in our notation as 'high rising');

(2) any preceding syllables are usually pitched somewhat below the mid-point, those that are stressed either being level or having a slightly falling pitch;

(3) any following syllables are pitched at or near the bottom of the compass.

25.24 The general impression of this melodic contour, therefore is of a sudden rise followed by a sharp descent.[1] This contour is not used in normal English non-specific questions and some learners find it slightly embarrassing to use the high-rising pitch. It is of course essential to overcome any such embarrassment, since this contour is highly characteristic of Russian.

25.25 *Examples*

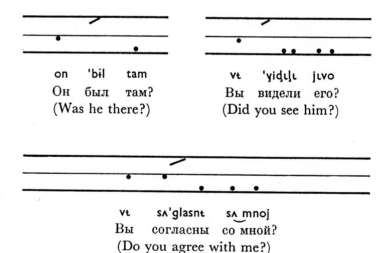

on	'bɨl	tam		vɨ	'ɣidɨlɨ	jɪvo
Он	был	там?		Вы	видели	его?
(Was he there?)				(Did you see him?)		

vɨ	sʌ'glasnɨ	sʌ mnoj
Вы	согласны	со мной?
(Do you agree with me?)		

---

[1] The descent often begins in the last part of the syllable bearing the high-rising pitch but this is, as it were, 'accidental'. The student should simply aim to pitch unstressed syllables after the high-rising pitch at the bottom of his compass.

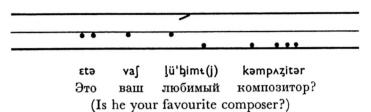

εtə   vaʃ   ʃü'ḩimɩ(j)   kəmpʌʑitər

Это   ваш   любимый   композитор?

(Is he your favourite composer?)

25.26 Here too the location of the last stressed syllable and the accompanying pitch can be varied, according to where the logical weight falls (cf. §§ 25.15, 19).

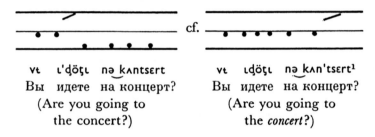

cf.

vɩ   ɩ'd̦ö̞ţɩ   nə̧ kʌntsɛrt   vɩ   ɩd̦ö̞ţɩ   nə̧ kʌn'tsɛrt[1]

Вы   идете   на концерт?   Вы   идете   на концерт?

(Are you going to   (Are you going to
the concert?)   the *concert?*)

3. Tentatives

25.27 Under 'tentatives' we include requests (in which the verb is in the imperative), suggestions to another person (in which the verb is in the conditional), inclusive suggestions, i.e. suggestions that the speaker and another person or other persons should do something together (in these the verb is in the first person plural fut. pfv. or, if it is a verb of motion, in the first person plural pres.)[2] and doubting questions (in which the verb is in the second person, is negated and is followed by the particle ʃɩ ли).[3]

25.28 The general characteristics of the melodic contour of tentatives are as follows:

(1) the accented syllable of the logically weighted word has

---

[1] The shift of logical weight can be, and often is, conveyed by a change of word-order, thus:

  vɩ nə̧ kʌn'tsɛrt ɩd̦ö̞ţɩ   Вы на концерт идете?

[2] With different contours such sentences could be plain statements or non-specific questions.

[3] With a different contour such sentences could be non-specific questions.

25. INTONATION

a rising-falling pitch, the highest point being slightly above or at the mid-point of the compass and the starting point slightly below this; from its highest point the rising-falling pitch descends to the bottom of the compass (the fall is thus greater than the rise) and any following unstressed syllables remain at the bottom of the compass;[1]

(2) preceding syllables are pitched about the middle of the compass, any that are stressed having a slight rise, which usually ends about as high as the highest point of the rising-falling pitch.

25.29   Tentatives in English have a rising pitch at the end of the sentence and are thus quite different in melodic contour from tentatives in Russian.

25.30   *Examples*

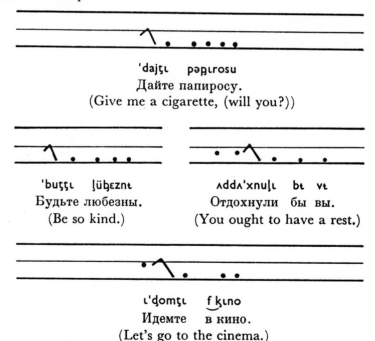

'dajʈɪ   pəɓɪrosu
Дайте папиросу.
(Give me a cigarette, (will you?))

'buʈʈɪ   ǀübɛznɪ
Будьте любезны.
(Be so kind.)

ʌddʌ'xnuǀɪ   bɪ   vɪ
Отдохнули бы вы.
(You ought to have a rest.)

ɪ'domʈɪ   f kɪno
Идемте   в кино.
(Let's go to the cinema.)

---

[1] The rising-falling pitch appears in fact to be a falling pitch modified initially by a slight 'kick-up'.

ɳι xʌ'ʈiʈι lι sʌ‿mnoj
Не хотите ли со мной?
(Don't you want to come with me?)

4. *Emphasis*

25.31 Emphasis for purposes of expressing such emotions as surprise, indignation, anger, etc., is usually achieved by uttering the appropriate accented syllable with greater force than normally, i.e. the stress is heavier or stronger than usual. At the same time any fall or rise usually stretches over a wider range than in non-emphatic utterance. Emphatically accented syllables are often longer than normally accented syllables. Sometimes, however, emphatically accented syllables may be shorter than normally accented syllables. Pronunciation in such a way may convey brusqueness, but the difference in meaning between long and short emphatically accented syllables is not yet fully known.

25.32 The rising-falling pitch (§ 25.28) is also used for certain emphatic purposes. In this event, however, it is not surprise, indignation, anger, etc., which are expressed but certain kinds of admiration, appeal or persuasiveness. It is impossible at present to be more specific about the emphatic function of this pitch.

25.33 Examples of this melodic contour for emphasis in Russian are:

ʌna 'otʃιɳ krʌʂivəjə
Она очень красивая.
(She's very beautiful.)

v lιsu 'otʃιɳ prιjatnə
В лесу очень приятно.
(It's lovely in the woods.)

25. INTONATION

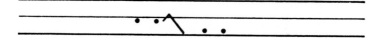

ja ʃuˈbʃu oʃɪŋ

Я люблю осень.

(I adore autumn.)

25.34 Emphasis for warning has a different melodic contour, of which the principal characteristic is that the accented syllable of the logically weighted word has a falling-rising pitch. This pitch descends nearly to the bottom of the register from a point slightly above the bottom and then rises to the mid-point or higher (in the latter event the starting-point may be just below the mid-point). There is thus a greater rise than fall. Any un-stressed syllables after the falling-rising pitch continue to rise slightly.

25.35 Warnings often contain a verb in the imperative and it is usually, though not always, the imperative which carries the falling-rising pitch, as the following examples show.

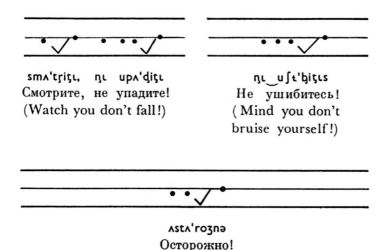

smʌˈtɾiʃɪ, ŋɪ upʌˈdiʃɪ

Смотрите, не упадите!

(Watch you don't fall!)

ŋɪ uʃɪˈb̦iʃɪs

Не ушибитесь!

(Mind you don't bruise yourself!)

ʌstʌˈroʒnə

Осторожно!

(Do be careful!)

229

5. *Further types of question*

25.36 In sections 1 (*b*) and 2 of this chapter we described the melodic contours of respectively specific questions and non-specific questions. In this section we describe three further types of question.

25.37 (*a*) *Reduced questions*

By 'reduced question' we mean here a question consisting of the conjunction a a (and) followed by a noun (or noun-phrase) or adverb (or adverbial phrase). There is never a verb in this kind of question.[1] A reduced question may be supplementary to a preceding question, to which an answer may have been received, or it may be an independent question, arising from a statement made by the speaker or his interlocutor.

25.38 The general characteristics of the melodic contour of a reduced question are as follows:

(1) the conjunction is usually pitched at about the mid-point of the compass;

(2) if the stressed syllable in what follows the conjunction is final it has a rising pitch, starting slightly below the mid-point and rising higher than the mid-point; if, however, it is non-final it has a level pitch,[2] slightly below the mid-point, and the following unstressed syllables gradually rise in pitch until the last reaches a point higher than the mid-point;

(3) any unstressed syllables intervening between the conjunction and the stressed syllable are pitched at the same level as the beginning of the stressed syllable.

25.39 Thus the general shape of this melodic contour is

---

[1] Though it may be followed immediately by a *separate* question not of the 'reduced' type.

[2] It may rise slightly at the end but we shall mark it as level.

25. INTONATION

25.40 In the examples which follow we give the preceding context of the reduced questions, but melodic contours are given only for the reduced questions themselves.

mɪ 'fʂɛ ɪ'dom 'f park
Мы все идем в парк.
(We are all going to the park.)

a 'kaʈə
А Катя?
(And what about Katya?)

a ʌ'na
А она?
(And what about her?)

pʌj'du pəxʌ'ʒu pʌ 'ɣerɪgu
Пойду похожу по берегу.
(I'm going for a walk on the beach.)

a ɪ'gzamɪnɪ
А экзамены?
(And what about your exams?)

25. INTONATION

ʂɪvodɳə ˈyetʃɪrəm ja budu rʌˈbotəʈ
Сегодня вечером я буду работать.
(This evening I'm going to work.)

a ˈzaftrə
А завтра?
(And tomorrow?)

a ˈzaftrə yetʃɪrəm
А завтра вечером?
(And tomorrow evening?)

25.41 (b) *Repeat-questions*

By 'repeat-question' here we do not mean repetition of the entire original question, but repetition of *part* of the original question (often only one word), when the questioner has either not heard or understood the answer or for some other reason wishes the answer to be confirmed or refuted. In form the repeat-question consists *either* of the interrogative word (or a few words including the interrogative word) from an original specific question, *or* of the logically weighted word (or a few words including this word) from an original non-specific question.

25. INTONATION

25.42 In the latter case, the high-rising pitch is used, just as in the original non-specific question. Thus:

vɪ tʃɪ'taʃɪ ɛtu kɲigu
Вы читали эту книгу?
(Have you read this book?)

tʃɪ'tal
Читал.
(Yes.)

tʃɪ'taʃɪ
Читали?
(You have read it?)

25.43 We shall not further illustrate this type of repeat-question.

25.44 In the case of a specific repeat-question a mid-rising melodic contour, similar to that described in §§25.38, 39 for reduced questions, is used[1] (whereas the original specific question has a melodic contour with a falling pitch, see §25.17).

25.45 The examples which follow are expansions by means of answer and repeat-question of examples given in §§25.18, 19. We give the melodic contour only for the repeat-question.

'kto ʌna?
kʌ'ʂirʃə
Кассирша.
(The cashier.)

kto
Кто?
(Who?)

---

[1] The conjunction a a, with a middle pitch, is of course absent.

kʌg'da vɨ 'yidɨʃɨ jɨvo?
ftʃɨ'ra
Вчера.
(Yesterday.)

	or	

kʌg'da
Когда?
(When?)

kʌg'da yidɨʃɨ
Когда видели?
(When did you see him?)

'kak ɛtə nəzɨva(j)ɨtsə pʌ'ruskɨ?
kərʌn'daʃ
Карандаш.
(Pencil.)

	or	

kak
Как?
(What?)

'kak nəzɨva(j)ɨtsə
Как называется?
(What is it called?)

25.46 (c) Echo-question

By 'echo-question' we mean here a repetition of the question by the person to whom the original question has been put. In echoing a question, first person pronouns and verb forms may have to be changed to second person or vice versa, plural forms to singular forms or vice versa, etc. An example of such a change is

'skoɭkə vɨ zəplʌ'ʃiɭɨ?
Сколько вы заплатили?
(How much did you pay?)

'skoɭkə ja zəplʌ'ʃil?
Сколько я заплатил?
(How much did I pay?)

25. INTONATION

25.47 If the original question is a non-specific question then the echo-question has to have the interrogative particle ʮ ли, as in

> vɛ ɪ'döʝɪ f ḵɪ'no?
> Вы идете в кино?
> (Are you going to the cinema?)

> ɪ'du ʮ ja f ḵɪ'no?
> Иду ли я в кино?
> (Am I going to the cinema?)

25.48 All echo-questions have the high-rising pitch on the accented syllable of the logically weighted word. This applies whatever the type of the original question—non-specific question, specific question, reduced-question or repeat-question. The point is that with an echo-question one is in fact asking 'Is *this* your question?' or 'Is *this* what you are asking?' and 'this' is expressed by the original question, grammatically modified if necessary (see § 25.46). These questions are therefore a variety of non-specific question.[1]

25.49 Examples of echo-questions are

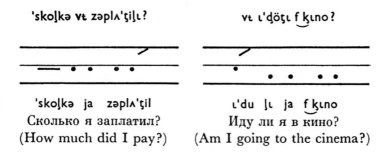

| 'skoʮkə vɛ zəplʌ'ʈiʮɪ? | vɛ ɪ'döʝɪ f ḵɪno? |

'skoʮkə ja zəplʌ'ʈil
Сколько я заплатил?
(How much did I pay?)

ɪ'du ʮ ja f ḵɪno
Иду ли я в кино?
(Am I going to the cinema?)

---

[1] An echo-question may be used as a rhetorical question, i.e. may not in fact be an 'echo' of a question put by another person.

25. INTONATION

a 'kaʈə?   kʌg'da yidʲɪʲlʲɪ?

a 'kaʈə   kʌg'da yidʲɪl
А Катя?   Когда видел?
(And what about Katya?)   (When did I see him?)

Compound sentences

25.50 The variety of structures of compound sentences is quite considerable and all the details of their intonational characteristics cannot be dealt with in this book. We shall limit our remarks, which will be of a broad nature, to some sentence-types in which there are only two clauses. In sentences of this kind one clause may contain new information, the other given information (i.e. information which is already known or is not presented as new information) or both clauses may contain new information.

1. *Statement*

25.51 If a two-clause sentence is a statement, then the general melodic characteristics are as follows:

(1) any clause containing new information has the falling pitch on the stressed syllable of the logically weighted word;

(2) any clause containing given information has the mid-rising pitch at the end, if it is the first clause (and the last rising pitch is *higher* than any preceding ones, subsequent unstressed syllables continuing to rise), but a low level melodic contour if it is the second clause.

25.52 In the following sets of examples, the phonetic transcription, orthographic version and English translation are given once for each set and over them are placed three different melodic contours. In the first contour the second clause contains the new information while the first contains given information;

236

in the second contour the situation is reversed; and in the third contour both clauses contain new information. A vertical line, which is not to be taken as indicating a pause, separates the contours of the two clauses and the symbols G ('given information') and N ('new information') are placed above the contours. In the third contour an optional pause is indicated by ⦙.

25.53 The first sentence illustrated is one consisting of two co-ordinate clauses.

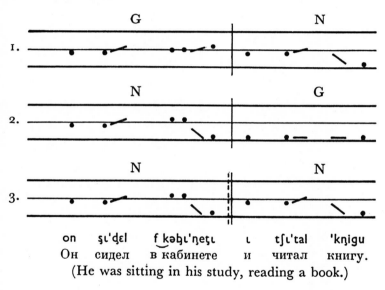

on	ʂɪ'dɛl	f kəʜɪ'ɲeʈɪ	ɪ	tʃɪ'tal	'knigu
Он	сидел	в кабинете	и	читал	книгу.

(He was sitting in his study, reading a book.)

1. I.e. What he was doing was reading a book, while (as we know) sitting in his study. With this contour, however, the information of the entire sentence may be new, though there still seems to be more 'weight' attached to the clause with the falling contour.

2. I.e. What he was doing was sitting in his study, while (as we know) reading the the book.

3. I.e. What he was doing was sitting in his study and reading a book (neither of which facts we knew before).

25.54 In the next sets of examples the sentences consist of two clauses, one of which is subordinate to the other. In set (a) the

25. INTONATION

subordinate clause is first, in set (*b*) the subordinate clause is second. The illustrations are set out as above (§§25.52, 53).

25.55   (*a*)

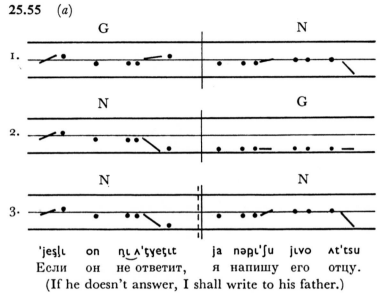

'jeʃʟ   on   n̩ʟ ʌ'ʈɣeʈʟ   ja   nəɹ̩'ʃu   jʟvo   ʌt'tsu
Если   он   не ответит,   я   напишу   его   отцу.
(If he doesn't answer, I shall write to his father.)

1. I.e. If he doesn't answer (which we have postulated) then what I shall do is write to his father. Cf. also note 1, § 25.53.

2. I.e. I shall write to his father (a step which has been mentioned) in the event of his not answering.

3. I.e. There is the possibility that he will not answer and in that event I shall write to his father (and neither of these facts was known before).

25. INTONATION

25.56 (*b*)

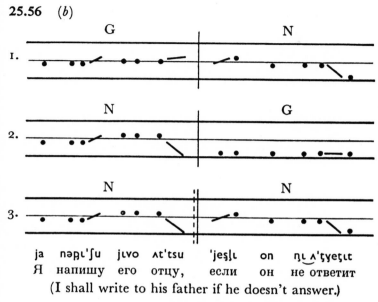

ja	nəɐ̩ɬ'ʃu	jɩvo	ʌt'tsu	'jeʂɬ	on	ɳɬ ʌ'ʈyeʈɩt
Я	напишу	его	отцу,	если	он	не ответит

(I shall write to his father if he doesn't answer.)

1. I.e. I shall write to his father (which has been mentioned) in the event of his not answering.

2. I.e. What I shall do is to write to his father in the event (which has been mentioned) of his not answering.

3. I.e. Neither the writing to his father nor the possibility of his not answering has been mentioned before or even implied.

2. *Specific question*

25.57 Two-clause sentences which are specific questions show the same general melodic characteristics as statements (§25.51). If the clauses are co-ordinate, then the likelihood is that both are asking for new information and the melodic contour will be

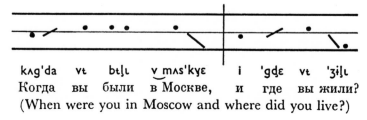

kʌg'da	vɛ	bɛɬɩ	v mʌs'kyɛ	i	'gdɛ	vɛ	'ʒɨɬɩ
Когда	вы	были	в Москве,	и	где	вы	жили?

(When were you in Moscow and where did you live?)

239

25. INTONATION

25.58 With a subordinating structure we observe the same patterns as in statements with subordinating structure.

25.59 (*a*)

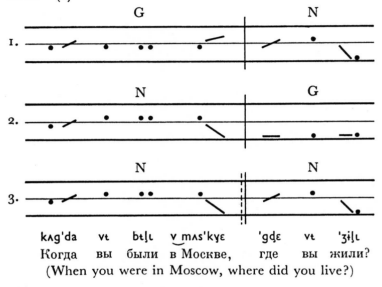

kʌgˈda	vɪ	btʃʊ	v mʌsˈkүɛ	ˈgdɛ	vɪ	ˈʒiʃʊ
Когда	вы	были	в Москве,	где	вы	жили?

(When you were in Moscow, where did you live?)

    1. I.e. I know you were in Moscow, but where did you live?
    2. I.e. But where did you live when you were in *Moscow*?
    3. I.e. When you were in Moscow (which has not yet been mentioned) where did you live (which I haven't yet asked you)?

25.60   (*b*)

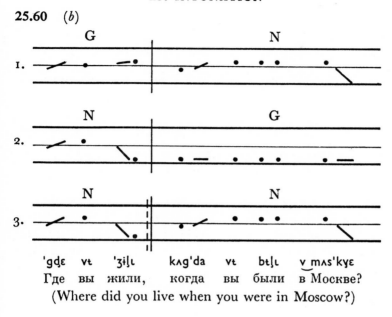

'gdɛ	vɪ	'ʒɨlɪ	kʌg'da	vɪ	bɪlɪ	v mʌs'kʏɛ
Где	вы	жили,	когда	вы	были	в Москве?

(Where did you live when you were in Moscow?)

1. I.e. Where did you live when you were in *Moscow*?
2. I.e. I know you were in Moscow, but where did you live?
3. I.e. Where did you live (a question I have not yet put)—
when you were in Moscow, I mean?

3. *Non-specific question*

25.61   When two non-specific questions are linked by 'and'
the high-rising pitch occurs in both clauses:

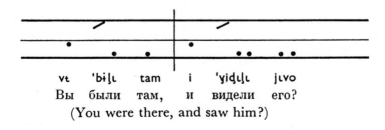

vɪ	'bɨlɪ	tam	i	'ʏidɪlɪ	jɪvo
Вы	были	там,	и	видели	его?

(You were there, and saw him?)

25. INTONATION

25.62 When linked by 'or', however, the high-rising pitch occurs in the first clause, but the falling pitch in the second clause:[1]

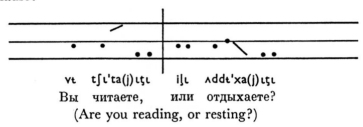

vɪ tʃɪ'ta(j)ɪtʲɪ   iɭɪ   ʌddɪ'xa(j)ɪtʲɪ

Вы читаете,   или отдыхаете?

(Are you reading, or resting?)

25.63 In non-specific questions with a subordinating structure, the main clause has the high-rising pitch if it is concerned with the new information, the subordinate clause has a low level melody if it is second but, if it is first, it has a higher level melody, level with the beginning of the main clause.

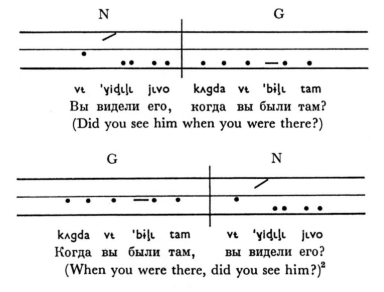

N   G

vɪ 'yidɪɭ jɪvo   kʌgda vɪ 'biɭɪ tam

Вы видели его,   когда вы были там?

(Did you see him when you were there?)

G   N

kʌgda vɪ 'biɭɪ tam   vɪ 'yidɪɭ jɪvo

Когда вы были там,   вы видели его?

(When you were there, did you see him?)[2]

---

[1] More generally, the clause after 'or' has the falling pitch, and each preceding clause which is a non-specific question has the high-rising pitch.

[2] I.e. I know you were there but what I'm asking is 'did you see him'?

25.64 If the *subordinate* clause is concerned with the new information, then the situation is reversed and the subordinate clause has the rising pitch:

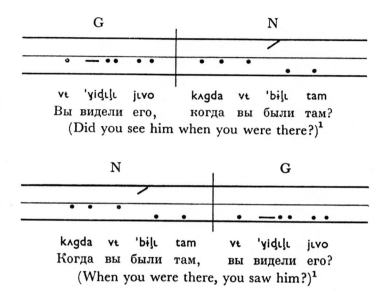

vɨ 'ɣidɨlɨ jɨvo   kʌgda vɨ 'bɨlɨ tam
Вы видели его,   когда вы были там?
(Did you see him when you were there?)[1]

kʌgda vɨ 'bɨlɨ tam   vɨ 'ɣidɨlɨ jɨvo
Когда вы были там,   вы видели его?
(When you were there, you saw him?)[1]

25.65 Finally, if both main clause and subordinate clause are concerned with new information then the main clause has the high-rising pitch and the subordinate clause has the falling pitch:

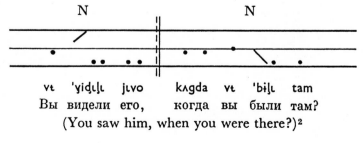

vɨ 'ɣidɨlɨ jɨvo   kʌgda vɨ 'bɨlɨ tam
Вы видели его,   когда вы были там?
(You saw him, when you were there?)[2]

---

[1] I.e. It was when you were there that you saw him?
[2] I.e. What I'd like to know is 'did you see him'? I mean when you were there?

25. INTONATION

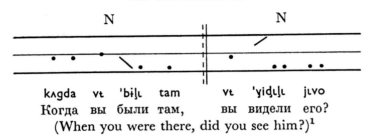

kʌgda vɪ 'biɟʟ tam   vɪ 'yiɟʟɟʟ jʟvo
Когда вы были там,   вы видели его?
(When you were there, did you see him?)[1]

Further remarks

1. *Enumerations*

25.66 By 'enumeration' we mean a series of items, each having
the same syntactical role. Each item may be a single word, as in

(fʂʟvʌ'zmoʒnt(j)ʟ 'fruktɪ) — 'jabləkʟ, ʌpʟ'ʂint, 'pɛrʂʟkʟ, bʌ'nant
(Всевозможные фрукты) — яблоки, апельсины, персики,
бананы.
((All sorts of fruit)—apples, oranges, peaches, bananas.);

or a group of words (adjective and noun, adverbial phrase,
etc.); or even a clause, as in

stʌ'ju nə plʌt'formʟ, tʃʟ'taju gʌ'ʐɛtu, 'papkə pəd' miʃkəj,
pʌ'txoɟʟt 'po(j)ʟst, vɪ'xoɟət 'ʟüɟʟ
Стою на платформе, читаю газету, папка под мышкой,
подходит поезд, выходят люди.
   (I stand on the platform, read my paper, my document-case
is under my arm, the train comes in, out get the people.)

25.67 If the series is closed (indicated in print by a stop after
the last item) there are three possible melodic contours for
enumerations:
   (1) all the items except the last, which has the falling pitch,
       have the mid-rising pitch;
   (2) all the items, except the last, which has the falling pitch,
       have the high-rising pitch;
   (3) all the items have the falling pitch.

25.68 When the items consist of more than one word, the
significant pitch occurs of course on the logically weighted word

[1] See footnote 2, p. 243.

25. INTONATION

in each item. If the series is open (indicated in print by dots after the last item) then the falling pitch is absent from variants (1) and (2), all items having the mid-rising or high-rising pitch.

25.69 It is not entirely clear what is the difference in meaning between these variant contours. Ye. A. Bryzgunova[1] considers that contour (2) is simply a 'more colloquial' variant of contour (1). This is not to say, of course that contour (1) is excluded from normal conversational style or from the reading aloud of printed passages. In the opinion of the present writers, contour (3) in conversation sometimes seems to convey more of an impression that the series is being improvised as the speaker utters it, whereas with contours (1) and (2) (in the event at least of their being closed) there is more of an impression that the speaker already knows beforehand what and how many items he is going to enumerate.

2. *Interpolations*

25.70 By 'interpolation' we mean here a phrase (rarely only one word) or an entire clause which is inserted into a sentence and interrupts, without otherwise changing it, the normal melodic contour of the sentence. Interpolations usually contain some explanatory matter, added as a parenthesis.

25.71 The intonational characteristics of an interpolation lie in the fact that it is spoken with a low, level contour (at or near the bottom of the compass) and at a somewhat faster speed than the surrounding sentence. There is often little stress differentiation, all the syllables being spoken with more or less equal stress, though vowel quality and length distinguish the accented syllables (see §§24.8, 46).

25.72 The items in square brackets in the following sentences are interpolations:

'doktər, [kʌtortʲ(j) znal ɛtə,] nʲ ʌ'tɕyetʲːl

Доктор, [который знал это,] не ответил.

(The doctor, [who knew this,] did not answer.)

---

[1] In *Практическая фонетика и интонация русского языка*.

25. INTONATION

'pavləvə, [ɪʒɣɛs(t)nəjə ruskəjə bə⎸ɪɾinə,] uʒɛ 'viʃlə nʌ‿'pɛnʂⱡju

Павлова, [известная русская баллерина,] уже вышла на пенсию.

(Pavlova, [the well-known Russian ballerina,] has already retired.)

'zojə, — [tɪ pomnⱡʃ jⱡjo,] — mʌja ʒt'na, 'utʃɪtsə f‿'ʃkoⱡɪ

Зоя, — [ты помнишь ее,] — моя жена, учится в школе.

(Zoya, my wife—[you remember her]—teaches in school.)

25.73 Often enough, an interpolation may be identical in form with an apposition or a subordinate descriptive clause, as in the first two examples above. Appositions and subordinate descriptive clauses are, however, distinguished from interpolations by being uttered at normal speed, with normal rhythm and with a mid-rising pitch or a falling pitch, depending on the circumstances.

25.74 Items such as the equivalent of 'he said', 'she announced', occurring *after* the words spoken, are also usually treated as interpolations, as in

pʌ'ra ⱡtʃ'ʈi, [skʌzal on]

— Пора идти, [сказал он].

(—It's time to go, [he said]).

nⱡ 'duməju, [ʌtʃyeʈⱡlə ʌna]

— Не думаю, [ответила она].

(—I don't think so, [she answered]).

3. The levelling-out pitch

25.75 One more type of contour must be mentioned. It is used in statements (and enumerations) but differs from that described in § 25.13. The falling pitch is replaced by a *level* pitch, which is not usually quite as low as the low point of the falling pitch. Preceding syllables are pitched about the mid-point or slightly higher. If a mid-rising pitch precedes the levelling-out pitch and there are intervening unstressed syllables, the latter remain at the same level as the end of the mid-rising pitch. Following unstressed syllables at the end of the contour remain on the same low level pitch, which we call here the 'levelling-out' pitch.

25. INTONATION

25.76 Examples of the levelling-out pitch are:

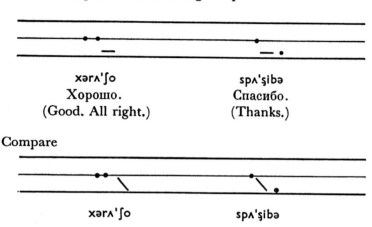

xərʌ'ʃo
Хорошо.
(Good. All right.)

spʌ'şibə
Спасибо.
(Thanks.)

Compare

xərʌ'ʃo

spʌ'şibə

25.77 The difference in meaning between the levelling-out pitch and the falling pitch is not clear as yet. Students will certainly notice this pitch in conversation and it may strike them as 'peculiarly Russian'. Nevertheless they should certainly not 'overwork' it, as it is not as common as the falling pitch. A few examples of it are in the passages for practice in chapter 26.

26

PASSAGES FOR PRACTICE

The passages for practice given in this chapter are intended to be used after the entire book, in particular chapter 25, has been studied. The student may, however, wish to make at least occasional use of the passages before studying chapter 25, in order to practise groups of words or entire sentences. In this case he will have to interpret the special accent-marks (see below) as simple stress-marks and either use his normal English melodic contours, in so far as this is possible, or imitate the pronunciation of a native speaker or at least a competent teacher.

The accent-marks used in the following transcriptions have a two-fold function. They indicate both stress and the pitches described in chapter 25. In addition to these accent-marks, which are described below, we use a vertical bar | to indicate the end of a melodic contour. Where there is a slight pause at the end of a contour in the recordings made for this chapter, this is shown by an additional, broken vertical line, thus ⦙. A longer pause is shown by a double vertical bar, thus ‖. This is usually found at the end of a sentence, though occasionally elsewhere too. Thus the 'bar-marks' demarcate the 'intonational stretches', within which the accent-marks show the intonational characteristics (i.e. both melodic contour and rhythm).

The functions of the accent-marks are as follows:

(a) ˋ indicates the falling pitch (§ 25.13), as in xərʌˋʃo Хорошо (Good. All Right).

(b) ˍ indicates the levelling-out pitch (§ 25.75), as in xərʌˍʃo Хорошо (Good. All right).

(c) ′ indicates the high-rising pitch (§ 25.23), as in on ′bɨl tam Он был там? (Was he there?).

(d) ˄ indicates the rising-falling pitch (§ 25.28), as in ˄dajtɪ Дайте... (Do give me...) or kak krʌ˄şivə Как красиво! (How beautiful!).

(e) ˊ indicates a slightly rising pitch. On the one hand it indicates the mid-rising pitch of reduced questions (§ 25.37), as in a ˊtaɳə А Таня? (And Tanya?) The pitch of the surrounding unstressed syllables is then understood to be as described in § 25.38 and it should particularly be remembered that the pitch continues to rise in unstressed syllables following the mid-rising pitch of reduced questions. The same symbol ˊ also indicates the slightly rising pitch occurring on stressed syllables in other types of sentence, as in

rʊstʌˊran jeşţ nʌ ˊpɛrvəm t nə ʃtʌˊrom ttʌˋʒax
Ресторан есть на первом и на втором этажах.
(There's a restaurant on the first and second floors.)

In such a sentence, or more strictly in such an intonational stretch, each of the slightly rising pitches after the first is slightly lower than the preceding one, so that they form a descending scale of slightly rising pitches. If however the *last* pitch in a stretch is a rising one, the pitch rises through the accented syllable and any subsequent unaccented syllables until it is slightly higher than the initial rising pitch in the stretch. Such a melodic contour is usually a 'non-final' contour, i.e. indicates that the sentence is not yet finished. An example is

prɪslʌˇŋaləs ˉmaʟɪŋkəjʟ ˉrozəvəjʟ ˉʟitʃʟkə ⫽ z̯ gəluˉbɨmʟ yʟˇʃoʟtmʟ glʌˇzamʟ

...прислонялось маленькое розовое личико, с голубыми веселыми глазами.

(...was pressed her rosy little face, with its merry blue eyes.)

Two more accent-marks are used in addition to the above. The raised vertical tick ' indicates a stressed syllable occurring after a rising pitch and remaining, with no appreciable change of pitch, as high as the end-point of the rising pitch. Intervening and subsequent unstressed syllables are at the same pitch, as in yʟˇʃoləjə tʌ'kajə веселая такая (so cheerful). The lowered vertical tick ˌ indicates a stressed syllable occurring after a falling or levelling-out pitch and remaining, with no appreciable change of pitch, as low as the end-point of the preceding pitch. Intervening and subsequent unstressed syllables are at the same pitch, as in yʟˇʃoləjə tʌˌkajə, or a ɪnʌgˇda ʌ̯dʲin toʟkə ˌxvost a иногда один только хвост (and sometimes only the tail). The same symbol also indicates a low-pitched stressed syllable occurring in the same contour after the high-rising pitch, as in

u‿vas ˉjeʂ svʌˌbodnɨ(j)ʟ nəmɪˌra
У вас есть свободные номера?
(Have you any rooms free?)

The system of transcription used cannot represent the into-nation with great delicacy. It cannot, for example, show the relative height of slightly rising pitches in one stretch nor the relative height or speed of different stretches. The system can, however, give a good general impression of Russian intonation, the more so if the help of a native speaker or competent teacher is engaged.

Passage 6 was not recorded specially for this book. All the others were recorded specially for this book, each by two different native speakers. Differences in their intonation and occasional other differences in their pronunciation of the texts are shown by means of parallel transcriptions in places. Alternative pronunciations with or without j between two vowels and at the end of words after ι and t, and also, occasionally, with or without ι before j, are shown by brackets, as elsewhere in this book, whether or not the speakers pronounced j or ι in these positions. It is advisable to practise each entire passage in one variant at a time. Subsequently, a comparison of the two versions will give some additional idea of the variations possible in Russian intonation. For the most part the differences in intonation reveal the different interpretations placed on the passages by the two speakers.

TEN PASSAGES FOR PRACTICE

1

prʊˈɣetstyɩjə‖

1 ˈzdrastvujʈɩ‖; ˈzdrastvuj‖

2 ˈdobrə(j)ɩ ˈutrə‖
   ˈdobrə(j)ɩ ˌutrə‖

3 ˈdobrɩ(j) ˈɣetʃɩr‖
   ˈdobrɩ(j) ˌɣetʃɩr‖

4 spʌˈkojnəj ˈnotʃɩ‖

5 ˈkak vɩ pəʒtˈva(j)ɩʈɩ‖

6 spʌˈʂibə ⁝ xərʌˈʃo‖
   spʌˈʂibə xərʌˌʃo‖

7 a ˈkak ˈvɨ‖

8 ŋɩtʃɩˈvo ʂɩ̞ɛ‖

9 fʂɛ u̯ vaz zdʌˈrovɩ domə‖

10 ˈda‖ fʂɛ ˈʒɨvɩ ɩ zdʌˈrovɩ‖
    ˌda‖ ˈfʂɛ ˈʒɨvɩ ɩ zdʌˈrovɩ‖

11 pɩrɩˈdajʈɩ pʌʒalstə prʊˈɣet ʌt m̩ɩŋa‖

12 ŋɩprɩˈmɛnnə‖; ʌb̞ɩˈzaʈɩɭnə‖
    ŋɩprɩˌmɛnnə‖;

252

1

Приветствия

1 Здравствуйте! Здравствуй!
2 Доброе утро.
3 Добрый вечер.
4 Спокойной ночи.
5 Как вы поживаете?
6 Спасибо, хорошо.
7 А как вы?
8 Ничего себе.
9 Все у вас здоровы дома?
10 Да, все живы и здоровы.
11 Передайте пожалуйста привет от меня.
12 Непременно *or* Обязательно.

Greetings

1 How do you do (*plural or singular formal*); How do you do (*singular familiar*).
2 Good morning.
3 Good evening.
4 Good night.
5 How are you?
6 Well, thank you.
7 And how are you?
8 Not so bad *or* All right.
9 Is everybody well at home?
10 Yes, they're perfectly well.
11 Give them my regards, please *or* Do remember me to them.
12 Certainly.

26. PASSAGES FOR PRACTICE

13 zəxʌˇdiʈɩ k̯ nam‖

14 s̯ udʌˇvoɭʂʈyɩ(j)ɩm‖

15 də̯ ʂyɩˇdaŋ(ɩ)jə‖

16 prʌʃˇtʃæjʈɩ‖; prʌʃˇtʃæj‖

17 pʌˇka‖
    pʌ‿ka‖

18 fʂɩˇvo xʌˇroʃtvə‖; fʂɩˇvo ˇdobrəvə‖

19 ʃtʃɩˇʂɭivəvə puˇʈi‖

2
rəzgʌˇvor nʌ ˇuɭɩtsɩ‖

1 ʂɩrˇg̩ej‖ ɛtə ˈtɨ‖ ˇzdrastvuj‖

2 ˇzdrastvuj ˇpayɩl‖ ˇskoɭkə ˇɭɛt ŋɩ yɩˇdaɭɩʂ‖ ˇkak tɩ ʒɩˇyoʃ‖
   ˇzdrastvuj‖ ˇpayɩl‖ ˇskoɭkə ɭɛt ŋɩ ˇyidɩlɩʂ‖

3 xərʌ‿ʃo ⁝‖ spʌ‿ʂibə‖ aˇtɨ‖
   xərʌˇʃo ⁝‖ spʌˇʂibə‖

4 ˈja ˇtoʒɩ xərʌˇʃo‖ ˇgdɛ tɩ rʌˇbotə(j)ɩʃ‖
   ˈja ˇtoʒɩ xərʌʃo‖

254

13 Заходите к нам.
14 С удовольствием.
15 До свидания.
16 Прощайте; Прощай.
17 Пока.
18 Всего хорошего *or* Всего доброго.
19 Счастливого пути.

13 Do call on us.
14 I shall be glad to (*literally* 'With pleasure').
15 Goodbye ('Au revoir').
16 Goodbye (*plural or singular formal*); Goodbye (*singular familiar*).
17 So long.
18 Cheerio.
19 Have a good journey ('Bon voyage').

2

Разговор на улице

1 — Сергей, это ты? Здравствуй!
2 — Здравствуй, Павел! Сколько лет не видались/виделись! Как ты живёшь?
3 — Хорошо, спасибо, а ты?
4 — Я тоже хорошо. Где ты работаешь?

Conversation in the street

'Sergei, is it you? Hello!'
'Hello, Pavel! It's ages since we met! How are you (getting on)?'
'Well, thank you, and you?'
'I'm well too. Where are you working?'

5   nə‿zʌˈvodɪ| v‿ləbərʌˈtoʃɪ(j)ɪ‖ aˈti‖

6   ˈja rʌˈbotəju nʌ‿ˈfabɽɪkɪ‖ ˈja ţɪpeʃ ˈglavnt(j) ɪnჳtŋer ˈfabɽɪkɪ‖

                                  ˈja ţɪpeʃ ˈglavnt(j) ɪnჳtˈŋer ‚fabɽɪkɪ‖

7   ˈnu ⁞ a ˈkak şɪˈmja‖

    a ˈkak şɪˈmja‖

8   ʌˈţʲlitʃnə‖ ˈdeţɪ rʌs‿tut‖ ˈstarʃt(j) ˈigəʃ uჳε ˈutʃɪtsə f‿ˈʃkoｌɪ‖

    ˈdeţɪ rʌsˈtut‖ ˈstarʃt(j) ⁞ ˈigəʃ ⁞

9   ˈmlat-ʃt(j)| vʌˈlodə| pʌka ˈxodɪt v‿ˈdɛtskɪ(j) ˈsat‖ ˈzojə ⁞ tɪ ˈpomŋɪʃ

    ˈmlat-ʃt(j) ⁞   ˈzojə ⁞ tɪ ˈpomŋɪʃ

10   jɪjo ⁞ mʌˈja ჳtˈna ⁞ pɽɪpədʌˈjot f‿ˈʃkoｌɪ‖ ʌna uˈtʃiţɪｌ̥ŋɪtsə‖ ˈnu ⁞ a tɪ

    jɪjo ⁞ mʌja ჳtˈna ⁞ pɽɪpədʌˈjot f‿ˈʃkoｌɪ‖   a ˈti ⁞

11   ჳt ˈŋilşə ⁞ iｌɪ ˈfşo jɪʃtʃo xəlʌsˈtoj‖

12   ჳt‿ŋilşə‖ jɪʃˈtʃo f‿ˈproʃləm gʌ‿du‖

    ჳtˈŋilşə‖ jɪʃtʃo f‿ˈproʃləm gʌˈdu‖

13   ˈkto tvʌja ჳt‚na‖

    ˈkto tvʌja ჳtˈna‖

14   mʌˈja ჳtna ‿vratʃ‖ ʌna rʌˈbotə(j)ɪt v‿ˈdɛtskəj pəｌɪˈkｌiŋɪkɪ‖ şɪjˈtʃas

    mʌja ჳtˈna ˈvratʃ‖   ‖ şɪjˈtʃas

15   ʌna ŋɪ rʌˈbotə(j)ɪt ⁞ pətʌˈmu ʃtə mɪ ˈჳdom ɽɪˈɦonkə‖ pɽɪ(j)ɪჳˈჳaj

    ʌna ˈŋε rʌˈbotə(j)ɪt| pɽɪ(j)ɪჳˈჳaj

16   kʌ‿mŋε v ‚goşţɪ ⁞ ja pəznʌˈkomｌu ţɪɦa ჳ ჳtˈnoj‖

    kʌ‿mŋε v ˈgoşţɪ

26. PASSAGES FOR PRACTICE

5 — На заводе, в лаборатории. А ты?

6 — Я работаю на фабрике. Я теперь главный инженер фабрики. 7 Ну, а как семья?

8 — Отлично. Дети растут...Старший, Игорь, уже учится в школе. 9 Младший, Володя, пока ходит в детский сад. Зоя, — ты помнишь 10 ее — моя жена, преподает в школе. Она учительница. Ну, а ты 11 женился или все еще холостой?

12 — Женился. Еще в прошлом году.

13 — Кто твоя жена?

14 — Моя жена врач, она работает в детской поликлинике. Сейчас 15 она не работает, потому что мы ждем ребенка. Приезжай 16 ко мне в гости, я познакомлю тебя с женой.

'In a works, in the laboratory. And you?'
'I'm working at a factory. I'm chief factory engineer now. Well, how is your family?'
'Fine. The children are growing up. The older one, Igor, is already at school. The younger one, Volodya, is still at the kindergarten. Zoya—you remember her—my wife, is teaching in a school. She's a schoolmistress. Well, are *you* married, or are you still a bachelor?'
'I'm married. Last year.'
'What does your wife do?'
'My wife is a doctor, she works in a children's clinic. At present she's not working, because we're expecting a baby. Come and visit me—I'll introduce you to my wife.'

17 spʌˈʂibə ‖ ʌɦɩˈzaʈɩɭnə prɩˈjedu‖ k̬ səʒʌˈɭeŋɩju mʌja ʌstʌˈnofkə‖

   ʌɦɩˈzaʈɩɭnə prɩ͵jedu‖

18 də ʂyɩˈdaŋ(ɩ)jə‖ pɩrɩˈdaj prɩyɛt ˈʒojɩ| i ˈdeʈəm‖

   ‖ pɩrɩˈdaj prɩˈyɛt ˈʒojɩ ɩ ˈdeʈəm‖

19 fʂɩˈvo xʌˈroʃtvə‖

       (ˈɛs xʌˈvroŋɩnə‖ gəvʌˈʂiʈɩ pʌˈrusǩɩ‖)

        3

     v̬ gʌʂˈʈiŋɩtsɩ‖

1 ˈzdraʂʈɩ‖ skʌˈʒiʈɩ| u̬ vas ˈjeʂʈ svʌ͵bodnɩ(j)ɩ nəmɩ͵ra‖

2 ˈjeʂʈ‖ kʌˈkoj ˈnomɩr vam ˈnuʒɩn ‖ nʌ ʌdnʌˈvo ‖ iɭɩ nə̬ dvʌˈjix‖

 _jeʂʈ‖ kʌˈkoj nomɩr vam ˈnuʒɩn ‖ nʌ ʌdnʌˈvo iɭɩ nə dvʌˈjix‖

3 nʌ ʌdnʌˈvo ʒɩ͵laʈɩɭnə ‖ s̬ ˈvannəj ɩ ʈɩɭɩˈfonəm‖

4 u̬ ˈnas fʂɛ nəmɩˈra s̬ u̬ˈdopstvəmɩ‖

 u̬ nas ˈfʂɛ nəmɩra s̬ u̬͵dopstvəmɩ‖

5 a ˈskoɭkə ˈsto(j)ɩt nomɩr‖

 a ˈskoɭkə ˈsto(j)ɩt ͵nomɩr‖

6 ˈtʂi pɩdɩˈʂat‖

7 ˈɛtə mɩŋa usˈtra(j)ɩvə(j)ɩt‖

26. PASSAGES FOR PRACTICE

17 — Спасибо, обязательно приеду, К сожалению, моя остановка.

18 — До свидания! Передай привет Зое и детям.

19 — Всего хорошего.

(С. Хавронина, *Говорите по-русски*)

'Thanks, I'll certainly come. I'm sorry, this is my stop.'
'Goodbye! Remember me to Zoya and the children!'
'Cheerio!'

(S. Khavronina, *Russian as we Speak it*)

3

В гостинице

1 — Здравствуйте! Скажите, у вас есть свободные номера?

2 — Есть. Какой номер вам нужен — на одного или на двоих?

3 — На одного, желательно, с ванной и телефоном.

4 — У нас все номера с удобствами.

5 — А сколько стоит номер?

6 — Три пятьдесят.

7 — Это меня устраивает.

In a hotel

'How do you do! Tell me, have you any rooms vacant?'
'Yes. What type of room do you need—single or double?'
'Single, preferably, with bath and telephone.'
'All our rooms have (such) facilities.'
'How much does a room cost?'
'Three fifty.'
'That suits me.'

26. PASSAGES FOR PRACTICE

8   kag ˈdolgə vɛ prʌˈbudɨʒɨ u‿nas‖

     ˈkag dolgə vɛ prʌˈbudɨʒɨ ‖ u‿ˏnas‖

9   ŋɨˈdelɨ pəltʌˈrɨ ˈdɣɛ‖ ja prɨˈjɛxələ f‿kəməŋdɨˈrofku‖

     ŋɨˈdelɨ pəltʌˈrɨ‖ ˈdɣɛ‖

10   mʌˈgu prɨdlʌˈʒɨʈ vam ˈnomɨr nʌ‿ˈdvatsəʈ vʌˈʂmom ttʌˈʒɛ‖

11   ˈja sʌˈglasnə‖

12   pʌˈʒalstə ‖ zʌˈpolnɨʈɨ ɭɨsˈtok dɭɨ prɨ(j)ɨʒˈʒajüʃtʃɨx‖

13   xərʌˈʃo‖ ˈtak‖ fʌˈmɨɭɨjə‖ ˈimə‖ ˈoʈtʃɨstvə‖ nʌ‿skoɭkə ˈdŋej‖ ˈvot|

     xərʌ_ʃo‖ _tak‖ fʌ_mɨɭɨjə‖ _imə‖ _oʈtʃɨstvə‖ nʌ‿ˏskoɭkə _dŋej‖

14 pʌˈʒalstə‖

15   ˈnomɨr vaʃtj ˈkomnətɨ dvatsəʈ ˈvoʂɨm dvatsəʈ ˈpæʈ‖ vʌˈʒmɨʈɨ

     'nomɨr[1] vaʃtj ˈkomnətɨ ‖ dɣɛ ˈtɨʃtʃɨ vəʂɨm ˈsot ˈdvatsəʈ ˈpæʈ‖

16 ˈkɭütʃ‖

17   spʌˈʂibə‖ skʌˈʒɨʈɨ| nə‿kʌˈkom ttʌˈʒɛ pərɨˈkmaxɨrskəjə ‖

18   nʌ‿ˏpɛrvəm‖

19   a ˈgdɛ moʒnə pʌʌˈḥedəʈ‖

---

[1] Stressed syllable pitched at or slightly above mid-point, with no appreciable changes in pitch until high-rising pitch is reached.

260

26. PASSAGES FOR PRACTICE

8 — Как долго вы пробудете у нас?

9 — Недели полторы-две. Я приехала в командировку.

10 — Могу предложить вам номер на двадцать восьмом этаже.

11 — Я согласна.

12 — Пожалуйста, заполните листок для приезжающих.

13 — Хорошо. Так...фамилия...имя...отчество. На сколько дней...Вот... 14 пожалуйста.

15 — Номер вашей комнаты 2825. Возьмите 16 ключ.

17 — Спасибо. Скажите, на каком этаже парикмахерская?

18 — На первом.

19 — А где можно пообедать?

'How long will you be staying here?'
'One-and-a-half to two weeks. I'm on business.'
'I can offer you a room on the twenty-eighth floor.'[1]
'I'll take it.'
'Will you fill in the visitor's form, please?'
'All right. Let's see...surname...forename...patronymic. How many days...There you are.'
'Your room is number 2825. Here's the key.'
'Thank you. Tell me, what floor is the hairdresser's on?'
'The first floor.'
'And where can I eat?'

[1] In Russian hotels the numbering of the floors begins with the ground floor, which is called the 'first floor'. Subtract one from the above floor numbers to obtain the English equivalent.

20 ɾʊstʌˈran jeʂ nʌ ˈp̲ervəm t nə ftʌˈrom ɪtʌˈʒax‖ ˈsliʃtʂʊ ˌmuzɪku‖

ɾʊstʌˈran jeʂ nʌ ˈp̲ervəm│ t nə ftʌˈrom ɪtʌˌʒax‖

21 ɛtə v ɾʊstʌˈraɲʊ‖ ˈkroɱʊ tʌvo│ nʌ ˈkaʒdəm ttʌˈʒɛ jeʐ buˈʃɛt‖ ʊ ˈm̥ejʂʊ

ˈkroɱʊ tʌvo ┊ ʊ ˈm̥ejʂʊ

22 y̲ yʊˈdu ┊ u ˈnas jeʐ ɦuˈro ʌpˈsluʒɪvəŋ(ʊ)jə ‖ ˈtam vɛ ˈsmoʒɪʂʊ zəkʌˈzaʂ

y̲ yʊˈdu ┊ ˈtam vɛ ˈsmoʒɪʂʊ zəkʌˈzaʂ

23 ɦʊ̣ɛt f kʊˈno ┊ f ʈ̥ʊˈatɾ̥ ┊ ι dəgəvʌˈɾitsə ʌb ɪksˈkurʂʊ(j)ι pə m̲ʌsˈkyɛ‖

ɦʊ̥ˈɛt f kʊˈno ┊ f ʈ̥ʊ̣atɾ̥ ┊

24 fʂo ɛtə ˈotʃʊŋ uˈdobnə‖

fʂo ɛtə ˈotʃʊŋ uˈˇdobnə‖

25 ˈjeʂ̣ʊ vam ˈʃtoɲʊbuʂ pʌˈnadəɦʊtsə ┊ ʌbrʌˈʈiʂʊz g ˈgorɲʊtʃnəj ʊ̣ʊ

ˈjeʂ̣ʊ[1] vam ˈʃtoɲʊbuʂ[1] pʌˈnadəɦʊtsə ┊ ʌbrʌˈʈiʂʊz g ˈgorɲʊtʃnəj │ ʊ̣ʊ

26 d̥ʊˈʒurnəj pʌ ʊtʌˈʒu‖

d̥ʊˈʒurnəj pʌ ʊtʌˈʒu‖

27 bləgədʌˈɾu vas‖ vɛ ˈotʃʊŋ ̣ʊ̈ˈɦɛznt‖

28 pʌˈʒalstə‖ ˈ̣ift nʌˈpravə‖

29 grʌʒˈdankə‖ yʊrˈɲiʂʊs‖ vɛ zʌbɨ̣ʊ ˈḳütʃ‖

vɛ zʌˈbɨ̣ʊ ˈḳütʃ‖

30 ˈax spʌˈʂibə‖ rʌʂˈʂejənəʂʈ‖

ˈax│ spʌˈʂibə‖

(ˈruskʊ jʊˈzik pʌ ˈrad̥ιo‖)

_____

[1] Stressed syllable pitched at or slightly above mid-point, with no appreciable changes in pitch until high-rising pitch is reached.

20 — Ресторан есть на первом и на втором этажах. Слышите музыку? 21 Это в ресторане. Кроме того, на каждом этаже есть буфет. Имейте 22 в виду, у нас есть бюро обслуживания. Там вы сможете заказать 23 билет в кино, в театр, и договориться об экскурсии по Москве.

24 — Все это очень удобно.

25 — Если Вам что-нибудь понадобится, обратитесь к горничной или 26 дежурной по этажу.

27 — Благодарю Вас. Вы очень любезны.

28 — Пожалуйста. Лифт направо.

[Пауза]

29 — Гражданка! Вернитесь! Вы забыли ключ.

30 — Ах, спасибо. Рассеянность...

(Русский язык по радио)

'There's a restaurant on the first floor and another on the second floor. Can you hear the music? That's in the restaurant. Apart from that there's a buffet on each floor. Bear in mind, we have a service bureau. You can order tickets for the cinema or the theatre there, or make arrangements for a trip round Moscow.'

'It's all very convenient.'

'If you need anything, ask the chambermaid or the floor supervisor.'

'Thank you. You're very kind.'

'Not at all. The lift is on the right.'

[Pause]

'Madam! Come back! You've forgotten the key.'

'Oh, thank you. I'm so absent-minded...'

(Russian by Radio)

4

1 ˘vot ˉtak vot ɩ ˎjɛʒʒu‖ ˉɣɣɛrx i ˘vɳis ‖ z gʌˉrɨ də ˘na gəru‖ i ˉtak ‖
   vot ˉtak vot ɩ ˎjɛʒʒu‖ ˉɣɣɛrx i ˘vɳis‖   ɩ ˉtak

2 ˉfşu ˘ʒɨʒɳ‖ fpɩrɩˉḑi ˍxvost‖ ˉzzaḑɩ pəsʌˉʒɨr‖ a ɩnʌgˉda ʌˍḑin tolkə
   fşu ˘ʒɨʒɳ‖ fpɩrɩˉḑi ˘xvost‖   a ɩnʌgˉda ʌ˘ḑin tolkə

3 ˌxvost ‖ a ˉzzaḑɩ ɳɩkʌ˘vo‖ ˉbɨlə nas kʌg'datə ˘mnogə‖ a ʈɩˉpeɽ ˉşeɱ
   ˌxvost ‖   bɨlə nas kʌgˉdatə ˘mnogə‖

4 tʃɩlʌˉɣɛk ʌsˌtaləş‖ ʌfˉtobustɩ‖ a ˉʃto ʒʌ ɩɳʈɩˉɽɛs nʌ ʌfˌtobuşɩ‖ ˉʃto

5 u˘ɣiḑɩʃ‖ vot ˉmɨ s vaɱɩ ˉjeḑɩm ‖ a zəxʌˉʈim ‖ ʌstʌˍnoɣɩmşə ‖ ˍvɨjḑɩm ‖
   ˘vot mɨ s vaɱɩ ˉjeḑɩm ‖ a zəxʌˊʈim ‖ ʌstʌˉnoɣɩmşə ‖ ˘vɨjḑɩm ‖

6 pəşɩˍḑim ‖ pʌˉsmotrɩm ˌna məɽɩ‖ ˉvɨ ʃtoɳɩbuʈ pəşɳɩˍma(j)ɩʈɩ‖ a ˉtam‖
   pəşɩˉḑim ‖ pʌˉsmotrɩm ˉna məɽɩ‖ ˉvɨ ʃtoɳɩbuʈ pəşɳɩˉma(j)ɩʈɩ‖ a ˉtam‖

7 ˉtɽi ɱɩˉnutɩ ‖ i ˉkapɽɩ‖ jɩʃˉtʃo tɽi ɱɩˌnutɩ ‖ ˉanə'kapɽɩ‖ zʌˉvaļətsə
   tɽi ɱɩˉnutɩ‖ ˉi ˉkapɽɩ‖ jɩʃˉtʃo tɽi ɱɩ'nutɩ ‖ ʌnʌˉkapɽɩ‖ zʌˉvaļətsə

8 v rɩstʌˉran ‖ i ˉpjut‖ ˘ax ‖ ˘kak krʌˉşivə‖   ˘kak krʌˉşivə‖ a ɩz rɩstʌˍ
   v rɩstʌˉran ‖ ˉi ˉpjut‖ ˘ax ‖ kak krʌˉşivə‖ ˘ax ‖ kak krʌˉşivə‖ a ɩz rɩstʌˍ

9 ˘ranə ‖ ˉɳi nʌ ˉʃak‖ ˘vɨskətʃət nə ɱɩˌnutku‖ ˉkupət suɣɩˉɳɩrɩ ‖ ˉi
   ˉranə ˉɳi nʌ ˉʃak‖ ˘vɨskətʃət nə ɱɩˉnutku ‖ ˉkupət suɣɩˉɳɩrɩ ‖

10 nʌ˘zat‖

             (ˉɣiktər ɳɩˉkrasəf‖ ˉpervəjɩ znʌˉkomstvə‖)

26. PASSAGES FOR PRACTICE

4

1 — Вот так вот и езжу. Вверх и вниз, с горы да на гору. И так 2 всю жизнь. Впереди хвост, сзади пассажир. А иногда один только 3 хвост, а сзади никого...Было нас когда-то много, а теперь семь 4 человек осталось. Автобусы...А что за интерес на автобусе? Что 5 увидишь? Вот мы с вами едем, а захотим — остановимся, выйдем, 6 посидим, посмотрим на море, вы что-нибудь поснимаете. А там? 7 Три минуты — и Капри, еще три минуты — Анакапри. Завалятся 8 в ресторан и пьют. ,,Ах, как красиво, как красиво!'' — а из ресто- 9 рана ни на шаг. Выскочат на минутку, купят сувениры — и 10 назад.

(Виктор Некрасов, *Первое знакомство*)

Well, this is how I ride around. Up and down, down one mountain and up another. And it's been like that all my life. The (horse's) tail in front, a passenger behind. And sometimes there's only the tail, and nobody behind...There used to be a lot of us but now there are only seven left. It's the buses...And what interest is there on a bus? What do you see? Here you and I are driving along, and if we want, we can stop, get out, have a sit down, have a look at the sea, and you can take a picture of something. But on the buses? Three minutes—and that's Capri, another three minutes—Anacapri. They crowd into the restaurant and drink. 'Oh, how lovely, oh, how lovely!'—but they never set foot outside the restaurant. They'll hop outside for a minute to buy souvenirs—and then back inside again.

(Victor Nekrasov, *First Acquaintance*)

5

1 ˋsluʃəj‖ ˋtut u‿nas| pʌˋpalsə tʌˊkoj ˋkoɱιk¦| uˋmŗoʃ‖ ʃɨˋpnul mɲι

ˊtut u nas pʌˊpalsə tʌˊkoj ˋkoɱιk¦|

2 ˊɲɛmə| i pəkʌˊzal glʌˊzaɱι nʌ‿ˊparɲə v‿ʐιˊļonəj ruˋbaʃķι‖

3 zdʌˆrovə ˌdruk¦| skʌˌzal ja¦| i prəţιˊnul ˊruku ɛtəmu ʃuˋtu‖ ˋjasnəjə

zdʌˋrovə ˌdruk¦| ι prəţιˊnul ˋruku ɛtəmu ʃuˌtu‖ ˋjasnəjə

4 u‿ɲιvo| bɨˊla ˋroļ‖

u‿ɲιvo bɨla ˌroļ‖

5 ˋɣiktər¦| ˊbɨstrə skʌˋzal on‖ ɱιˋtroxιn‖

ˌbɨstrə skʌˌzal on‖

6 sprʌˋşi u‿ɲιˌvo| ˊkto on tʌˋkoj¦| ʃɨˊpnul mɲι ˋɲɛmə‖

sprʌˊşi u‿ɲιvo| ʃɨˌpnul mɲι ˌɲɛmə‖

7 ˊnu| ˆladnə¦| skʌˌzal ja‖ ˊtɨ ˋkto tʌkoj| ˋdruk‖

nu ˋladnə¦| tɨ ˊkto tʌˋkoj druk‖

8 ˊja ˋsam ιs‿sɣιr‿dlofskə¦| ˌbɨstrə ʌˌţɣeţιl on‖ prιˊʃloş mɲι ˊʐḑeş

ˊja ˈsam ιs‿sɣιrˋdlofskə¦|

9 ɓιŗιˊʒɨţ tŗιnətsəţιˊḑɲɛvnuju ιkənʌˊɱitʃιskuju blʌˋkadu‖

10 ˊţɛ ˋtrojι¦| i ḑιˊɣitsɨ| i ˊɲɛmə| i pʌˊtaɲιn| i ˊtaɲə¦| ˊƥŗamə zʌˋʃļiş

ţɛ ˊtrojι¦|

11 ʌt‿ˌşɱɛxə‖

26. PASSAGES FOR PRACTICE

5

1 — Слушай, тут у нас попался такой комик, умрешь, —
шепнул мне 2 Нема и показал глазами на парня в зеленой
рубашке.

3 — Здорово, друг, — сказал я и протянул руку этому
шуту — ясная 4 у него была роль.

5 — Виктор, — быстро сказал он. — Митрохин.

6 — Спроси у него, кто он такой, — шепнул мне Нема.

7 — Ну ладно, — сказал я. — Ты кто такой, друг?

8 — Я сам из Свердловска, — быстро ответил он. — При-
шлось мне здесь 9 пережить тринадцатидневную эконо-
мическую блокаду.

10 Те трое, и девицы, и Нема, и Потанин, и Таня прямо
зашлись 11 от смеха.

'Listen, we've got a real comic here. You'll kill yourself,'
Nema whispered to me and indicated with her eyes a fellow in
a green shirt.

'Hello, old man,' I said, and thrust my hand out to this joker
—it was clear what his role was.

'Victor,' he said quickly. 'Mitrokhin.'

'Ask him who he is,' Nema whispered to me.

'All right then,' I said. 'Who are you, old man?'

'I'm from Sverdlovsk (myself),' he answered quickly. 'I've
had to endure a thirteen-day economic blockade here.'

Those three, and the girls, and Nema, and Potanin, and
Tanya were quite helpless with laughter.

12 ˈtr̝eʈɯ(j) ˇras| uʒɛ rʌsˈkaztvə(j)ɯt| t ˈslovə fˇslovə ‖ ʃtˈpnul mn̩ɯ

ˈtr̝eʈɯ(j) ˇras uʒɛ rʌsˌkaztvə(j)ɯt ‖ t ˈslovə fˇslovə ‖ ʃtˌpnul mn̩ɯ

13 ˈn̩ɛmə‖

ˌn̩ɛmə‖

14 ˈpar̝ɯn s ˈpolnəj ʂɯˈr̝joznəʂʈju prədʌlˈʒal‖

15 kʌˈn̩ɛʃnə ‖ ˈtrudnə pr̝ɯxodɯtsə tʃɯlʌˈɣɛku| kʌɡˇda u n̩ɯvo ɦɯn̩ˈʒin

ˈtrudnə pr̝ɯxodɯtsə tʃɯlʌˈɣɛku| kʌɡda u n̩ɯˇvo ɦɯn̩ˈʒin

16 nə nʌˈlɛ‖ ˈzna(j)ɯʃ| ˈʃto tʌkoji ɦɯn̩ˈʒin nə nʌˈlɛ‖ n̩ɯ ˈto ʃtə sʌfˈʂem n̩ɛt‖

nə nʌˌlɛ‖ | ʃto tʌˇkojɯ ɦɯn̩ˈʒin nə nʌˌlɛ‖ n̩ɯ ˈto ʃtə sʌfʂem ˈn̩ɛt ‖

17 a ˈtak ‖ nʌˇdva ˈtr̝i ˇvɨxləpə‖ no ˈja n̩ɯ ʈɯˈr̝alʂə‖ ˈutrəm ‖ nədɯˇvaju

a ˈtak‖ nʌˇdva ˈtr̝i ˇvɨxləpə‖ ˈutrəm nədɯˇvaju

18 ˌʂɣɛʒuju ruˈbaʃku ‖ pəkuˈpaju ˌʂɣɛʒuju ɯsˌtonskuju ɡʌˈʒetu ‖ t ɯˇdu

ˌʂɣɛʒuju ruˈbaʃku ‖

19 nə vʌˈgzal k pr̝ɯˈxodu |ɯn̩ɯnˈgratskəvə ˈpo(j)ɯzdə‖ stʌˈju ‖ tʃɯˈtaju

tʃɯtaju

20 ɡʌˈʒetu ‖ ˈkoʒənəjə ˈpapkə pʌd ˈmiʃkəj ‖ pən̩ɯˈma(j)ɯʃ‖ pʌˈtxodɯt

ɡʌˈʒetu ‖ pʌˈtxodɯt

21 ˌpo(j)ɯst ‖ ɯʒ n̩ɯˇvo vɯˈxodɯt dəbrəpʌˈr̝adətʃnəjə ʂɯˈmja ‖ ˈpapə|

ˈpo(j)ɯst ‖ ˈpapə ‖

22 ˈmamə| ˈdotʃkə ɣɯˈʂma ʂɯmpʌˈʈitʃnəjə‖

ˈmamə ‖ ˈdotʃkə ‖ ɣɯˈʂma sɯmpʌˈʈitʃnəjə‖

23 ˈslovə fˇslovə ‖ stʌˈnal mn̩ɯ nʌˇuxə ˈn̩ɛmə‖

nu ˈslovə fˇslovə| stʌˌnal mn̩ɯ ˌna uxə ˌn̩ɛmə‖

12 — Третий раз уже рассказывает, и слово в слово, — шепнул мне 13 Нема.

14 Парень с полной серьезностью продолжал:

15 — Конечно, трудно приходится человеку, когда у него бензин 16 на ноле. Знаешь, что такое бензин на ноле? Не то что совсем нет, 17 а так, на два-три выхлопа. Но я не терялся. Утром надеваю 18 свежую рубашку, покупаю свежую эстонскую газету и иду 19 на вокзал к приходу ленинградского поезда. Стою, читаю 20 газету, кожаная папка под мышкой, понимаешь? Подходит 21 поезд, из него выходит добропорядочная семья: папа, 22 мама, дочка, весьма симпатичная...

23 — Ну, слово в слово, — стонал мне на ухо Нема.

'That's the third time he's told the story and it's word for word the same,' Nema whispered to me.

The fellow went on perfectly seriously:

'Of course it's difficult for a man when his petrol's down to zero. You know what "petrol down to zero" means? Not exactly right out but just enough for the engine to give two or three coughs.[1] But I didn't lose my head. In the morning I put on a clean shirt, buy the latest Estonian newspaper and go to the station, to the Leningrad bay. I stand and read my paper, my leather document-case under my arm, get it? In comes the train and out gets a respectable family: dad, mum and the daughter, a very nice girl...'

'Word for word,' Nema groans into my ear.

[1] Lit. 'for two or three puffs [from the exhaust]'.

24 jıʃˈʈeʂʈyʊnə ǁ ʌˈŋi rʌʂˈʈeɾənt‖ ŋʊznʌˈkomʊ(j) ˈgorət ǁ ŋʊznʌˈkoməjə

ŋʊznʌˈkomʊ(j) ˈgorət ǁ ŋʊznʌˈkoməjə

25 ˌretʃ‖ f ˈtot mʌˈmɛnt kʌgda ʌŋi prʌˈxodət ˈmimə mʊˌŋa ǁ ja ʌpusˈkaju

ˈretʃ‖ f ˈtot mʌˈmɛnt ǁ kʌgda ʌŋi prʌˈxodət mimə mʊˈŋa ǁ ja ʌpusˈkaju

26 gʌˈʐetu ǁ ʊ gəvʌˈɾu ǁ zʌˈmeʈ| pʌˈrusḳʊ‖ ˈǀubʌ_pitnə¹‖ kʌˈŋeʃnə ʌŋi

gʌˈʐetu ǁ ʊ gəvʌˈɾu ǁ   ˈǀubʌˈpitnə¹‖ kʌˈŋeʃnə ǁ ʌŋi

27 brʌˌsajutsə kʌ mŋɛ s vʌˈprosəmʊ ǁ i ˈtut səyʊrˈʃennə sluˈtʃæjnə

brʌˈsajutsə kʌ mŋɛ s vʌˈprosəmʊ ǁ i ˈtut səyʊrˈʃennə sluˈtʃæjnə ǁ

28 vtjʊˈʂŋæ(j)ʊtsə ʃtə u mʊˈŋa jeʂʈ svʌˈbodnəjʊ ˈvɾemə‖

vtjʊˈʂŋæ(j)ʊtsə ʃtə u mʊˈŋa ˈjeʂʈ svʌˈbodnəjʊ ˈvɾemə‖

(vʌˈʂiǀʊ(j) ʌˈkʂonəf‖ pʌˈra moj ˌdruk ǁ pʌˈra‖)

6²

1 vt ˈpomŋʊʈʊ ǁ ˈɛtə bʊlə ˈɲatəvə ˈmartə‖ vt pɾʊglʌˈʂiǀʊ nas f ʈʊˈatɾ|

2 ʃtobʊ ʌˈʈmeʈʊʈ ˈdeŋ vʌˈʂmovə ˈmartə‖

3 kʌˈŋeʃnə| ja ˈpomŋu‖ vam pʌˈnrayʊlsə spʊkˌtakǀ‖

4 ˈotʃʊŋ‖ ˈkromʊ fʂʊvo ˈprotʃʊvə ɛtə bʊlə ˈotʃʊŋ pɾʊˈʲjatnə ǁ ʃtə bʊl

5 ʌˈtmetʃʊn ˈnaʃ ˈdeŋ‖

6 a f kʌˈtorʊ(j) ˈras vt ˈbiǀʊ nʌ ɛtəm bʌˈǀeʈʊ‖

7 ˈɛtəd bʌˈǀɛt ja smʌˈtɾelə və ftʌˈroj ras‖ ˈpɛrvʊ(j) 'ras ǁ ɛtə ˈbilə

8 v ǀʊŋʊnˈgradʊ ǁ ʊ ftʌˈroj v mʌsˈkyɛ‖

¹ Spoken by the informants with two stresses, as if two words, and with all vowels somewhat lengthened.

² Two extracts from a recorded conversation. The paragraph divisions represent the alternation between the two speakers.

24 — Естественно, они растеряны — незнакомый город, нез-
накомая 25 речь. В тот момент, когда они проходят мимо
меня, я опускаю 26 газету и говорю, заметь, по-русски:
,,Любо-пыт-но``. Конечно, они 27 бросаются ко мне с
вопросами, и тут совершенно случайно 28 выясняется,
что у меня есть свободное время.

(Василий Аксенов, Пора, мой друг, пора)

'Naturally, they feel lost—don't know the town, don't know
the language. Just as they're going past me, I lower the paper
and say—in Russian, mark you—"Ve-ry cu-rious". Of course
they descend on me and pepper me with questions and then it
turns out, quite by chance, that I have some free time.'

(Vasily Aksyonov, It's Time, my Friend, it's Time)

6

1 — Вы помните, это было пятого марта? Вы пригласили
нас в театр, 2 чтобы отметить день восьмого марта.
3 — Конечно, я помню. Вам понравился спектакль?
4 — Очень. Кроме всего прочего, это было очень приятно,
что был 5 отмечен наш день.
6 — А в который раз вы были на этом балете?
7 — Этот балет я смотрела во второй раз. Первый раз, это
было 8 в Ленинграде, а второй в Москве.

'Do you remember?—It was on the fifth of March. You had
invited us to the theatre to celebrate Woman's Day.'[1]
'Of course I remember. Did you like the performance?'
'Very much. Apart from anything else, it was very pleasant
to celebrate our day.'
'How many times have you seen that ballet?'
'That was the second time I saw that ballet. The first time
was in Leningrad and the second time in Moscow.'

[1] Lit. 'the eighth of March', which is celebrated as Woman's Day in the
U.S.S.R.

26. PASSAGES FOR PRACTICE

9 a ˈja bɪl pʌˈʒaluj daʒ¹ ˈŋɛskəˌkə ˈras| ɪ fʂæ̣ķ̣ɪ(j) ˈras| kʌgda ja

10 smʌˈtʃu ɛtət bʌˈɛt ⫶ on mŋ̣ɪ fʂo ˈbolʃt ɪ ˈbolʃt ˈnrayɪtsə‖

.   .   .   .   .   .

11 vot ˈmɨ ˈkaktə s ̣vaṃɪ fʂo ˈvʃemə səħ̣ɪˈra(j)ɪmsə pʌˌjɛxəʈ f ˈķ̣in ⫶

12 v ̣ˈdommu'ʐej tʃɪjˈkofskəvə‖ ɪ ˈfʂo ŋ̣ɪˈkak ŋ̣ɪ səħ̣ɪˈʃomsə‖ ɪ pʌˈʒaluj bɪ

13 ˈsto(j)ɪlə ɛtə ˌʐdɛləʈ‖

14 no vɪ ʒɪ ˈzna(j)ɪʈɪ| pəʈʃ̣ɪmu ɛtə ŋ̣ɪ ˈviʃlə‖ ja ˈduməju ʃtə mɪ

15 səħ̣ɪˈʃomsə yɪˈsnoj ⫶ kʌgda zəʐ̣ɪ̣ɪˈŋejut ɖ̣ɪˈʃeyjə‖

16 ˈda| ɪ ˈnuʒnə ʌħ̣ɪˈzaʈ̣ɪˌnə pʌˈjɛxəʈ tuˈda| pəʈʌˈmuʃtə ˈmuzɪku

17 ḳ ɛtəmu bʌˈɛtu| tʃɪjˈkofskɪ(j) nəp̣ɪˈsal ˈiṃɪnə f ķ̣ɪˈnu‖

18 a vɪ ˈzna(j)ɪʈɪ| kʌgˈda ˈsmotʃɪʃ ɛtəd bʌˈɛt ⫶ ˈto ˈkaʒttsə| ʃtə

19 vʌˈzmoʒnəṣʈ̣ɪ ˌmuzɪ̣ḳɪ ˈŋɛ ɪʃˈtʃerpənt ˌtantsəmŋ̣ɪ‖

20 ˈda| ˈfʂotəḳɪ tʃɪj'kofskɪ(j) ɖ̣ɪ̣ʃˈ̣yiʈ̣ɪˌnə ⫶ ʌstʌˈjotsə ŋ̣ɪpʃɪvzʌjˈdonnɪm

21 kəmpʌˌʐitərəm‖ ŋ̣ɪpʃɪvzʌjˈdonnɪm ˈiṃɪnə ˈvot ˈv ̣obləṣʈ̣ɪ bʌˈɛtə‖

22 ɛtə vaʃ ǀü'ħ̣imɪ(j) kəmpʌˌʐitər‖

23 ˈtrudnə skʌˌzaʈ...m̩²...ˈtrudnə nʌzˌvaʈ...m̩²...ˈimə ǀüˈħ̣iməvə

24 kəmpʌˈʐitərə ⫶ no pʌˈʒaluj səyɪrˈʃɛnnə sprəyɪˈḍǀivə bɪlə bɪ skʌˈzaʈ|

¹ *sic*, final vowel omitted by speaker.
² m̩ signifies a 'syllabic' m, used here as a 'hesitation particle'. It was
uttered with a fairly low, level pitch. The dots represent pauses interrupt-
ing contours.

26. PASSAGES FOR PRACTICE

9 — А я был, пожалуй, даже несколько раз, и всякий раз, когда я 10 смотрю этот балет, он мне все больше и больше нравится.

. . . . . .

11 — Вот мы как-то с вами все время собираемся поехать в Клин, 12 в дом-музей Чайковского. И все никак не соберемся. И пожалуй бы 13 стоило это сделать.

14 — Но вы же знаете, почему это не вышло. Я думаю, что мы 15 соберемся весной, когда зазеленеют деревья.

16 — Да, и нужно обязательно поехать туда, потому что музыку 17 к этому балету Чайковский написал именно в Клину.

18 — А вы знаете? — Когда смотришь этот балет, то кажется, что 19 возможности музыки не исчерпаны танцами.

20 — Да, все-таки Чайковский действительно остается непревзойденным 21 композитором. Непревзойденным именно вот в области балета.

22 — Это ваш любимый композитор?

23 — Трудно сказать...м...трудно назвать...м...имя любимого 24 композитора, но пожалуй совершенно справедливо было бы сказать,

'And I've seen it—oh—several times, and every time I see that ballet I like it more and more.'

. . . . . .

'You know, you and I are always intending to go to Klin, to the museum in Chaikovsky's house. And yet we never manage it. And it would probably be worth going.'

'But you know why we never made it. I think we shall manage it in the spring, when the trees start to turn green.'

'Yes, and we really must go there, because it was in Klin that Chaikovsky composed the music to that ballet.'

'You know what? When you see that ballet, you feel that the dances don't exhaust all the possibilities of the music.'

'Yes, whatever one may say, Chaikovsky really remains unsurpassed as a composer. I mean precisely in the field of ballet.'

'Is he your favourite composer?'

26. PASSAGES FOR PRACTICE

25 ʃtə tʃʊjˈkofskɪ(j) ʌˈdin ɪsˈsamɪx ǀüˈbimɪx mʌ(j)ix kəmpʌˈʑitərəfǁ

26 mɳɛ ˈotʃʊɳ 'nrayɪtsə jivo ʂɪmfʌˈɳitʃɪskəjə ˌmuzɪkə ǁ ˈotʃʊɳ 'nrayɪtsə

27 jɪvo bʌˈǀɛtnəjə ˌmuzɪkəǁ ˈpravdə[1]

28 a ˈopɪrnəjəǁ

29 ˈopɪrnəjə kʌˈɳɛʃnəǁ ˈɳikəvəjə ˈdaməǁ pʌˈʑaluj nʌɪˈboǀɪ(j)ɪ znʌ-

30 ˈtʃiʦɪǀnəjə ɪz jɪvo ˈopɪrǁ

(ɪz zvukʌˈzapɪʂɪ rəzgʌˈvorəǁ)

7

1 yɪrˈʃiɳɪnǁ ˈʃtoʃǁ ˈjeʂǀɪ ɳɪ dʌ'jut ˈtʃæju ǁ to dʌˈvajʦɪ ˈxoʦ pəʃɪlʌ-

jeʂǀɪ ɳɪ dʌˈjut ˌtʃæju ǁ to dʌˈvajʦɪ xəʦ pəʃɪlʌ-

2 ˈsofstvu(j)ɪmǁ

ˈsofstvu(j)ɪmǁ

3 tuʑɪnˈbaxǁ   dʌˆvajʦɪǁ ʌ ˈtʃomǁ

dʌ_vajʦɪǁ

4 yɪrˈʃiɳɪnǁ   ʌ ˈtʃomǁ   dʌˈvajʦɪǀ   pəmɪtʃˈta(j)ɪm ǁ   nəprɪˈmɛr ʌ toj

dʌˈvajʦɪ   pəmɪtʃˈta(j)ɪm ǁ

5 ˈʑiʑɳɪ ǁ kʌˈkajə budɪt ˈpoʂǀɪ ˈnas ǁ ˈǀɛt tʃɪrɪʑ ˈdyeʂʦɪ ˈtristəǁ

6 tuʑɪnˈbaxǁ   ˈʃtoʃǁ poʂǀɪ ˈnas budut ǀɪˈtaʦ nə vʌzˈduʃnɪx ʃʌˈrax ǁ

7 iˈʑmɳeɳətsə ɳɪd-ʑʌˈki ǁ ʌtˈkrojut moʑɪd 'biʦ ʃtsˈtoji ˈtʃufstvə ǁ ɪ

ʌtˈkrojut bɪʦ ˈmoʑɪt ʃtsˈtoji ˈtʃufstvə ǁ

[1] Melodic contour unfinished, interrupted by other speaker.

25 что Чайковский один из самых любимых моих композито-
ров.   26 Мне очень нравится его симфоническая музыка,
очень нравится   27 его балетная музыка. Правда...
28 — А оперная?
29 — Оперная, конечно. ,,Пиковая дама'' — пожалуй, на-
иболее зна-   30 чительная из его опер.

(Из звукозаписи разговора)

'It's difficult to say—er—It's difficult to name—er—your
favourite composer but it would probably be quite true to say
that Chaikovsky is one of my very favourite composers. I like
his symphonic music very much and I like his ballet music very
much too. True...'
'And his operatic music?'
'His operatic music, of course. "The Queen of Spades", I'd
say, is the most important of his operas.'

(From a recorded conversation)

7

1 *Вершинин.* Что ж? Если не дают чаю, то давайте хоть
пофило-   2 софствуем.
3 *Тузенбах.* Давайте. О чем?
4 *Вершинин.* О чем? Давайте помечтаем...например, о той
5 жизни, какая будет после нас, лет через двести-триста.
6 *Тузенбах.* Что ж? После нас будут летать на воздушных
шарах,   7 изменятся пиджаки, откроют, может быть/быть
может, шестое чувство и

Vershinin: Well, if they won't give us tea, let's at least do a bit
  of philosophizing.
Tuzenbakh: All right. What about?
Vershinin: What about? Let's dream, for example, about what
  life will be like after we're gone, in two or three hundred
  years.
Tuzenbach: Well, after we're gone they'll fly in balloons, they'll
  change the cut of their coats, they'll discover a sixth sense,

26. PASSAGES FOR PRACTICE

8 rəzʌˈyjut jɪ'vo‖ no ˈʒɨʒn̩‖ ʌsˈtaɳɪtsə fʂo ˈta ʒɬ ‖ ʒɨʒn̩ ˈtrudnəjə|

ʌsˈtaɳɪtsə fʂo ˈta ʒɬ ‖

9 ˈpolnəjə ˈtajn ‖ ɩ ʃtʃɩˈʂļivəjə‖ɩ tʃɩlʌˈyɛk tʃɩɽɩsˈtɨʂətʃu ˈļɛt ‖ tʃɩlʌˈyɛk

ɩ tʃɩlʌˈyɛk tʃɩɽɩsˈtɨʃtʃu ˈļɛt ‖

10 budɩt ˈtag ʒɬ vzdɬˏxaʈ‖ ˈax ‖ ˈʈaʃkə ˏʒɨʈ‖ ɩ ˈvm̩ɛʂʈɩ ş ˈʈɛm totʃnə ˈtag

ˈʈaʃkə ˈʒɨʈ‖ ɩ ˈvm̩ɛʂʈɩ ş ˈʈɛm ‖ totʃnə ˈtag

11 ʒɬ ‖ kak ʈɩˈpeɽ ‖ on budɩt bʌˈjatsə ɩ ɳɩ xʌˈʈeʈ ˈʂm̩erʈɩ‖

ʒɬ ‖ kak ʈɩˈpeɽ ‖ on budɩt bʌˈjatsə| ɩ ɳɩ xʌˈʈeʈ ˏʂm̩erʈɩ‖

12 yɩrˈʃɨɳɩn‖ pʌˈduməf‖ ˈkak vam skʌˏzaʈ‖ ˈmɳɛ ˈkaʒɬtsə ‖ ˈfʂo nə ʒɩˈm̩ļɛ

ˈkak vam skʌˈzaʈ‖ ˈfʂo nə ʒɩˈm̩ļɛ

13 dʌlʒno ɩʒm̩ɩˈɳitsə ˏmaləpʌˏmalu ‖ ɩ uˈʒɛ m̩ɩˈɳæ(j)ɩtsə nʌ ˏnaʃtɣ

dʌlʒno ɩʒm̩ɩˈɳitsə maləpʌˈmalu ‖ ɩ uˈʒɛ m̩ɩˏɳæ(j)ɩtsə‖ nʌ ˏnaʃtɣ

14 glʌˏzax‖ tʃɩɽɩʒˈdyeʂʈɩ ˈtɽistə ‖ nəkʌˈɳɛts ˈtɨʂətʃu ˈļɛt ‖ ˈdɛlə ɳɩ

glʌˈzax‖

15 f ˈsroɋɩ ‖ nʌsˈtaɳɩt ˈnovəjə ʃtʃɩˈʂļivəjə ˈʒɨʒn̩‖ uˈtʃastvəvəʈ v ɛtəj

nʌsˈtaɳɩt ˈnovəjə| ʃtʃɩˈʂļivəjə ˏʒɨʒn̩‖

16 ˏʒɨʒn̩ɩ| mɬ ɳɩ ˈbudɩm kʌˏɳɛʃnə ‖ no mɬ dļɩ ɳɩˈjo ʒɬˈyom ʈɩˈpeɽ ‖

17 rʌˈbotə(j)ɩm ‖ ˈnu ‖ strʌˈda(j)ɩm ‖ mɬ tvʌˈɽim jɩˏjo ‖ ɩ ˈv ɛtəm

ɩ ˈv ɛtəm|

18 ʌˈdnom ‖ ˈtseļ naʃtvə bɬʈɩˈja ‖ i ˈjeşɩ xʌˈʈiʈɩ ‖ ˈnaʃɬ ˈʃtʃæʂʈjɩ‖

(ˈa ˈpɛ ˈtʃɛxəf‖ ˈtɽi ʂɩsˈtɽɨ‖)

8 разовьют его, но жизнь останется все та же, жизнь трудная,
9 полная тайн и счастливая. И человек через тысячу лет,
человек   10 будет так же вздыхать: ,,ах, тяжко жить! ''—
и вместе с тем точно так   11 же, как теперь, он будет
бояться и не хотеть смерти.

12 *Вершинин* (*подумав*). Как вам сказать? Мне кажется, все
на земле   13 должно измениться мало-помалу и уже
меняется на наших   14 глазах. Через двести-триста,
наконец, тысячу лет, — дело не   15 в сроке, — настанет
новая счастливая жизнь. Участвовать в этой   16 жизни
мы не будем, конечно, но мы для нее живем теперь,
17 работаем, ну, страдаем, мы творим ее — и в этом
18 одном цель нашего бытия и, если хотите, наше счастье.

(А. П. Чехов, Три сестры)

perhaps, and develop it, but life will still remain the same—
difficult, full of mysteries and yet happy. And man in a
thousand year's time, man will still sigh:—'Oh! how hard
life is!'—and at the same time he'll be afraid of death and
want to go on living, just as he does today.
Vershinin (*after a moment's thought*): How shall I put it to you?
I think that everything on earth is bound to change gradually,
and is changing before our very eyes. In two or three hundred
years—a thousand years, if you like—it's not a matter of how
long—a new, happy life will come. Of course we won't take
part in that life, but we're living for it now, working and
suffering for it, we're creating it—and in that alone lies the
point of our existence and, if you like, our happiness.

(A. P. Chekhov, The Three Sisters)

26. PASSAGES FOR PRACTICE

8

1 no ˈkromʮ ˌpeʂʮn ‖ u‿ˈnaz bʮlə jʮʃˈtʃo| ˈŋetʃtə xʌˈroʃtjʮ ‖ ˈŋetʃtə

  u‿ˈnaz bʮlə jʮʃtʃo ˈnetʃtə xʌˈroʃtjʮ ‖

2 ʝüˈhiməjʮ ˌnamʮ ‖ ʮ ˈmoʒʮdbʮʇ zəmʮˈŋafʃtjʮ nam ˈsontst‖ və‿ftʌˈrom

3 ʮtʌˈʒɛ naʃtvə ˈdomə pəmʮʃˈtʃaləs zələtʌˈʃyejŋə‖ i v‿ˈŋej ‖ sʮʮdʮ

  i v‿ˈŋej ‖ sʮʮdʮ

4 ˈmnog,ʮx ˈdɛvuʃtk məʂʮˈrits ‖ ʒʮˈla ʃʮsnətsəʇʮˈlɛʇŋəjə ˈgorŋʮtʃnəjə

  ˈmnog,ʮx ˈdɛvuʃtk məʂʮˈrits ‖

5 ˈtaŋə‖ ˈkaʒdəjʮ ˈutrə ‖ k ʂʮˈklu ʌˈkoʃttʃkə ‖ pʮʮslʌˈŋaləs ˈmaʝʮŋkəjʮ

  pʮʮslʌˈŋaləs ˈmaʝʮŋkəjʮ

6 ˈrozəvəjʮ ˈʝitʃʮkə ‖ z gəluˈbimʮ yʮˈʂoltmʮ glʌˈzamʮ ‖ ʮ ˈzvonkʮ(j)

  ˈrozəvəjʮ ˈʝitʃʮkə ‖

7 ˈlaskəvʮ(j) ˈgoləs kʮʮˈtʃal nam‖

8 ʌʮʮsˈtaŋʇʮkʮ‖ ˈdajʇʮ kʮʮŋdʮˈʝetʃkəf‖

  ʌʮʮsˈtaŋʇʮkʮ‖ ˈdajʇʮ kʮʮŋdʮˈʝötʃkəf‖

9 mʮ ˈfʂɛ ʌbʌˈratʃʮvəʝʮs nʌ‿ɛtət ˈjasnʮ(j) ˈzvuk ‖ ʮ ˈradəs(t)nə dəbrʌ-

  mʮ ˈfʂɛ ʌbʌˈratʃʮvəʝʮs nʌ‿ɛtət 'jasnʮ(j) 'zvuk ‖ ʮ ˈradəs(t)nə ‖ dəbrʌ-

10 ˈduʃnə smʌˈtʮeʝʮ nʌ‿ˈtʃistəjʮ ˈdɛyʮtʃjʮ ʝʮˈtso ‖ ˈslavnə ultˈbafʃtjʮʂə

  ˈduʃnə ‖ smʌˈtʮeʝʮ nʌ‿ˈtʃistəjʮ ˈdɛyʮtʃjʮ ʝʮˈtso ‖

11 nam‖ ˈnam bʮlə pʮʮˈjatnə| yidʮʇ pʮʮˈpʝusnutʮ(j) k ʂʮˌklu ˈnos ‖ ʮ

  ˈnam bʮlə pʮʮˈjatnə ˌyidʮʇ pʮʮˌpʝusnutʮ(j) k ʂʮˌklu ˈnos ‖ ʮ

12 ˈmɛlkʮjʮ ˈhɛltjʮ ˈzubʮ| bʝʮʂˈʇɛfʃtjʮ ʮspʌd‿ˈrozəvʮɣ ˈgup| ʌtˈkritʮx

  ˈmɛlkʮjʮ ˈbɛltjʮ ˈzubʮ|

278

8

1 Но, кроме песен, у нас было еще нечто хорошее, нечто
2 любимое нами и, может быть, заменявшее нам солнце. Во
втором 3 этаже нашего дома помещалась золотошвейня,
и в ней, среди 4 многих девушек-мастериц, жила шест-
надцатилетняя горничная 5 Таня. Каждое утро к стеклу
окошечка...прислонялось маленькое 6 розовое личико
с голубыми веселыми глазами, и звонкий 7 ласковый
голос кричал нам:
8 — Арестантики! дайте кренделечков!
9 Мы все оборачивались на этот ясный звук и радостно,
добро- 10 душно смотрели на чистое девичье лицо, славно
улыбавшееся 11 нам. Нам было приятно видеть приплю-
снутый к стеклу нос и 12 мелкие белые зубы, блестевшие
из-под розовых губ, открытых

But apart from singing we had something else that was good,
something which we loved and which perhaps took the place of
the sun for us. On the second[1] floor of our house there was a
gold-embroidery workshop and among the many embroideresses
who worked there there lived a sixteen-year-old maidservant
called Tanya. Every morning, she would press her rosy little
face, with her merry blue eyes, against the glass of the small
window and her sweet, clear voice would call out to us:
'Convicts, dear convicts! May I have some pretzels, please?'
We would all turn round when we heard this limpid sound
and joyfully, benignly look at the pure girlish face smiling so
wonderfully at us. We loved to see her nose pressed to the glass
and her little white teeth gleaming behind her pink lips, opened

[1] Cf. the note to passage 3, p. 261.

13 u˙lĭpkəj‖ mι brʌˉsaʃιʂ ʌtˉkrĭʈ jej ˉd̦yeɾ| tʌlˉkajə drug ˉdrugə ‖ i ˉvot

   mι brʌˉsaʃιʂ ʌtˉkrĭʈ jej ˉd̦yeɾ ‖ tʌlˉkajə drug ˉdrugə ‖ i ˉvot

14 ʌˉna| yιˉʃoləjə tʌˈkajə| ˉm̦iləjə ‖ ˉfxodιt k ˈnam| pətstʌˉvʃæjə svoj

   ʌna| yιˉʃoləjə tʌˌkajə ‖ ˉm̦iləjə ‖ ˉfxodιt k ˉnam ‖ pətstʌˉvʃæjə svoj

15 p̦ιˉɾedn̦ιk‖ stʌˉ(j)it p̦ιɾιd ˉnam̦ι ‖ sklʌˉn̦if n̦ιmnogə ˉnabək svʌju

   p̦ιˉɾedn̦ιk ‖ stʌˉ(j)it p̦ιɾιd ˈnam̦ι ‖ sklʌˉn̦if n̦ιmnogə ˉnabək svʌju

16 gʌˉlofku ‖ stʌˉ(j)it ‖ i ˉfʂo ultˉba(j)ιtsə‖

   gʌˉlofku ‖

   (mʌˉkʂim ˉgoɾk̦ι(j)‖ ˉdvatsəʈ ˉʃeʂʈ ι ʌˉdna‖)

9

1   n̦ι ˉto ʃtop on bιl tak truˉʂʃif| i zʌˉḫit‖ sʌfˉʂɛm daʒι nʌˉproʈιf‖ no

   ʃtəb

2 ʂ ˉn̦ɛkətərəvə ˉvɾem̦ιn̦ι ‖ on bιl v rəzdrʌˉʒĭʈιʃnəm i nəpɾιˉʒonnəm

3 səstʌˉjæn̦(ι)jι pʌˉxoʒιm nʌ ιpʌˉxondɾιju‖ on də tʌˉvo ugluˉḫilsə

4 f ʂιˉḫa ‖ i ujιdιˉn̦ilsə ʌt ˉfʂɛx ‖ ʃtə bʌˉjalsə daʒι ˉfʂakəj ˉfstɾetʃι ‖ n̦ι

   ‖ i ujιdιˉn̦ilsə ʌt ˌfʂɛx ‖ ʃtə bʌˉjalsə   ˉfʂakəj ˌfstɾetʃι ‖

5 ˉtoʃkə ˌfstɾetʃι s xʌˌʐæjkəj‖ on bιl zʌˉdavʃιn ˉḫednəʂtju‖ no daʒι

                                                            no daʒι

6 ʂʈιˉʂn̦onnəjι pəlʌˉʒen(ι)jι ‖ p̦ιɾιsˉtalə f pʌʂʃedn̦ι(j)ι ˉvɾemə ʈιgʌˉʈiʂ

   ʂʈιˉʂn̦onnəjι pəlʌˉʒen(ι)jι p̦ιɾιsˉtalə f pʌʂʃedn̦ι(j)ι ˉvɾemə ʈιgʌˉʈiʂ

7 jιvo‖ nʌˉsuʃtʃnιm̦ι d̦ιˉlam̦ι svʌ(j)im̦ι| on sʌfˉʂɛm p̦ιɾιsˉtal i n̦ι xʌˉʈɛl

   jιvo‖ nʌˉsuʃtʃnĭm̦ι d̦ιˉlam̦ι svʌ(j)im̦ι| on sʌfˉʂɛm p̦ιɾιsˉtal i n̦ι xʌˉʈɛl

13 улыбкой. Мы бросались открыть ей дверь, толкая друг друга, и — вот 14 она, — веселая такая, милая, — входит к нам, подставляя свой 15 передник, стоит перед нами, склонив немного набок свою 16 головку, стоит и все улыбается.

(Максим Горький, *Двадцать шесть и одна*)

in a smile. We would rush to open the door for her, jostling each other, and in she would come, so cheerful, so sweet, holding out her apron, and stand in front of us, her little head tilted slightly to one side—she would stand there, all smiles.

(Maxim Gorky, *Twenty-six Men and a Girl*)

9

1 Не то чтоб он был так труслив и забит, совсем даже напротив; но 2 с некоторого времени он был в раздражительном и напряженном 3 состоянии, похожем на ипохондрию. Он до того углубился 4 в себя и уединился от всех, что боялся даже всякой встречи, не 5 только встречи с хозяйкой. Он был задавлен бедностью; но даже 6 стесненное положение перестало в последнее время тяготить 7 его. Насущными делами своими он совсем перестал и не хотел

It was not that he was so cowardly and downtrodden, indeed quite the contrary; but for some time he had been in an irritable, tense state, like a morbid depression. He had so withdrawn into himself, had so secluded himself from everybody, that he was afraid of any encounter, not merely an encounter with his landlady. He was crushed by poverty; but even his straitened circumstances had lately ceased to hang heavy upon him. He had completely ceased to bother himself about the necessities of

26. PASSAGES FOR PRACTICE

8 zəŋɩˌmatsə‖ ŋɩkʌˇkoj xʌˇʒæjk̩ɩ| f ˌsuʃtʃnəs̩tɩ on ŋɩ bʌˇjalsə‖ ʃto bɩ ˇta

zəŋɩˇmatsə‖ ŋɩkʌˇkoj xʌˇʒæjkɩ f ˌsuʃtʃnəs̩tɩ on ŋɩ bʌˇjalsə‖

9 ŋɩ zəmtˇʃ|alə proȶ̩ɩf ŋɩvo‖ no ʌstʌˇnav|ɩvətsə nʌ ˬ|eʃ̩ŋɩtst‖ ˇsluʃəȶ

‖ no ʌstʌˇnav|ɩvətsə nʌ ˬ|eʃ̩ŋɩtst‖

10 fŞækɩ(j) ˇvzdor‖ prʌˬɛtu fŞu ʌˇbɨd̩ɩnuju dɽɩȟ̩ɩˇdeŋ| də k̩ʌ'torəj jɩmu

prʌˇfŞu ɛtu ʌˇbɨd̩ɩnuju dɽɩȟ̩ɩˇdeŋ‖ də k̩ʌˇtorəj jimu

11 'ŋɛt ŋɩkʌ'kovə 'd̩ɛlə‖ ˇfŞɛ eȶ̩ɩ pɽɩstʌˇvaŋ(ɩ)jə ʌ p̩|ʌȶɩˇʒɛ| u'grozɩ|

ˇŋɛt ŋɩkʌˇkovə ˇd̩ɛlə‖ ˇfŞɛ eȶ̩ɩ pɽɩstʌˇvaŋ(ɩ)jə ʌ p̩|ʌȶɩˇʒɛ‖ uˇgrozɩ‖

12 'ʒaləbɩ‖ i pɽɩ ˬɛtəm səmʌˇmu ɩzvʌˇratʃ|ɩvətsə‖ ɩzyɩˇŋatsə‖ ˇ|gaȶ‖

ˇʒaləbɩ‖

13 ˇŋɛt‖ uʃ ˇlut-ʃɩ prʌskʌ|ˇznuȶ kakŋɩbuȶ ˇkoʃkəj pʌ 'leʃ̩ŋɩtst i u|ɩˇznuȶ‖

‖ uʃ ˇlut-ʃɩ prʌskʌ|ˇznuȶ kakŋɩbuȶ ˇkoʃkəj pʌ ˌleʃ̩ŋɩtst| i u|ɩˇznuȶ

14 ʃtəbɩ ŋɩkˇto ŋɩ yɩˇdal

(ˇɛf ˇɛm dəstʌˇjɛfsk̩(ɩ)j‖ pɽɩstuˇp̩|eŋ(ɩ)jɩ ɩ nəkʌˇzaŋ(ɩ)jɩ|‖)

10

1 ʌˇgromnɩ(j) kəȟ̩ɩˇŋɛt bɩl nʌˇpolŋɩn yɩʃˇtʃamɩ ʌtʃɩˇyidnə ȟɩspɽɩs-

ʌˇgromnɩ(j) kəȟ̩ɩˇŋɛt bɩl nʌˇpolŋɩn yɩʃˇtʃamɩ‖ ʌtʃɩˇyidnə ȟɩspɽɩs-

2 ˇtannə upətɽɩˇb|æ(j)ɩmɩm̩ɩ‖ bʌ|ˇʃoj ˬstol| nə k̩ʌˌtorəm |ɩˌʒa|ɩ ˇkŋigˌɩ ɩ

ˇtannə upətɽɩˇb|æ(j)ɩmɩm̩ɩ‖ bʌ|ˇʃoj ˇstol‖ nə k̩ʌˇtorəm |ɩˇʒa|ɩ ˇkŋigˌɩ| ɩ

3 ˇplanɩ‖ vɩˇsokɩ(j)ɩ ş̩ɩˇk|annɩ(j)ɩ ʃkʌˇfɨ ȟɩb|ɩʌˇȶekɩ| s k̩|üˇtʃæmɩ

ˇplanɩ‖ vɩˇsokɩ(j)ɩ ş̩ɩˇk|annɩ(j)ɩ ʃkʌˇfɨ ȟɩb|ɩʌˇȶekɩ‖ s k̩|üˇtʃæmɩ

4 v 'd̩yɛrtsəx‖ vɩˇsokɩ(j) ˇstol| d̩|ɩ pɩ'saŋ(ɩ)jə f stʌ'jætʃ|ɩm pəlʌ'ʒeŋ(ɩ)jɩ|

v ˇd̩yɛrtsəx‖ vɩˇsokɩ(j) ˇstol| d̩|ɩ pɩˇsaŋ(ɩ)jə f stʌˇjætʃ|ɩm pəlʌˌʒeŋ(ɩ)jɩ‖

26. PASSAGES FOR PRACTICE

8 заниматься. Никакой хозяйки в сущности он не боялся, что бы та 9 ни замышляла против него. Но останавливаться на лестнице, слушать 10 всякий вздор про всю эту обыденную дребедень, до которой ему 11 нет никакого дела, все эти приставания о платеже, угрозы, 12 жалобы, и при этом самому изворачиваться, извиняться, лгать, — 13 нет, уж лучше проскользнуть как-нибудь кошкой по лестнице и улизнуть, 14 чтобы никто не видал.

(Ф. М. Достоевский, Преступление и наказание)

life and had no desire to. He was not in fact afraid of any land-lady, whatever she might design against him. But to stop on the stair, to listen to all sorts of nonsense about all these mundane trivialities, which did not in the least concern him, all these demands for rent, threats, complaints, and at the same time to have to resort to various shifts, to find excuses, to lie—no, he preferred to slip up the stair somehow, like a cat, to steal past, so that nobody saw him.

(F. M. Dostoyevsky, Crime and Punishment)

10

1 Огромный кабинет был наполнен вещами, очевидно беспрес- 2 танно употребляемыми. Большой стол, на котором лежали книги и 3 планы, высокие стеклянные шкафы библиотеки с ключами 4 в дверцах, высокий стол для писания в стоячем положении,

The huge study was full of things which were obviously in constant use. The large table, on which there lay books and plans, the tall, glass-fronted book-cases, with keys in the doors, the tall desk for writing standing up, on which there lay an open

26. PASSAGES FOR PRACTICE

5 nə kʌˈtorəm ǀɩˈʒalə ʌtˈkritəjə ʦɩˈtraʦ ‖ tʌˈkarnt(j) stʌˈnok ‖ s̠ rʌˈzlo-

nə kʌˈtorəm ǀɩʒalə ʌtˈkritəjə ʦɩˈtraʦ ‖ tʌˈkarnt(j) stʌˈnok| s̠ rʌˈzlo-

6 ʒtntmɩ ɩnstruˈmɛntəmɩ ‖ ɩ s̠ rʌsˈsɩpəntmɩ kruˈgom ˈstruʃkəmɩ ‖ ˈfʂo

ʒtnɩmɩ ɩnstruˈmɛntəmɩ ɩ s̠ rʌsˈsɩpəntmɩ kruˈgom ˈstruʃkəmɩ ‖

7 vtˈkaztvələ pəstʌˈjannuju rəznʌʌˈbraznuju ɩ pəˈɾadətʃnuju ˈdejəʦɩ-

8 nəʂʦ‖ pə dyɩˈʒeɳɩjəm ɳɩbʌǀˈʃoj nʌˈg̠ɩ ‖ pʌ ˈʦyordəmu nəǀɩˈgaɳɩju

pə dyɩˈʒeɳɩjəm ɳɩbʌǀʃoj nʌˈg̠ɩ ‖ pʌ ˈʦyordəmu nəǀɩˈgaɳɩju

9 ˈʒiǀɩstəj suxʌʃˈtʃavəj ruˈķi ‖ yɩˈdna bɩla fˈknæʒɩ jɩʃtʃo uˈpornəjə ɩ

ˈʒiǀɩstəj suxʌʃˈtʃavəj ruˈķi ‖ yɩˈdna bɩla f ˈknæʒɩ jɩʃtʃo uˈpornəjə ɩ

10 ˈmnogə vtˈderʒɩvəjüʃtʃəjə ˈʃilə ˈʂyɛʒej ˈstarəʂʦɩ‖ ˈʒdɛləf ˈɳɛskəǀkə

mnogə yɩˈderʒɩvəjüʃtʃəjə ˈʃilə ˈʂyɛʒəj ˈstarəʂʦɩ‖ ˈʒdɛləf ɳɛskəǀkə

11 kruˈgof ‖ on ˈʂɳal ˈnogu s̠ ɳɩˈdaǀɩ stʌnˈka ‖ ʌpˈʦor stʌˈmɛsku ‖ ˈķinul

kruˈgof ‖ ˈķinul

12 jɩjo f ˈkoʒənt(j) kʌrˈman| pɾɩˈdɛlənt(j) k̠ stʌnˈku ‖ ɩ pədəjˈda k̠ stʌˈlu|

jɩjo f ˈkoʒənt(j) kʌrˈman|

13 pədʌzˈval ˈdotʃ‖ on ɳɩkʌgˈda ɳɩ bləgəslʌˈvǀal svʌjiẏ dɩ,ʦej ‖ ɩ ˈtoǀkə

ɩ ˈtoǀkə

14 pət-sˈtayɩf jɩj ʃtʃɩˈʦiɳɩstuju| jɩʃtʃo ɳɩ ˈbrituju ˈniɳtʃɩ ˈʃtʃoku| skʌˈzal ‖

pət-sˈtayɩf jɩj ʃtʃɩˈʦiɳɩstuju jɩʃtʃo ɳɩ ˈbrituju niɳtʃɩ ˈʃtʃoku ‖

15 ˈstrogə ɩ vmɛʂʦɩ ş ˈʦem vɳɩˈmaʦɩǀnə ˈɳɛʒnə ʌgǀɩˈdɛf jɩjo‖

ˈstrogə ɩ ˈvmɛʂʦɩ ş ʦem vɳɩˈmaʦɩǀnə ˈɳɛʒnə ʌgǀɩˈdɛf jɩjo‖

16 zdʌˈrovə‖ ˈnu ‖ ˈtak sʌˈdiʂ‖

tak sʌˈdiʂ‖

(ˈeǀ ˈɛn tʌlsˈtoj‖ vʌjˈna i ˈmir‖)

5 на котором лежала открытая тетрадь, токарный станок, с разло- 6 женными инструментами и с рассыпанными кругом стружками, — все 7 выказывало постоянную, разнообразную и порядочную деятель- 8 ность. По движениям небольшой ноги...по твердому налеганию 9 жилистой, сухощавой руки видна была в князе еще упорная и 10 много выдерживающая сила свежей старости. Сделав несколько 11 кругов, он снял ногу с педали станка, обтер стамеску, кинул 12 ее в кожаный карман, приделанный к станку, и, подойдя к столу, 13 подозвал дочь. Он никогда не благословлял своих детей и только, 14 подставив ей щетинистую, еще не бритую нынче щеку, сказал, 15 строго и вместе с тем внимательно-нежно оглядев ее:

16 — Здорова?...ну, так садись!

(Л. Н. Толстой, *Война и мир*)

exercise-book, the lathe, with tools set out and shavings scattered around—all bespoke a constant, varied and orderly activity. The movements of the small foot and the firm pressure of the lean, sinewy hand showed that the prince had the still resilient, tenacious vigour of an active old age. He made a few more turns of the lathe and then removed his foot from the pedal, wiped his chisel, dropped it into a leather pocket attached to the lathe, and going over to the table summoned his daughter. He had never been in the habit of blessing his children and so he merely offered her his bristly cheek, as yet unshaven that day, and, eyeing her sternly and yet with attentive tenderness, said:

'You well?...Right, sit down then.'

(L. N. Tolstoy, *War and Peace*)

EAR-TRAINING EXERCISES

A 1.1 The teacher of Russian phonetics should make his pupils thoroughly familiar with the acoustic qualities of the Russian vowels. To this end he should say the vowels aloud a large number of times in a fixed order. He should number the vowels and give the pupils the phonetic symbols, and each pupil should have a copy of the following list in a place where he can refer to it constantly:

i	ɨ	ʟ	t	ɛ	e	a	æ	ʌ	ə	o	ö	u	ü
1	2	3	4	5	6	7	8	9	10	11	12	13	14

A 1.2 This list contains only the vowels to which distinct symbols are constantly allotted in the phonetic transcriptions in this book. The other vowel sounds, to which distinct symbols were assigned only in discussing particular points of pronunciation, may be introduced when the pupils can recognize all the above vowels with certainty, both in isolation and in fairly difficult combinations.

A 1.3 When the teacher has said these fourteen vowels a large number of times in the above order, he should then say them in mixed order and ask the pupils to give the numbers of the vowels dictated.

A 1.4 When the pupils can give the numbers correctly, the teacher should begin dictating sequences of sounds, introducing consonants in order of difficulty. The words which he dictates should be written down phonetically by the pupils. It does not as a rule seem necessary to number the consonants.

A 1.5 When a new consonant is introduced for the first time, it should be repeated a number of times by itself and in combinations with various vowels.

A 1.6 The following are some examples to illustrate the sort of 'words' that should be dictated by the teacher:

(1) With easy consonants (p, b, t, d, k, ķ, g, g̦, m, n, r, f, v,

A 1. EAR-TRAINING EXERCISES

s, z, ʃ, ʒ, ts, dz, tʃ, dʒ, j, ɲ, ɥ, m̥, f, ɣ): pagˌɛno, muḳida, ʃɛvatu, sɨboma, gˌemɨʒɛ, raḳivt, guʃɨft, tsɨmotku, kɨfadzɛ, nədʒɨpu, vəbutʃkʌʒ, tsɛdnamʃʌg, ɦejudʌrtʃ, fmˌɛgortstn, dʒɨyjɨtnuɲ, rɨfemtsarv, ʒutsnərɦor, m̥üʃæɦjond, grʌməskrɨʃk, tʃætʃɨfḳigʒ, ɲjöyjatnəʃ, jejümˌokn, ʃtʃüdnəbkrɨ, fnɨʃtʃɛznært.

(2) With difficult consonants (l, ḷ, ṭ, ḍ, ṇ, ṣ, ẓ, ṛ, x, χ): ʌldurgˌɛʃ, laʒrtḷaʃt, ṭæḷɛdnoʒ, lɨdütʃtorg, mtṇüʃtʃöṭ, ṛɛʒdoṇtl, ploxatsṭɛrnə, taṛuvnʌg, fjeṣoxarlɨ, bʒolχüyjöṇ, ẓeḷdæχɨr, xəʃloʃtʃeẓṇi, m̥üḷaʒdöṛ, krutaẓḷɨtst, ɲjɨṛɛdzdyöṛṭ, fstglɛbnujə, kxoχɨbaḷ, mḷardnəjüṣṭɨ.

(3) With diphthongs: ḍatnəjvlux, blʌjṇɛdtj, vḷöṭʃtʃüjfjɨməj, skroʒʒejmjeṛ, lujdʒntjɦöṣ, tʃtzzəjvuṭṭɛl.

A 1.7 The teacher should invent some hundreds of such words, adapting them to the needs of his various pupils.

REMARKS ON RUSSIAN ORTHOGRAPHY[1]

A 2.1 Throughout this book phonetic forms are followed by orthographic versions of words, and before the sections illustrating the various sounds there are remarks on their orthographic representation. Although the system of Russian orthography could largely be pieced together from this material and from chapter 23 (Similitude and Assimilation), this appendix gives, in more easily accessible form, the general principles of Russian orthography.

[1] Students of the Russian language will already be familiar with the principles of Russian orthography. Students of phonetics may not be: this appendix is included largely for their benefit. More detailed discussion (in English) of Russian orthography will be found in D. Ward's *The Russian Language Today* (Hutchinson, 1965), pp. 69–77, and 'A Critique of Russian Orthography' (in *In Honour of Daniel Jones*, ed. D. Abercrombie et al.), pp. 384–94.

The syllabic mode

A 2.2   The Russian alphabet has thirty-two letters, viz.:

Upper case	Lower case	Italic upper case	Italic lower case	Upper case	Lower case	Italic upper case	Italic lower case
А	а	*А*	*а*	Р	р	*Р*	*р*
Б	б	*Б*	*б*	С	с	*С*	*с*
В	в	*В*	*в*	Т	т	*Т*	*m*
Г	г	*Г*	*г*	У	у	*У*	*у*
Д	д	*Д*	*д*	Ф	ф	*Ф*	*ф*
Е	е	*Е*	*е*	Х	х	*Х*	*х*
Ж	ж	*Ж*	*ж*	Ц	ц	*Ц*	*ц*
З	з	*З*	*з*	Ч	ч	*Ч*	*ч*
И	и	*И*	*и*	Ш	ш	*Ш*	*ш*
Й	й	*Й*	*й*	Щ	щ	*Щ*	*щ*
К	к	*К*	*к*	Ъ	ъ	*Ъ*	*ъ*
Л	л	*Л*	*л*	Ы	ы	*Ы*	*ы*
М	м	*М*	*м*	Ь	ь	*Ь*	*ь*
Н	н	*Н*	*н*	Э	э	*Э*	*э*
О	о	*О*	*о*	Ю	ю	*Ю*	*ю*
П	п	*П*	*п*	Я	я	*Я*	*я*

A 2.3   Eight of these letters are vowel-letters, viz.: а, е, и, о, у, э, ю, я; one, й, represents the phoneme j, usually as the end-point of a diphthong, occasionally as a consonant before a vowel; two, ъ and ь, are 'auxiliary' signs, having no phonetic value on their own (their function is described below); and the remaining twenty-one are consonant letters.

A 2.4   This apparent deficiency of an alphabet of thirty-two letters, in face of the larger number of phonemes, is made good by the fact that most of the consonant letters represent either hard consonants or palatalized (soft) consonants, depending on what follows, and that several of the vowel-letters have a two-fold function. They indicate not only a certain vowel value but also the fact that the vowel sound is preceded by j if there is no consonant letter immediately preceding the vowel-letter, or that certain consonant letters immediately preceding the vowel-letter in the same word represent palatalized consonants. The vowel-letters which indicate that certain preceding consonant letters represent palatalized consonants, and which may conveniently be called 'softening vowel-letters',[1] are e, и, ю and я. Thus:

	'sadu	саду	(garden, *dat. sing.*),
but	'ṣadu	сяду	(I shall sit)
and	jat	яд	(poison);
	tuk	туг	(tight, *sh. fm. masc.*),
but	ṭuk	тюк	(bale)
and	juk	юг	(south);
	nos	нос	(nose),
but	ŋos	нес	(carried)
and	joʃ	еж	(hedgehog).

A 2.5 The letter e, when accented, represents either the vowel-phoneme o, as in the preceding example, or the vowel-phoneme e. In the latter case the corresponding non-softening vowel-letter is э. This letter, however, does not occur in many words and in most of them it is in initial position. An example of the contrasting function of э and e is, however, provided by

	sɛr	сэр	(sir),
but	ṣɛr	сер	(grey, *sh. fm. masc.*)
and	jɛst	ест	(eats).

A 2.6 The letter и is also a softening vowel-letter, corresponding to the non-softening vowel letter ы. There are two points to be noted with regard to this pair of letters. First, while ы always represents the non-front allophones ɨ and ᵼ of the i-phoneme, и represents the front allophones i and ɩ except after the letters ж, ш and ц and in certain compounds (see p. 295), and, sometimes, at word juncture (see §§ 12.31, 47). Thus

	sɨt	сыт	(satiated, *sh. fm. masc.*),
but	ṣit	сит	(sieve, *gen. pl.*).

Secondly, the letter и has the twofold value ji or jɩ only *within*

---

[1] The term 'soft vowel-letters', which is often used, is not appropriate since neither the vowel-letters nor the vowels which they represent can be said to be soft (palatalized).

a word when not immediately preceded by a consonant letter. In absolute initial position it does not have this twofold value (with one set of exceptions; see below) but simply the value i or ι. Thus

	mʌ'jix	моих	(my, *gen.*, *prep. pl.*),
but	'igəɾ	Игорь	(Igor)
and	ι'van	Иван	(Ivan).

The words их, им, ими (they, resp. *gen.-prep.*, *dat.*, *instr.*) are usually pronounced ix, im, 'iɱι but have an alternative pronunciation jix, jim, 'jiɱι.

A 2.7 The other softening vowel-letters do not have this restriction on their twofold value, as may be seen from the examples given in preceding paragraphs.

A 2.8 From preceding paragraphs and from remarks and illustrations elsewhere in this book it is evident that the phonetic value of, say, the letter т depends on what other letters it is associated with. Thus, in та (that, *nom. fem.*) the letter т = t, but in те (those, *nom.*) т = ţ. This feature of Russian orthography may be conveniently referred to as a 'syllabic mode'.

A 2.9 The letter ь, called in Russian 'ɱaxķι(j) znak мягкий знак (soft sign), indicates that the preceding consonant letter represents a palatalized consonant. It occurs in three positions:

(*a*) At the end of a word, as in

| | oş | ось | (axle), |
| cf. | os | ос | (wasp, *gen. pl.*). |

(*b*) Between two consonant letters, where it indicates the 'independent' softness of the first consonant, as in

	'reţkə	редька	(radish),
cf.	'rɛtkə	редко	(rarely)
and	'poļkə	полька	(Polishwoman),
cf.	'polkə	полка	(shelf).

(*c*) Between a consonant letter and one of the softening vowel-letters, where it indicates both that the consonant letter represents a palatalized consonant (see, however, p. 296) and that the vowel-letter has the twofold value of j + vowel-sound, as in

	'goʂtjə	гостья	(guest, *fem.*)
(cf.	'goʂtə	гостя	(guest, *gen. sing. masc.*))
and	ljot	льет	(pours),
(cf.	lot	лед	(ice)).

A 2.10 In the last case, while indicating the occurrence of a palatalized consonant, the soft sign also has the function of 'separating' sign, called in Russian rəzdɪ'ḷiʈɪḷnt(j) znak разде-лительный знак.

A 2.11 This is the sole function of the letter ъ, called in Russian 'ţyordɪ(j) znak твердый знак (hard sign). It occurs only between a consonant letter and a softening vowel-letter,[1] its function being to indicate that while the vowel-letter has the twofold value of j + vowel-sound, the consonant letter represents a hard consonant (see, however, p. 298), as in

	ʌ'tjɛst	отъезд	(departure),
(cf.	ʌ'ţɛts	отец	(father))
and	ʌ'bjɛtkɪ	объедки	(leavings)
(cf.	ʌ'ḃɛt	обед	(dinner)).

The morphophonematic principle

A 2.12 A perusal of the examples given in chapter 23 (Similitude and Assimilation) will reveal that Russian orthography does not register similitudes and assimilations, i.e. it does not indicate either the vowel substitutions brought about by a shift in the position of the accent nor consonant substitutions brought about by the influence of neighbouring consonants. Thus, by and large, Russian orthography registers morphemes[2] in their 'basic' phonematic form, stripped, as it were, of any changes brought about in their constituent phonemes by accent-shift and consonantal influence. This feature of Russian orthography may be called the 'morphophonematic principle'.

---

[1] In the 'Old Orthography' (pre-1917) it also occurred at the end of every word which did not end in a vowel letter or ь. Some émigré publications still adhere to this convention.

[2] A 'morpheme' is, roughly speaking, an ultimate lexico-grammatical unit of a language. By 'ultimate' here we mean that it cannot be further reduced without loss of or change in its lexical and/or grammatical meaning.

A 2. REMARKS ON RUSSIAN ORTHOGRAPHY

A 2.13 Operating together with the syllabic mode, the morphophonematic principle results in the continuing orthographic identity of one and the same morpheme in varying phonetic conditions, as may be illustrated by the following table, where column 1 gives the orthographic form, with meaning in brackets, column 2 the phonetic form, and column 3 the phonematic form.

1		2	3
(*morpheme 'carry'*)			
носка	(carrying)	'noskə	'noska
носит	(carries)	'noʂɪt	'noʂit
носить	(to carry)	nʌ'ʂiʈ	na'ʂiʈ
вынос	(carrying out)	'vɨnəs	'vinas
выносить	(to give birth to)	'vɨnəʂɪʈ	'vinaʂiʈ
(*morpheme 'perfective'*)			
сыграть	(to play)	sɨ'graʈ	si'graʈ
сбалансировать	(to balance)	zbəlʌn'ʂirəvəʈ	zbalaŋ'ʂiravaʈ
сделать	(to do)	'zdɛləʈ	'zdelaʈ
сшить	(to sew)	ʃʃiʈ	ʃʃiʈ
сжать	(to reap)	ʒʒaʈ	ʒʒaʈ

Further points

A 2.14 Once the syllabic mode and the morphophonematic principle of Russian orthography are understood, then the overwhelming majority of orthographic forms is phonetically lucid, *if the position of the accent is known.* In normal Russian orthography the position of the accent is marked only to avoid ambiguity. Thus, the instrumental of 'sweat' may be written пóтом 'potəm in the rare event of a possibility of confusing it with потом pʌ'tom (then), and where the word 'what' may be confused with the conjunction 'that' it is provided with an accent-mark: чтó or чтò.

A 2.15 It has been calculated that in less than 10 per cent of all orthographic forms is the morphophonematic principle not adhered to. This is to say that in these instances, either the

A 2. REMARKS ON RUSSIAN ORTHOGRAPHY

orthography does register assimilative changes or that morpho-phonematic analysis of the contemporary language cannot support a particular spelling. Examples of the former case are provided by

'nozdrɪ	ноздри	(nostrils),

which may be compared with

	nos	нос	(nose)
and	'svaɖbə	свадьба	(marriage),

which may be compared with

svat	сват	(marriage-broker),

though it is probably true to say that, as far as the latter pair is concerned, the two elements свадь- and сват are now divorced and that the connexion between нос and ноздри is tenuous.

A 2.16 An example of a spelling which cannot be supported by morphophonematic analysis is provided by

bʌ'lotə	болото	(swamp)

since in no forms of this word or cognate words does the accent fall on the first syllable.[1] Such spellings may be said to be 'etymological', reflecting the pronunciation of past times.

A 2.17 Among other points which should be made are the following:

1. The genitive masculine and neuter ending of adjectives and some pronouns is written -oro and -ero, but here the letter г is purely 'etymological'—the pronunciation is with v, as in

'krasnəvə	красного	(red)
'şiɲɪvə	синего	(blue)
tʌ'vo	того	(that)
fşɪ'vo	всего	(all)

---

[1] The writing of the ending of болото by the letter o is in accordance with the morphophonematic principle, since this ending (a morpheme meaning 'nom.-acc. sing. neuter') is accented in many words and is pronounced o (e.g. ʌ'kno окно *window*).

The same applies where the accusative is identical with the genitive,

jɩ'vo его (him)

In a few words derived from pronouns the letter г also has the phonetic value of v, as in

ṣɩ'voɖŋə сегодня (today)
ɩtʌ'vo итого (altogether)

2. The reflexive particle is written -сь/-ся and was formerly pronounced with hard s. It is now quite common to pronounce the form -сь with palatalized ṣ

ṣmɩ'jöṭɩṣ смеетесь (you laugh)

In the infinitive and the third person singular and plural the reflective particle -ся is pronounced with hard s. This is usually so in the second person singular and past tense masculine too. In some other forms hard s is also heard, but there is a general tendency to adopt a spelling-pronunciation and to pronounce palatalized ṣ.

It should be noted that in the reflexive infinitive which ends -ться the soft sign has no *phonetic* function. In this form the ться and the тся in the third person singular and plural are all pronounced alike, as t-s or frequently, at normal conversational speed, as ts

ṣmɩ'jatsə смеяться (to laugh)
ṣmɩ'jotsə смеется (laughs)
ṣmɩ'jutsə смеются (they laugh)

3. It has already been pointed out above that the letter e in accented position may have the vowel value of the phoneme e or the phoneme o. In the latter instance it is provided with a diaeresis (ё) in normal printed Russian only to avoid ambiguity, thus

	fṣɛ	все	(everybody),
but	fṣo	всё	(everything);
	u'zna(j)ɩm	узнаем	(we shall learn),
but	uznʌ'jom	узнаём	(we learn).

In native words e (ë) can have the value jo, as in

| joʃ | еж | (hedgehog) |
| stˈrjo | сырье | (raw materials) |

but in loanwords jo is written ьо after consonants, otherwise йо, as in

pətʃtʌˈljon	почтальон	(postman)
ʃtˈnjon	шиньон	(chignon)
jot	йод	(iodine)
mʌˈjor	майор	(major)

4. The vowel-letters which occur after ш and ж are а, е, и, о and у but the softening vowel-letters е and и have no effect on the phonetic value of ш and ж. The sequences ʃo and ʒo are written ше and же in most words, but in a few words шо and жо are written, e.g.

ʃof	шов	(seam)
ʃorəx	шорох	(rustle)
ʒox	жох	(sly rogue)
ʌˈbʒorə	обжора	(glutton)

It is noteworthy that in some words verbal and nominal forms are distinguished *orthographically* by ше/же and шо/жо, thus

	ʌˈʒok	ожег	(charred, burnt)
	pʌˈd-ʒok	поджег	(set fire, to),
but	ʌˈʒok	ожог	(a burn, scald)
	pʌˈd-ʒok	поджог	(arson)

After ш and ж the letter и has the value ɨ or ɪ and the letter е in unaccented position has the value ɪ, thus

ʃɨʦ	шить	(to sew)
ʒɨʦ	жить	(to live)
ʒɪtˈvoj	живой	(lively)
ʒɪtˈna	жена	(wife)[1]

---

[1] The present orthographical rules also stipulate that after prefixes of foreign origin and in 'abbreviated compounds' the letter и is written (*without* the softening function) after other consonants—

| ˌpanɪslʌˈmjizm | панисламизм | (pan-Islamism) |
| gəsɪzˈdat | госиздат | (State Publishing House) |

A 2. REMARKS ON RUSSIAN ORTHOGRAPHY

The letters ш and ж are followed by other softening vowel-letters, again without effect on their phonetic value, in a very few words:

pərʌ'ʃut	парашют	(parachute)
brʌ'ʃurə	брошюра	(brochure)
ʒu'ʐi	жюри	(jury)

Like the softening vowel-letters the soft sign has no effect on the phonetic value of ш and ж. It occurs finally in

(a) some feminine nouns

voʃ	вошь	(louse)
loʃ	ложь	(lie)

(b) some imperatives singular

jɛʃ	ешь	(eat!)
ʐɛʃ	режь	(cut!)

(c) the second person singular of the verb

ɳ̩ɪ'ʂoʃ	несешь	(you carry)

(d) some adverbs

nʌ'otməʃ	наотмашь	(with the back of the hand)

and non-finally, with no phonetic function, before consonants, as in such imperatives plural as

'jɛʃʈɪ	ешьте	(eat!)
'ʐɛʃʈɪ	режьте	(cut!)

and, with 'separating function' (see § A 2.10), before vowels, as in

ʃjot	шьет	(sews)
'loʒju	ложью	(lie, *instr. sing.*)

5. The vowel-letters which occur after ц are a, е, и, о, у and ы, but the softening vowel-letters е and и have no effect on the phonetic value of ц. The sequence tso is rare and is spelt цо, the letter sequence це always having the phonetic value tsɛ, tse or, in unaccented position, tsɪ. Both ци and цы have the same phonetic values, the present orthographical rules stipulating that цы is written only in endings and suffixes:

| ʌfˈtsɨ | овцы | (sheep, *gen. sing.*) |
| bɪlʌˈlitst(j) | белолицый | (white-faced) |

and in a few isolated words (and derivatives)

tsɪˈgan	цыган	(gypsy)
ˈtsɨpətʃkɪ	цыпочки	(tip-toes)
tsɪˈplonək	цыпленок	(chicken)
ˈtsɨtsˈtsɨts	цыц-цыц	(chuck-chuck)
ˈtsɨkət	цыкать	(to hush)
fˈtsɨpkəx	в цыпках	(chapped)

In transliterated foreign names, other softening vowel-letters may occur after ц, again without phonetic effect on ts, as in

| ˈtsjurɪx | Цюрих | (Zurich) |

6. The vowel-letters which occur after ч and щ are a, е, и, о and у. These two letters always represent palatalized consonants and their phonetic value is therefore unaffected by the preceding non-softening vowel-letters a, o and y. The letter o is in any case rare after ч and щ, the phoneme o here being represented in most instances by the letter e.

Both letters may be followed by the soft sign, either at the end of a word, when it has no phonetic function, as in

(*a*) feminine nouns such as

| retʃ | речь | (speech) |
| yeʃtʃ | вещь | (thing) |

(*b*) imperatives such as

| platʃ | плачь | (weep!) |

(*c*) infinitives, such as

| tetʃ | течь | (to flow) |

(*d*) adverbs, such as

| protʃ | прочь | (away) |

or non-finally, with no phonetic function, before consonants, as in the imperative plural

| ˈplatʃtɪ | плачьте | (weep!) |

or the imperative singular reflexive

| 'prætʃsə | прячься | (hide!) |

and, with 'separating' function (see above) before vowels, as in

| tʃja | чья | (whose, *nom. sing. fem.*) |
| 'poməʃtʃju | помощью | (help, *instr.*) |

7. After c and з the hard sign, ъ, may have the same function as the soft sign:

| 'sjɛxəʈ | съехать | (to ride down) |
| ɩ'zjæʈ | изъять | (to withdraw) |

This also applies to some loanwords with the hard sign:

| ʌdju'tant | адъютант | (adjutant) |

8. The morphophonematic principle is not adhered to in the orthography of prefixes which in their 'basic' form end in z— they are written with c, not з, before letters representing voiceless consonants. Thus, the prefixes (o)без-, воз-/вз-, из-, низ-, раз-/роз- and через- are written (o)бес-, вос-/вс-, ис-, нис-, рас-/рос- and черес- in such words as

bɪs'krɨlɪ(j)	бескрылый	(wingless)
vʌs'xot	восход	(rise)
ɩspus'kaʈ	испускать	(to emit)
ɳɪsprəyɪr'gaʈ	ниспровергать	(to overthrow)
rəspɪ'satsə	расписаться	(to sign)
tʃɪrɪşşɪ'deɭɳɪk	чересседельник	(girth)

Chart of Russian Consonant Phonemes

	Bilabial		Labio-dental		Dental	Denti-alveolar	Alveolar		Post-alveolar	Palatal	Velar	
		palatalized		palatalized				palatalized				palatalized
Plosive	p b	pʲ bʲ				t d		ʈ ɖ			k g	kʲ
Fricative			f v	fʲ vʲ			s z	sʲ zʲ	ʃ ʒ		x	
Affricate							ts	tʃ*				
Nasal	m	mʲ				n		nʲ				
Lateral					l			lʲ				
Rolled/Flapped							r	rʲ				
Semi-vowel										j		

* Described by some as 'palato-alveolar'.

INDEX OF PHONETIC SYMBOLS

The symbols in the chart on p. 299, together with the others used in this book, are indexed below, separately from English words. Symbols which are similar to or are modified forms of letters of the English alphabet follow the appropriate letters of the alphabet. Thus ɪ comes below i and ɨ comes below ɪ, etc. Symbols which are very different from any letter of the English alphabet are placed at the end of this part of the Index, in the sequence ə, əː, əj, ɔ, ɔː, ɣ, ʌ, ʌj, θ, ɷ, ɷj, ɷu, ö, öj.

For spelling of individual phonemes and difficulties of pronunciation, see under 'spelling' and 'difficulties' in the General Index.

INDEX OF PHONETIC SYMBOLS

GENERAL INDEX

LaVergne, TN USA
27 February 2011
218044LV00001B/38/P